i n s p i r e d
3D CHARACTER ANIMATION

inspired
3D CHARACTER ANIMATION

KYLE CLARK

Publisher: Stacy L. Hiquet

Marketing Manager: Heather Buzzingham

Managing Editor: Sandy Doell

Acquisitions Editor: Kevin Harreld

Senior Project Editor: Heather Talbot

Editorial Assistant: Margaret Bauer

Marketing Coordinator: Kelly Poffenbarger

Technical Reviewer: Steve Harwood

Development Editor: Kevin Harreld

Copy Editor: Jenny Davidson

Interior Layout: Bill Hartman

Illustrator: Jim van der Keyl

Cover Design: Michael Ford

Indexer: Sharon Shock

Proofreader: Mitzi Foster Koontz

ISBN: 1-931841-48-9

Library of Congress Catalog Card Number: 2001098232

Printed in the United States of America

02 03 04 05 SP 10 9 8 7 6 5 4 3 2 1

This book is dedicated to my wonderful wife Jennifer and daughter Peyton. Thanks for being patient. I love you both very much.

Foreword

By Tom Sito
Animation Director

We are a nation of tinkerers. We were recognized as such in the earliest days of our existence. Napoleon called America "that nation of clockmakers and shop-keeps." Our faith in the promise of technology and our desire for change is dogmatic and absolute.

Hollywood (the name used here as a symbol for all the visual entertainment industry) in particular embraces continual technological change. 1908: Narrative Film; 1913: The Feature Length Format; 1927: Sound; 1934: Color; 1940s: Television and Videotape; 1952: 3D; 1960s: Documentary-Style Handheld Cutting Techniques; the 1990s: Computer Generated Imaging. Tinseltown loves to periodically turn itself upside down with revolution after revolution.

Some might feel that our ever-improving digital innovations make the older traditional skills of character animation and storytelling obsolete. I can't count how many times someone has said to me *"Animation; isn't that all done by computers now?"*

So is there still room for the artist among all these lab coats?

Despite all the headlines and articles about technological complexity, movies and television are still a form of storytelling—an art that traces back before Homer. The heroes of our newest sci-fi blockbusters would not be that unfamiliar to someone who read *Gilgamesh, Die Nibelungenlied,* or *Sir Gawain and the Green Knight* when they were first published.

Do you remember the films *Tron, The Last Starfighter, Young Sherlock Holmes, Death Becomes Her, This Is Cinerama, Bwana Devil, The Rescuers Down Under, What Dreams May Come, Final Fantasy?* How about *Pinnochio, Bambi, Gone with the Wind, Citizen Kane, The Searchers, The Godfather, 101 Dalmations, Psycho, Beauty and the Beast?* What is the difference between the former set and the latter? The earlier group were all touted in their time as breakthrough innovations yet they are now mostly forgotten. The latter group of films live in our collective memory as fresh as the day they first debuted.

The cold, hard fact is no matter how excited professionals get over some new whizz-bang, after about 30 seconds the audience forgets the look and watches the story. And if the story is not good or the performance unclear, the movie fails.

We refer to a piece of music, art, or film as Classic when it achieves a mastery of performance and technique that reaches us on a basic human level. The scene with Dumbo meeting his mother in chains from Walt Disney's 1941 *Dumbo* still triggers tears after more than 60 years. Hard to believe that whole sequence was once blank paper. The innocence of Pinnochio, the antics of Bugs and Daffy, the foibles of Fred Flintstone still entertain no matter how long ago they were created. One of the reasons we are always drawn back to Shakespeare's plays is that you can stage them in space suits, underwater, or in the hood, and they stay Shakespeare. Shakespeare's portrayals of universal human behavior transcend his time period and any medium that is used to present them.

Did you ever notice how Hollywood has a preference for British actors and actresses at Oscar time? Many were trained in the Royal Shakespeare Company stage work and they are thoroughly grounded in the basic fundamentals of classical acting. They become adept at acting and can handle tragic dramas and broad slapstick with the same ease. I recall an interview with modern dance choreographer Twyla Tharp. She was asked what the requirements were for a new dancer to get into her troupe. Would it be helpful if they were familiar with the work of another innovator, say, Merce Cunningham? "No," Ms. Tharp replied. "I consider no one for my troupe who is not thoroughly grounded in classical French-Russian Corps-De-Ballet." Likewise, Henri Matisse disappointed many Fauvist and Cubist students when he made them first master painting in the most old-fashioned Beaux-Arts styles. You must know where we came from before you can interpret and do variations.

Some people ask me: "What's the big deal about being an animator? Someone else wrote the story, someone else designed the character, someone else times it out and records the actor, someone else sets the stage. So what is important about animating?" Some producers newly minted from business school have tried to reduce the animator's contribution to that done by a Third World laborer or some connect-the-dots software program. What is so special?

Continuing the example of Shakespeare, let's take for example Hamlet. In our minds now we all know what Hamlet said; we all know what happens to him; we all have an idea how he looks; we all know his personality. Yet what makes Lawrence Olivier's version of Hamlet different from Mel Gibson's, different from Leonardo DiCaprio, from John Gielgud, Ethan Hawke, Nicol Williamson, or John Barrymore? It's all about performance. The play's the thing. It's the same way some can tell a joke and others stumble even when using the same words. Facts are neutral—it's all in how they are presented. Likewise, anything can move. You can digitize a rock and make it dance the Mambo. Big deal. It's *How* things move and *When* they move—TIMING—that makes it a performance. That also sets apart Glen Keane from all the wannabe animators.

Many books on animation history go on about Walt Disney's passion for technological innovation, but not many mention how he sought to bolster his artists' traditional skills with classes in classic drawing and sculpture, bringing the finest artists of their time in to be guest speakers. Marc Davis told me Disney made all his artists go once a month to a little theater on Fairfax Boulevard to see the latest "Art Film" like *Un Chien Andalou* or *Bicycle Thief* and encouraged a discussion afterward. Top Disney animators, such as Art Babbitt the creator of Goofy or Bill Tytla the animator of the devil on Bald Mountain in *Fantasia*, taught that besides studying animation and drawing you should also read Stanislavsky's *An Actor Prepares* and *Acting: The First Six Lessons* by Ricard Boleslavsky.

In our own time we have seen the great success of John Lasseter and his Pixar studio. While it is sexier for periodicals to dwell on all the wonderful digital breakthroughs that Pixar has generated, John and Joe Ranft built the Pixar story department to be the best in the world, hiring classically trained artists who studied under Disney masters like Tee Hee, Eric Larson, Ken Anderson, and Vance Gerry.

Jim Hillin, a digital artist who held important positions at Disney and Digital Domain once summarized nicely the Pixar success: *"The best thing you can say about their films is ten minutes into the film you forget you are watching digitally generated images; you just want to know what happens to Woody & Buzz."*

Technological revolutions, like their political counterparts, raise up some and cast down others. When I began my career, my mentor was an old Disney animator and producer named Shamus Culhane. He told me stories about when the new technology was television, and he did some of the earliest commercials. He described how some agency errand boy would take a night class in television production and would overnight become the company's "TV Expert" and a producer. I saw equally meteoric advancements in the digital revolution. But the record shows that after all the overnight experts, posers, and fakers take their shot and fade away, the artists and real filmmakers remain.

As of this writing, in my opinion digital animation and filmmaking is about where sound filmmaking was in 1930. Sound technology was invented in the mid-1920s, gained prominence with *The Jazz Singer* in 1927, but still needed several more years to mature. The filmmakers had to endure new limitations and problems with the new technology stemming from the noise of camera motors and the placement of microphones. It wasn't until about 1934 that Hollywood managed to recover and amalgamate the sophisticated imagery of The Silent Era with the new sound technology and bring film into its greatest period.

Likewise, digital animation and imagery was developed in the 1980s, came to dominate in the late 1990s, and now we are learning to recoup and amalgamate our older traditional visual skills with the new technology. The general public won't forgive forever squared boxy fingers, lifeless plastic faces, and stiff floaty walks and bad direction just because it's CG. They'll just go rent another copy of *Bambi*.

New breakthroughs come and go. Today's innovation becomes tomorrow's screen saver. The artist whose training extends no further than mastery of a particular program soon finds himself as obsolete as a 2800BPS modem. But the artist who learns to use his digital tools not as a crutch to hide bad technique but to expand the scope of his traditional skills will be the artist who best succeeds and advances the art of animation into the future.

TS

About Tom Sito

Tom Sito is a veteran of animated film production. His screen credits include the Disney films *The Little Mermaid*, *Beauty and the Beast*, *Aladdin*, *The Lion King*, *Who Framed Roger Rabbitt?*, *Pocahontas*, *Dinosaurs*, and *Fantasia 2000*. At DreamWorks he contributed to *The Prince of Egypt*, *Antz*, *Paulie*, and *Spirit: Stallion of the Cimarron*, and for a time was head of story on the award-winning film *Shrek*. At Warner Brothers, he co-directed the animation for the film *Osmosis Jones* (2001), and presently is working on an as yet unnamed Looney Tunes feature length film.

Tom Sito has produced short films, taught at the University of Southern California and California Institute of the Arts, and written numerous articles on animation. He served three terms as president of the Motion Picture Screen Cartoonists' Union Local #839 and vice president of the International Animators' Society (ASIFA/Hollywood). He is a member of the Motion Picture Academy, the National Cartoonists Society, and Hollywood Heritage.

Acknowledgments

As Michael Ford and I sat there at lunch trying to convince each other that we had the time to actually write a book, I remember thinking we might need some help to finish the project. I didn't realize, however, how many people it would require to pull this thing off. Countless individuals and companies have contributed time, content, and advice to this book over the past 9 months.

I'd like to thank my family for being patient and understanding during the long nights and weekends it took to complete this project. I couldn't have done this without their support. Thanks to Michael Ford for helping seed the idea for the *Inspired* series and providing advice and inspiration along the way. A big thanks to Steve Harwood for his technical editing and for helping me organize my thoughts. This book would have been a jumbled mess without his help. And speaking of mess, the project staff at Premier did an excellent job of cleaning up my text. Heather Talbot and crew organized and edited the chapters and kept my grammar above that of a 3rd grader.

Many artists and animators contributed time to the effort. I'd like to thank all the interview candidates for letting me inundate them with questions about their work habits. Josh Scherr, Sean Mullen, Richie Baneham, and Mike Belzer provided invaluable insight to the world of animation. Huge thanks to Carlos Baena, Jim van der Keyl, and Glen McIntosh for letting me use their artwork. The images look great. In addition, the authors in the *Inspired* project need special recognition. Michael Ford, Alan Lehman, David Parrish, and Tom Capizzi helped create many elements necessary for this title.

And last, but definitely not least, Kevin Harreld for giving me the opportunity to write my first book. His commitment to and persistence on the *Inspired* series has made these books something we can be proud of.

About the Author

Kyle Clark was drawn to the world of movies and animation as a child watching *Stars Wars* and Ray Harryhausen films. Growing up in a small town in Texas, the idea of working in the movie industry was a bit out of reach. He entered Texas A&M University to study architecture. While working on his undergraduate degree, he was introduced to the world of computer graphics through a specialized master's program that had recently begun at the university. Students were using expensive software and hardware to produce short animated films. Soon after, *Jurassic Park* hit theaters and the decision was made. Kyle left Texas for the sunny skies of California to pursue a master's degree in film, video, and computer animation at the University of Southern California. While earning his two-year degree, he worked at Sony Imageworks, Cinesite Digital Studios, and Digital Magic on such titles as *Space Jam*, *The Cable Guy*, and *Mortal Kombat II*. He also produced a stop-motion animated short, *Switchback*, that won him a student academy award. Upon graduation, Kyle began work at Industrial Light & Magic in Marin County, California, as a digital character animator in the feature film division. During that time, he joined forces with Michael Ford to found Animation Foundation, an education-based animation consulting company. After completing work on the feature films *Star Wars Episode I: The Phantom Menace*, *Sleepy Hollow*, *Deep Blue Sea*, *The Adventures of Rocky and Bullwinkle*, and a *Glad* commercial, Kyle left for an animation company in Los Angeles, California. Mooncrescent Studios was started to produce the feature animated film *PC and the Web*. Kyle assumed the role as animation supervisor and began the process of building and designing an animation pipeline and recruiting talent. Mooncrescent Studios closed after a year in business and Kyle moved to Sony Imageworks to work as a lead character animator on the feature film *Harry Potter and the Sorcerer's Stone*. Currently, Kyle is the lead animator at Digital Anvil/Microsoft Studios on the Xbox titled *Brute Force*. In addition to time spent in production, Kyle has taught character animation classes at The Academy of Art—San Francisco, San Francisco State University, Texas A&M University, The University of Southern California, and UCLA.

About the Contributing Artists

This text was fortunate enough to have help from some of the industry's top artists. They contributed thoughts, artwork, and inspiration to this project. Their efforts are greatly appreciated. Below are a few of these fine folks.

Steve Harwood

Steve Harwood was first introduced to character animation shortly after receiving his B.A. in Cinema/Television from the University of Southern California. Enrolling in the digital arts program at San Francisco's Academy of Art College, he attended character animation courses instructed by members of the Pixar staff. He then returned to USC to complete his studies earning an M.F.A in film, video, and computer animation. Since then he has worked at several studios, including Cinesite Hollywood, Centropolis FX, and Sony Imageworks, on projects ranging from feature films to commercials and games. Some of the titles include *Space Jam*, *Mortal Kombat II*, *Stuart Little*, *The Patriot*, *The Tuxedo*, *McDonald's*, and *James Bond: Nightfire*.

Keith Lango

Keith Lango is currently the computer graphics supervisor of feature film at Big Idea Productions, Inc. in Chicago, makers of the top-selling children's video property *Veggietales* and *3-2-1 Penguins!*. Keith got his start in CG in the early '90s and has held positions as an illustrator, a senior animator, an animation supervisor, an assistant director, a CG supervisor, and a writer. Keith has also co-authored and co-illustrated a children's book as well as personally developed several award-winning short animated films. He lives happily with Kim (his wife of 14 years) and his three children: Candice, Laura, and John Mark.

Sean Mullen

Sean Mullen, a one-time student of the Cal Arts character animation program, began his career with two short, embarrassing films, *Oh Crappy Day* and *Horndog*, for the Spike & Mike Sick & Twisted Festival of Animation. After then working as a clean-up artist on various commercials and feature films such as *The Lion King*, he progressed to animating under his mentor, Dale Baer, on commercials featuring Tony the Tiger and Toucan Sam, among others, as well as films such as *Space Jam* and *Quest for Camelot*. Sean joined Sony Pictures Imageworks in 1998 to work on the original *Stuart Little*, for which he earned an Annie Award nomination for Outstanding Individual Achievement for Character Animation. Since that time he has been developing original feature film stories and artwork for Imageworks, as well as working as a supervising animator on *Stuart Little 2*.

Mike Belzer

Mike Belzer has been animating since he was 12 years old. He stumbled into an animation program in the Los Angeles area taught by Dave Master. This program not only taught him the fundamentals of animation, but it was through connections in the class that helped him get his first animation job on the *New Gumby Adventures* series in '87. He spent several years after *Gumby* animating after-school specials, TV pilots, and numerous commercials including such icons as Hershey's Kisses, Listerine bottles, and the Pillsbury Doughboy. Mike then began to animate on feature films. These films included *The Nightmare Before Christmas*, *James and the Giant Peach*, and most recently Walt Disney's *Dinosaur*. He's currently the supervising animator on a Jerry Bruckheimer film, *Down and Under*, due out in 2003.

Along the way, Mike has given many lectures and workshops in both stop-motion and computer animation. He has given these not only to numerous local schools, but also to studios and festivals as far away as London, Canada, Santo Domingo, Denmark, Germany, and Rio de Janeiro. He has been a spokesman for past Disney films in print and television as well as conventions.

Mike not only enjoys what he does for a living but also finds great pleasure in helping others to learn more about animation. He hopes to continue to grow in the field of animation while helping others along the way.

Josh Scherr

Josh Scherr has been working as an animator for the past seven years. The recipient of a master's degree in animation from USC's Cinema-TV School, Josh is currently employed at Naughty Dog—creators of the best-selling *Crash Bandicoot* series and the current PlayStation 2 hit *Jak and Daxter: The Precursor Legacy*. Josh's past jobs include stints at Disney Feature Animation, DreamWorks, Digital Domain, and various commercial production companies. He also was part of the small crew at Bonk Pictures—creators of the popular CG animated short *Los Gringos*. Josh has also taught Maya classes at Cal Arts the past two spring semesters, preparing the next generation of animators so they can steal his job out from under him.

Richie Baneham

Richie Baneham began his career in animation while studying at Ballyfermot College in Ireland in the late '80s. After completing his studies, he began work as an in-betweener at Don Bluth's studio in Dublin. He eventually left for the United States to work on *The Swan Princess* at Rich Animation. Richie then moved to Warner Brothers Animation to work on *Quest for Camelot*. His foray into computer graphics came during the production of *The Iron Giant*. He worked as both a traditional and CG animator using his knowledge to accomplish shots that involved Hogarth and the Giant. He carried that experience into work on *The Amazing Mr. Limpett* and *Osmosis Jones* before assuming the role as animation supervisor on *Scooby-Doo*. He currently resides in New Zealand and is the animation supervisor on the second installment of *The Lord of the Rings Trilogy*.

Carlos Baena

Carlos Baena has worked as a computer graphics animator at several studios. He began his career at Will Vinton Studios animating on M&M's commercials. He then spent time at several other companies such as Click3X, Dimension7, and Wildbrain, working on projects that ranged from commercials to documentaries, including Wildbrain's short film *Hubert's Brain*. In 2001, Carlos joined Industrial Light & Magic to work on films such as *Jurassic Park 3*, *Star Wars Episode II: Attack of the Clones*, and *Men in Black 2*. He was recently hired at Pixar Animation Studios. He can be reached at http://www.mclinn.net/~carlos.

Jim van der Keyl

Jim van der Keyl started his career in animation at the Disney Studios on *The Little Mermaid* as an in-betweener. Since then he has worked at many studios in Hollywood. His animation break came at Warner Brothers where he animated on the *The Iron Giant* and was nominated for an Annie Award. Afterward he made the transition to computer animation and those credits include *Harry Potter and the Sorcerer's Stone* and *Stuart Little 2*.

Glen McIntosh

Character animation lead **Glen McIntosh** has been in the film and animation business for ten years. After attending the classical animation program at Sheridan College, in 1991 McIntosh decided to immediately pursue his passion for art and film and moved from his childhood home in Calgary, Canada, to work for both Don Bluth Studios in Dublin, Ireland, and Twentieth Century Fox Studios in Phoenix, Arizona.

Driven by his desire to eventually work on films created by his two favorite directors, Steven Spielberg and George Lucas, McIntosh strove to perfect his skills as an animator and filmmaker. In 1998, he was hired by Industrial Light & Magic. At ILM, McIntosh has had the opportunity to turn his dreams into reality, creating animation for George Lucas' *Star Wars Episode I: The Phantom Menace* and the 20th anniversary re-release of Steven Spielberg's *E.T.: The Extra-Terrestrial*. Additional credits include *Jurassic Park III*, for which McIntosh was responsible for the unique behavior and movement of the raptors, *Deep Blue Sea*, and numerous commercials including Pepsi's *Playacting*, which received a Clio Award for Outstanding Character Animation. Most recently for *Star Wars Episode II: Attack of the Clones*, McIntosh oversaw the animation of the droid army for the end battle as well as helping conceptual designer, Doug Chiang, create the insect-like Geonosian aliens. McIntosh is currently working as a sequence lead animator on the feature film adaptation of *The Incredible Hulk* scheduled for a summer 2003 release.

Jason Owen

Jason Owen began his venture into the field of animation at the Art Institute of Dallas. In the summer of 2000, Jason graduated with an associate of applied science degree in computer animation and was awarded with a certificate for Best Animation Demo Reel. He then started his animation career in the gaming industry, working for Edge of Reality and contributed to the comic book hit *Spiderman* for the Nintendo 64. Jason soon thereafter began working at Digital Anvil—Microsoft's Austin-based Game Studio—where he is currently an animator on the anticipated squad-based shooter *Brute Force* for Microsoft's Xbox. Jason continues to enjoy experimenting with a variety of media including 2D work and life drawing, and he is interested in the possibility of film work sometime in his career.

Contents at a Glance

Contents

Introduction to *Inspired 3D Character Animation*

The world of animation is as popular as it ever has been. From the award-winning feature films to the fantastic worlds of video games, animation is taking people to places they've never been before. In the emerging market of animated content, computer-generated animation is leading the charge. Traditional methods of using pen and ink are falling to the mighty processor. Veteran artists are rethinking their approaches to generating imagery and incorporating new technologies into their skill sets. In addition, people of all ages are scrambling to learn the latest techniques as they prepare for a career in this exciting industry. As animation continues to be an integral part of our lives, the necessity to provide both veteran artists and the younger generation with a proper set of instructions becomes imperative.

The art and technology of creating computer animation is extremely intriguing. I was lured by the fantasy world *Jurassic Park* made in its debut in the summer of '95. Watching what appeared to be "real" dinosaurs was mesmerizing and inspiring. Nothing seemed more appealing to me than making giant creatures come to life and entertaining audiences of all ages. I made the decision to abandon my architecture plans and enter the life of working as a computer animator. After months of research, I decided to develop my skills at the University of Southern California. I assumed it was only a matter of learning the software and I'd be off to a career as a digital character animator.

It wasn't long before I realized there was much more to entering this field than just pushing buttons. Learning the software was the easy part. The real challenge was when I needed to apply the traditional fundamentals of animation that I had learned to this new technology. I looked to professors, fellow students, and industry acquaintances to find wisdom. In addition, I looked to books that had been authored by veteran Disney animators. All these sources were insightful, but none offered the complete answers to my questions. This world of computer animation had a different kind of process and no one seemed to have the solution.

After several years of working as a professional animator and teaching at various schools and universities, I began to see a common pattern. People that were new to computer graphics seemed to share the same stumbling blocks in creating believable characters within the digital environment. They understood the fundamentals, but had difficulty implementing their ideas. The tricks and techniques that had been prevalent for close to 100 years needed to be refined and rethought for the new age. *Inspired 3D Character Animation* intends to fill that void by providing both fundamentals of animation and how to implement those ideals into computer graphics software.

Computer Graphics Primer

This primer is a short description of some technical aspects surrounding the world of computer graphics. The concepts discussed are the backbone for how 3D software works. A basic understanding of these elements will be crucial to navigating the CG environment.

The Basics

The structure of the worlds that we create within 3D are complex systems that can be a little overwhelming. Whether you are new to 3D or need a quick guide to refresh your memory, use this primer as a reference to the basic elements of computer graphics. By understanding the basics of your 3D software, you can take your first steps toward developing your skills in the fascinating world of computer graphics.

Cartesian Coordinate System

The three-dimensional (3D) world in computer graphics applications is visualized using the Cartesian Coordinate System.

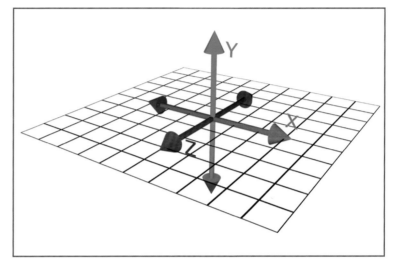

Figure I.1
The three components of the CCS system are X (width), Y (height), and Z (depth). The center of the 3D world (0, 0, 0) is referred to as the "origin."

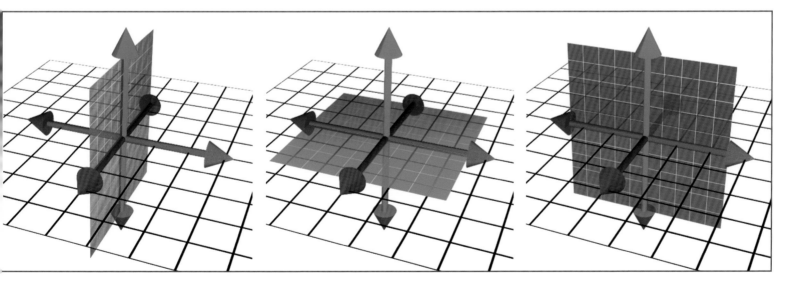

Figure I.2
The three major planes about the origin are the XY, XZ, and YZ.

Right- and Left-Handed Systems

The "hand" is a way to determine which direction of any component (x, y, or z) is positive or negative in relation to the others. To determine positive versus negative in either system, hold up the appropriate hand, palm toward your face. Stick your thumb out to the side; this represents positive X. Point your index finger straight up; this shows positive Y. Extend the middle finger toward your face; it's pointing out positive Z.

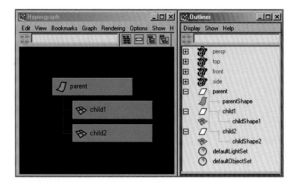

Figure I.4
A parent/child hierarchy.

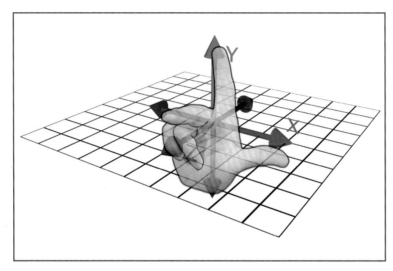

Figure I.3
Maya is a right-handed system.

Hierarchy

A hierarchy is a relationship of nodes to other nodes described in terms of parent, child, and sibling. By default, a child node will inherit what is done to its parent node, transforming along with it and maintaining the same spatial relationship.

Transformations (World, Local, Object, Gimbal)

The transform mode determines how you interactively manipulate nodes by changing what relationship you modify. **World space** manipulates an object with an axis of the same orientation as the world, regardless of the hierarchy. **Local space** is an alignment of the transform axis to the parent of the object. The transform channels of a node (rotate, translate, scale) are all stored in local space. **Object space** is the result of an object's transform in addition to the hierarchy above it.

Gimbal space is a breakdown of local space rotations. It displays each axis separately, showing you each rotation channel's actual orientation, rather than the accumulation of them as is shown in local space. Object rotation occurs one axis at a time. The **rotation order** (by default: x, y, z) specifies which axis rotates first, second, and third. Similar to a hierarchy built with the first axis on the bottom and last axis on top, the first axis inherits the rotation of the second and third. The second axis inherits the rotation of the third; the third axis inherits the rotations of the parent.

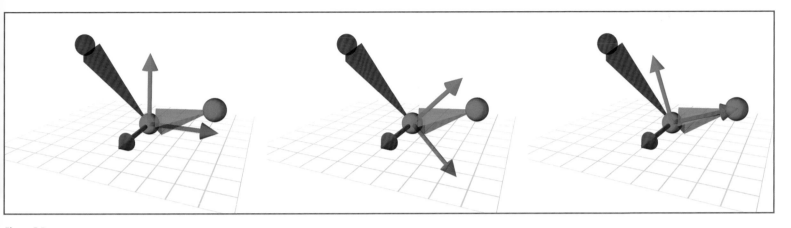

Figure I.5
World space, Local space, and Object space (from left to right).

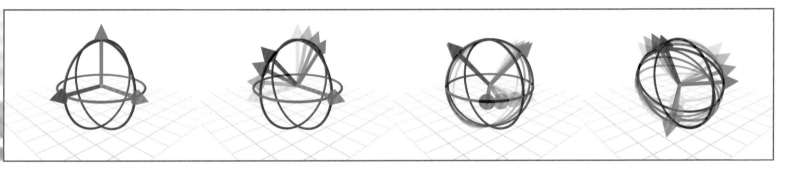

Figure I.6
Displaying Gimbal: no rotations, x rotation; adding y rotation; adding z rotations.

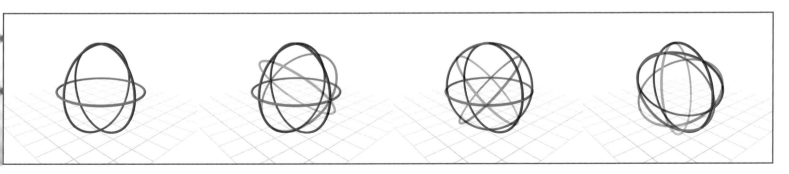

Figure I.7
The resulting local rotation rings over the Gimbal rings.

PART I

Overview

chapter 1
A Look Inside the Industry

State of the Industry

It's a great time for animation. There is tremendous opportunity for artists to display their talents. Once considered a child's medium, people of all ages are beginning to accept animation as a legitimate source of entertainment and information. Producers, directors, and businessmen are embracing the idea of using animation as a method of communicating to an audience. As technological advancements continue to grow, more arenas are going to be created for animation to be showcased.

Many entertainment and educational companies are using this platform to reach millions of viewers, and the numbers prove it. The value of global commercial computer animation production has increased from around 8 billion dollars in 1995 to more than 25 billion dollars in 1999, and is projected to grow to nearly 60 billion dollars by 2004. The overwhelming need for animation has created a great situation for animation artists. Benefits, work environments, and respect for personnel are stronger than ever. Companies understand the necessity to invest resources and time in talented animation artists in order to maintain a competitive production facility. As a result, artists are given an opportunity to work in a highly creative environment while earning an excellent living.

In the early '90s, the need for animators and 3D artists was due to a small supply of computer literate animators and artists who understood the complexities of high-end software packages. Due to competition, companies were forced to rapidly increase the salaries and benefits they were offering to employees. Studios began overloading their facilities with anyone who knew anything about 3D computer graphics and animation. Unfortunately, many of these companies were forced to close due to high overhead and the realization that many of the people they hired did not possess the skills needed to produce film-quality work. This feeding frenzy has calmed down and current hiring practices focus much more on talent and ani-

mation ability; however, competitive salaries and benefits still remain for those whose work meets the studio's level of quality. The hours are long and the work is challenging, but the fulfillment from both an artistic and a financial perspective can be quite rewarding. (See Figure 1.1.)

Along with these positive aspects, however, there are a few other things to consider. The animation industry tends to be cyclical in nature. There are periods when demand is high and you will have your choice of projects and generous salaries. Currently, film, commercial, and game companies are steadily increasing their workloads and many studios are hiring every animator within reach. However, there are times when production slows to a crawl and many of the shows that do get underway are cancelled shortly after. This can definitely create instability and a lack of job security. I have personally experienced two fully funded and green-lit projects being shut down in the middle of production because a boardroom full of businessmen decided that the 10 million dollars already spent was wasted. The way to stay on top is to work hard at every job and constantly look to increase your animation knowledge and skill level. A good artist will have very little trouble finding work, even in the most challenging times.

These production cycles have led animation toward an industry structure that is similar to live-action filmmaking, in which people are hired on a project-by-project basis. These productions assemble crews of people who are hired for a particular show. They are considered production hires and are either released after completion of the show or offered another project that the studio is currently working on or is about to begin production on. Downtime between projects can be anywhere from one week to six months. Although I do not personally like this process, it makes sense for production facilities to follow this format due to the high production costs of digital film elements and maintaining hundreds of artists on payroll.

3

Figure 1.1
Movies like *Jurassic Park* spawned the need for 3D animators. Copyright © 2002 by Universal Studios. Courtesy of Universal Studios Publishing Rights, a Division of Universal Studios Licensing, Inc. All rights reserved.

On the surface, this may not seem like an ideal situation for employment. Many animators, however, actually prefer this pattern. It does have its advantages. Artists aren't tied into long-term contracts at a facility they do not particularly like, and freedom to move and change is presenting itself on a regular basis allowing an animator to seek employment in other areas, such as gaming and commercials. In addition, the artist gets to experience a variety of show formats, supervisors, directors, and animation teams. This has great learning potential and provides you with a broader insight and understanding of the digital workplace, as well as an opportunity to make contacts for future projects and employment. Recommendations are a crucial part of the current hiring practices at most studios, so knowing someone definitely works in your favor.

The production cycle is just one thing to consider when attempting to enter or find work in the animation industry. Another important factor is the number of people interested in entering this field. Granted, more opportunities exist for animators, but that increased need has been met with an equal or greater number of individuals interested in computer animation. Special animation training and degree programs are available in most metropolitan areas and many universities and colleges have added an animation track to their curriculum. More schools mean more graduates and more graduates equal more competition.

Does that mean you should throw away your art supplies, sell your computer, and forget about becoming an animation artist altogether? Absolutely not. Just keep in mind that you're not guaranteed work just by attending the latest and greatest animation school. Nor will working at a renowned studio guarantee you longevity in this industry. Your success will ultimately come down to the quality of work you produce. Dedicate yourself to the craft, and most of all, master the fundamentals and their application.

All this being said, a career as a character animator is hard to match in terms of artistic fulfillment, excellent compensation, and just plain fun. It's an evolving world that combines art, technology, and emotion. An animator gets a chance to express himself physically and emotionally without the embarrassing nature of standing in front of a crowd. The chance to place a small portion of yourself on a movie screen or within a game played by millions of kids (and adults) is an exciting prospect.

Games, Commercials, and Features

Computer animation makes its presence in many forms of media including feature films, commercials, and video games. These types of entertainment and the facilities that create them make up the majority of the industry. It's important to understand the different working environments and expectations these areas carry with them.

Every animator has his or her dream project. This section isn't intended to promote or oppose any particular type of animation. Its sole purpose is to give the reader a better understanding of what to expect from working on a particular type of project. If you position yourself in a facility that's working in the style of animation you most enjoy, you should have a much more pleasant work experience.

Game Production

Game animation offers artists a great place to develop their skill set, as well as a format to produce quality motions. This area of animation has, perhaps, the most growth possibilities. We're just beginning to see the potential of real-time high-end graphics controlled by a game player. Recent advancements in the game industry provide game creators with the tools and technology to make images and characters that are extremely high in quality. Figure 1.2 shows two characters from *Oddworld Munch's Oddysee*.

Length of Production

Expect to spend approximately two years creating a game. This time frame can obviously vary depending on the project. I've seen games completed in 12 to 18 months and others that have been in production for more than four years. This may seem like ample time to comfortably create the necessary animation. However, the requirements of game production often make it difficult to deliver the proper number of motions in this time frame.

Games require enormous amounts of animation. A console game can contain 40 hours worth of animation. Compare that with 75 minutes for an animated feature and you'll quickly understand the fast pace that game animators must maintain in order to meet deadlines. Instead of taking four or five days to create a character's

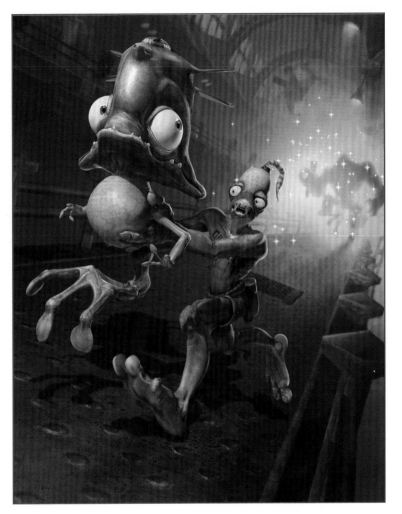

Figure 1.2
Abe and Munch present high-resolution characters and quality animation in this Xbox title.

walk cycle, a game animator might have to deliver the same cycle in half a day. Creating work at this pace requires a complete understanding of animation fundamentals and digital techniques.

Contributing to that pace is the size of the production staff. Games generally don't carry large animation teams. Three or four artists might be responsible for the entire set of motions. In addition, those artists might have to handle technical issues as well. Having the limited number of personnel and an overwhelming amount of animation to create usually means plenty of work to spread around.

Animation Style and Process

The majority of game animation is geared toward "player controlled" motions. This term refers to motions seen as a character runs around on the screen. If the control stick is moved left, the character will translate in that direction. If a particular button is pushed, the on-screen figure might jump. These actions are a direct result of the player's effort to win the game. That effort needs special consideration.

One of the main goals for game animation is to provide the player with the widest range of motions possible. For example, characters need to have the ability and agility to move in any direction. The animator must first create a simple run. That motion must then be given all the necessary variations to sprint left, right, and backward.

And that's just the start of it. On-screen characters potentially need the ability to jump, crouch, walk, dive, and roll. Each of these abilities will need multiple variations. In addition, these motions could potentially require additional work depending on the type of weapon the character is using. A walk with a pistol will be fairly different from one with a rifle. Because of this, the number of motions can add up. A character could have upward of 300 motions. Throw several characters into the mix and you've got a mountain of work. However, there are some positive aspects to this format of production.

Pros

Game production allows the animator a chance to animate many different motions on a range of characters. You might animate a four-legged beast in the morning and work on a human in the afternoon. This variation can help alleviate boredom and has some great benefits for the animator. Getting a chance to animate characters of assorted height, weight, and appendage count helps artists understand the way forms of all types move.

Part of the learning process for becoming a skilled animator involves repetition. You can read every text available, watch the entire library of animation and effects films, and take countless years of animation classes and still not be able to animate at the level required to establish a career in the field. I'm not suggesting that one can be a seasoned veteran by solely animating mass quantities of motions; it takes creating a motion, assessing its quality, and refining the movement. Just as a painter develops his skill set with each painting, every motion an animator completes moves him one step closer to success.

In addition to the opportunity to hone your skills via repetition, the style of animation created in games offers an excellent arena to master the fundamentals of motion. Running, walking, and jumping are basic movements that are physically based. Concepts such as timing, arcs, overlap, secondary, and balance are essential

to these actions. It's a great format to learn the craft of giving characters a believable sense of weight and timing. I'm not suggesting game animation is the only medium to hone these skills; rather, the emphasis in this type of production setting lends itself more toward development in these areas.

Another challenging aspect of game animation is the absence of a dedicated camera. In film productions, the director decides on a specific direction from which to film the action. Games do not have this convenience. The action happens in real time, and the game player controls the camera. This forces the animators to ensure that their animation works from every angle.

There is an exception to the parameters of game production mentioned previously. Many games have mini movies called *cut scenes*. They are small stories and introduce characters or events to better explain the game. Cut scenes are much closer to film production in format and process. Cameras are predefined and the animator has a specific action and emotion to convey within a given time frame. Animating these sequences offers a great opportunity to develop acting skills. This type of scenario, however, can be limited.

Cons

Minimal exposure to acting is probably the biggest downfall of working in games. The format doesn't typically lend itself to character development and emotion. (There are exceptions to the rule, as you'll learn in Chapter 3, "An Interview with Josh Scherr.") The lack of acting situations isn't due to an absence of story. In fact, story line has a strong presence in this style of production. The emphasis on strong performance, however, usually takes second seat to the game play motions.

Although acquiring acting skills is a tremendous plus, the environment of a game facility can definitely aid in the growth of a young animator. An artist can use the practices and standards of game production to develop an efficient and sound method of producing quality animation.

Commercials

Digital animation has a tremendous presence in the world of commercial production. As the technology came into focus, advertising agencies began using computer animation to produce eye-popping images to sell their products. The marriage was a good one. The advertising agencies got their amazing visuals and production companies filled their schedules with short projects. The viewers were treated to a host of new commercials that were a welcome replacement to the ads they were used to. (See Figure 1.3.)

Commercial production is a client-oriented industry. An ad agency hires a director or production facility to create its spot. The agency provides direction and can

Figure 1.3
Carl and Ray are photo-real digital characters created by Tippett Studios.

even create rough storyboards or concept drawings to convey the idea. The director and effects facility then work toward the goal of pleasing the client.

Length of Production

A typical commercial schedule ranges from six to nine weeks. During this time, models must be built, characters rigged, animation completed, and scenes lit and composited. This doesn't leave a tremendous amount of time to massage a piece of animation. An animator might get three days to complete a shot as opposed to three weeks on a feature. Aiding the shortened production schedule is the number of people commenting on the work. Directors, clients, and agencies all have a say in the creation of a spot. Animators often find themselves changing directions several times through the course of a commercial. Speed and an excellent understanding of technology are essential in hitting deadlines on a day-to-day basis.

One of the main advantages of this quick turnaround is the ability for an artist to work on many different projects. Instead of being married to a project for 24 months, animators can handle multiple characters and situations in a very short amount of time. Many artists love this aspect of commercial production and would never consider the long haul of features. This can drastically increase your exposure to various styles of animation and prove to be a great method for identifying the style of animation you'd most like to create.

Animation Style and Process

Commercials run the gamut on style and content. One of the most challenging aspects for a commercial animator is the ability to adapt her skill set frequently to meet the needs of each individual project. An artist might be faced with replicating a digital animal for one production and then be asked to create a six-legged Martian delivering a piece of dialogue in another. These tasks can include an equal

mixture of acting and physical animation. The animator must use every available resource to fulfill the requirements of the particular production.

Commercial production quality generally lies between that of games and features. Animators strive to obtain the excellence of feature films while working at a faster pace and with a smaller production staff. The final viewing platform is generally television where images are broadcast to millions of viewers. Images and animation need to be of the utmost quality.

Pros

Many commercial artists often wear multiple hats during a production. The artist usually assists in various facets of the production cycle. A person might rig a character, then animate it, then composite and light the scene. The exposure to a variety of jobs can help an animator understand the entire production process, and ultimately prepare him to generate higher quality motions. Knowing the limits of a set-up or how the final light pass will affect a pose can help the animator design the optimum scene.

Cons

Many commercial artists often wear multiple hats during a production. Yes, that is a repeat of the same sentence from above. The aspect that is one of the positives of commercials is also one of its downfalls. By not focusing on the specific aspects of character animation, an artist's ability to develop emotional performances can suffer.

Adding to the lack of job-specific duties is the notion that commercial production facilities generally don't employ an animation supervisor. Artists must look to fellow animators for feedback, inspiration, and refinement of their scenes. This can be a great way for an artist to learn from more experienced artists. Productions will often designate a lead animator to maintain the quality of animation. However, as with most productions, the real decision-making process usually comes from those writing the checks.

Animation for Feature Effects Films

In the early '90s, digital character animation dramatically changed the face of visual effects and feature films. *Jurassic Park* brought a never before seen realism to movie visuals and showed filmmakers what was possible with high-speed computers. Although digital technology had been used prior to this film, the effects and characters previously created had much less impact than a full-size T-Rex chasing a car. (See Figure 1.4.) No longer do directors and producers have to rely on actors in latex suits to bring these animals to life. They now utilize 3D technology to create much more realistic characters and creatures to interact with live-action elements.

Figure 1.4
Characters like the T-Rex from *Jurassic Park* were instrumental in merging animation with digital technology. Copyright © 2002 by Universal Studios. Courtesy of Universal Studios Publishing Rights, a Division of Universal Studios Licensing, Inc. All rights reserved.

Length of Production

Production cycles for effects films can vary from 1 month to 18 months. The shot difficulty, shot count, and budget all determine how long a facility will work on a project. In addition, the complexity of characters and situations affect the time a project can take. I've witnessed everything from 20 shots in 6 weeks to a marathon production of 2 years. The first scenario allowed animators between five and eight days to produce a shot. The second experience required significantly more work and allowed an artist an average of 10 days to complete his shots.

Animation Style and Process

There's a distinct difference in the nature and methods of animation produced for live-action films. Working in this photo-real environment generally forces the animator to approach his or her motions in a specific manner. The presence of real-life elements tends to influence the style. The animation must match actors, sets, and objects. Live-action films with CG integration are usually striving for photo-realism. They want the viewer to believe that the creature you are animating is a part of the world the filmmaker is creating. All these factors influence how the animation is approached and ultimately created.

It is true that many shots for effects films are completely digital. However, this involves creating a world that corresponds with elements from actual sets or locations and, therefore, keeps the animation in the same realm as if an actual set were being used.

In feature productions, shots are assigned to an artist as they become ready for animation. At this point, the animation supervisor, lead animator, or director will discuss the scene with the chosen animator. (Chapter 16, "Getting Started," discusses this more in detail.) Specific actions and emotions are decided upon and the artist is provided with any necessary reference footage. Storyboards, scripts, actor references, and a dialogue track might also be included. The artist will then begin to develop a plan toward solving the scene.

One of the major considerations for an animator working in this form of production is the material provided from the live-action film crew. It can ultimately determine what your scene can and cannot encompass. First, the camera operator usually predetermines the camera. This means the composition and length of a shot are going to be locked based on the actions from the physical set. For example, say the camera operator panned across the room from left to right and the shot calls for your character to walk across that same room. You'll have to animate a walk that keeps the character in frame and moves from left to right. The cinematographer has done his best to calculate the amount of time the specific character will take to move that distance. Your standard walk will probably not work in this situation. It may require some speed adjustment.

Now let's make it even more complicated. Throw an actor into the shot, and you really need to pay attention. If the digital character is reacting to something the live-action actor is saying, the timing for your animation is going to come directly from the actor's performance in the scene footage.

Here's an example:

This shot involves a live-action character named "Preston." Preston is yelling and pointing at a simple character. The animator is given this set of frames and asked to add a creature responding to Preston's actions. Preston begins the scene frame left and takes two steps toward screen right. At frame 98 he lifts his hand and firmly pokes the animator's character in the chest. (See Figure 1.5.) Surveying the action of Preston gives the animator an exact idea of when his character needs to react. The animator wants his character to take two steps back as Preston moves forward. It's necessary to break down the timing of Preston's steps in order to make the digital character travel at the same pace. In addition, the animator must ensure that his character's position matches Preston's finger at the designated frame. The finger must appear to touch the animator's character's chest and his character must react accordingly.

These restrictions can actually help the animator during his process of planning a scene. The action within the plate provides a reference for the digital character's actions. This creates a basic set of timings for the character to follow, and it provides a sense of what the animation needs to include.

Figure 1.5
The animation created must match the live-action photography.

Due to the complexity of creating photo-real visual effects, the animations created are usually shorter in length. However, as with everything in production, that's not always the case. Shot lengths can range anywhere from less than one second up to one minute in length. The average scene is probably about two seconds long and takes two weeks to finish. I know what you're thinking: How can you spend two weeks working on 48 frames of motion? Animating 48 frames can take a significant amount of time. Creating photo-realistic motion requires an understanding of motion and attention to the subtle details of movement.

In feature effects work, an animator usually works on all the characters in the shot. If two characters are exchanging dialogue, the animator will work on everything in that particular scene. In addition, artists will often animate multiple shots in a sequence. If action occurs over several shots, it benefits both the animator and production to have one person handle the character or characters. Continuity of action and emotion remains much more consistent. Special circumstances do arise, however. Having to deal with hundreds of creatures might warrant splitting up the shot between several people.

Cons

The only real downfall I've experienced when animating on effects films is the limitation on animation style. The presence of real-life physics from the actors or backgrounds taken on the set tend to require that the animation match those same sets of physics. It's much more difficult to take liberties with extreme timings or actions if you have a real actor standing in the scene. Can it happen? Certainly. However, remember that live-action films with CG integration are trying to accomplish a certain level of photo-realism. They want the viewer to believe the creature is a part of the world the filmmakers are trying to create.

The challenge of creating photo-real creatures and characters is extremely rewarding. There's a tremendous amount of enjoyment that comes from fooling a theater full of people into believing a digital character is alive and breathing. It provides a great opportunity for artists to emulate natural motions and bring a high level of subtlety into their work. And I'll be honest, seeing my name roll across the credits on a 40-foot screen is exciting.

Creating Believable Characters for Feature Animated Films

Feature animation is often considered the Holy Grail for an animation artist. It offers 75 minutes of animated characters. This format defined the standards for animation as entertainment dating back to the early days of Walt Disney. As a 2D medium, the films brought life and emotion to a world of characters that had existed only in our heads. These types of films are now being created entirely within a digital environment. Figure 1.6 shows a still from the popular film *Toy Story* from Pixar and Disney. It was the first computer animated feature film.

Length of Production

A typical production cycle for a 3D feature animated film is usually between 18 and 24 months. That doesn't necessarily include story development; rather, it encompasses the process of building models, animating shots, and lighting and rendering completed scenes. This schedule can obviously fluctuate depending on the facility and staff. However, creating an entire world of believable characters is time-consuming. You might consider it the marathon of filmmaking.

The pace of feature animation tends to be faster than effects films. Although the production time is usually longer, animators are producing a considerably larger amount of footage than an effects film. With crew sizes of 25 to 35 people, animators must push through the animation at a fairly rapid pace.

Many facilities require certain footage counts from their animators during the course of a week. This is a concept taken from the traditional process and refers to the number of frames or seconds an animator produces over a given time period. The counts can be anywhere from three to ten feet per week. A foot is based on the number of 35 mm film frames that span 12 inches. It works out to be 16 frames per foot. There are 24 frames per second in the film world. Do the math

Figure 1.6
A still from *Toy Story*. © DISNEY ENTERPRISES, INC./Pixar Animation Studios

and you'll see that animators are generally required to create anywhere from two to six seconds per week.

Animation Style and Process

Feature animation provides a giant canvas for creating complex, emotional characters and offers the animator the opportunity to showcase his skills in both a physical and emotional format. There are no live-action characters, backgrounds, or sets to influence the audience, and the life and performance of the entire cast must come from the animators.

The absence of a live-action element allows feature animation artists to take many more liberties with their animation. The animators must stay within the style of the film, but timings and poses can be much more extreme. The audience doesn't have an actual actor in the scene to compare the digital characters to. In addition, rendering objects in a stylized manner breaks the real-world connection often found in effects films. This is ideal for animators who enjoy exaggerated poses and timings.

As opposed to working with a digital plate, feature animation artists are handed a digital layout file that contains camera and set information. In addition, a basic choreography of the characters is often provided. This was created to give the director and animators a sense of how the shot will play alongside the ones around it. This doesn't necessarily lock the animators into the same timings as the layout, but does give the artists a general sense of what should be happening in the scene.

If the shot contains dialogue, animators are given a recording of the voice track. Animators use the dialect and tone of voice to decide what poses and attitude the character will have. Footage of the voice actor saying the lines can also provide valuable reference and subtleties of character. Many animated characters take on small actions of the actors providing the voice. (See Figure 1.7.) The presence of a dialogue track is extremely prevalent in feature-animated films. This format relies on the digital characters to tell the story.

Figure 1.7
A voice actor provides the sound track for an animated character.

Different facilities have various thoughts on how to divide the work among their artists. Disney, for example, follows the rules they set up for traditional films back in the '50s. They have leads that supervise a particular character in a film. That lead will have a team of animators who work on that character for the entire film. If a shot contains two characters, the work is split between two different teams. Other studios, however, break the animation into sequences and allow their artists to work on all of the characters in a shot. Whereas working on a single character for the entire film allows an animator to become extremely familiar with the nuances and emotional states that progress through the film, getting to animate several characters over the course of a feature provides a broader spectrum of acting styles. (Mike Belzer discusses this topic during his interview in Chapter 13.)

Pros

The biggest advantage to working in the medium is the emphasis placed on acting and emotion. Animators are generating the entire palette of a character's behavior. They are responsible for breathing life into three-dimensional geometry, and charged with the task of connecting the audience with the once static form. Getting

the opportunity to dedicate your entire day to this cause drastically increases your understanding of the heart and soul of animation.

Cons

The only negative aspect (and it isn't so much negative as it is challenging) is the level at which an animator in this medium must perform. Successfully animating for a feature length film is one of the most difficult tasks to accomplish. You are constantly judged on your ability to communicate effectively. As an animator, you must have total control of your character. The fundamentals of animation have to be second nature so the proper time can be spent on the acting and emotion of a scene. This is the most complicated aspect of animation and often makes or breaks a scene. Animators have to touch base with the emotional nature of humans and bring these characteristics to their scenes.

As you can see, there's a certain amount of crossover in the different types of animation production. Acting and emotion can be an integral part of feature effects films, whereas maintaining a believable physical presence is important for fully animated features. Game animation can be just as satisfying and challenging as feature animated work and creature animation can be as rewarding as an entertaining piece of acting. In the end, you as an artist must decide on what type of production you feel most matches your desires. Artists have distinct opinions about what they prefer to create. Find out what you like and pursue a career in that area.

Creature Versus Character

You might assume that moving objects around on the screen is essentially all the same. However, the type and style of animation between these two categories is fairly diverse. These categories comprise the majority of shots and scenes that character animation artists produce. In addition, there's a substantial difference in approach and style when animating creatures versus characters.

Creatures

The creature category includes beings such as dinosaurs, trolls, mummies, aliens, and animals. I would also include digital stuntmen in this category. These shows involve animating characters that don't have a major acting or emotional role in a film. The animation tends to be much more physically based and the characters have a non-speaking role.

These characters spend time destroying a city, jumping from building to building, or flying ships toward an enemy base. Some examples include the decaying human in *The Mummy*, the sharks in *Deep Blue Sea*, and Munch from the video game *Munch's Oddysee*. Figure 1.8 shows a few of these popular creatures.

Figure 1.8
Imhotep from *The Mummy* (Copyright © 2002 by Universal Studios. Courtesy of Universal Studios Publishing Rights, a Division of Universal Studios Licensing, Inc. All rights reserved) and Abe and Munch from *Munch's Oddysee* for the Xbox.

This style of animation is extremely challenging. Not only do you need to completely understand the fundamentals of animation and have a full understanding of the physical nature of these beasts, there's also an additional set of problems. These creatures often have skeletal systems that do not exist in nature. A designer might create a beast or being that has four joints in the arms. Where do you find reference footage for a fantasy character such as this? You don't. It's up to the animator to combine movements of things that currently exist and create a unique motion.

Characters

The character category would include Buzz and Woody from Pixar/Disney's *Toy Story* or the photo-real mouse in *Stuart Little*. These films rely on acting from their digital characters. This type of animation plays a more integral part in the plot development of a film and makes an attempt to connect on a personal level with the audience.

Character animation has a few similarities to creature animation, but adds another skill set to its creative process. The animator is dealing with motion that has more of an acting emphasis. This requires, as you might expect, extensive knowledge of acting and the ability to project feelings. As a villain actor creates a sense of animosity in a live-action drama, an animated villain must obtain the same level of dislike from the viewers. Anything less would leave the audience unfulfilled and uninterested.

Studio Life

Not many artists have the chance to make a decent living doing what they really love. Production settings provide a unique opportunity to develop artistically, as well as professionally. You can develop your animation skills, personal contacts, and resumè all under one roof.

Studios generally tailor the work environment to meet the needs of an artistic setting. Environments tend to be fairly loose and take on the personalities of the artist inhabiting them. Studios want employees to be comfortable and usually make every effort to accommodate their personnel. I've worked at several facilities and have yet to find even a mention of dress code.

On several occasions I've taken friends or family into the studio space where I'm currently working. They are amazed at the eccentric nature of these spaces. Decorations, posters, toys, and miscellaneous oddities bring the environment to life. I've seen everything from a full-service tiki bar to a room with a complete disco light setup. Artists make their work area unique and it really helps the creative flow (see Figure 1.9).

Figure 1.9
Artists' spaces from a few different facilities.

One of the most important aspects of working in a studio is the opportunity to learn from those around you. Studios make every effort to recruit the top talent in the industry. This will be an excellent time to draw on the experiences of people who are veterans in the industry or new animators who have a fresh approach to solving their scenes. I've learned a tremendous amount from seasoned professionals as well as students who've just begun their careers. I often recommend that people search out those interested in pushing their abilities and make an effort to routinely speak with them about your scenes. You'll find the results to be amazing.

Although extremely rewarding, the studio life can also be very tough. The number of work hours required and the level of stress can often be shocking to animators entering the industry. Don't count on many 9 to 5 days or Friday afternoons playing golf. Work isn't getting done unless the artist is in front of the computer. Directors and producers are constantly looking to reduce the cost of making their product. This forces production schedules to become tighter and requires personnel to push through the data.

Most digital productions fall into a similar pattern. For animators, the production cycle typically starts slow and ends at an accelerated pace. In the beginning, animators must wait for models to be created, scenes to be set up, and dialogue to be recorded. There are always setbacks in the completion of those tasks and this forces the delay of the actual animation. When shot production begins, an animator might be on a 9- or 10-hour per day schedule working 5 days a week. As the show moves closer to the deadline, these hours can change to 10 or 12 hours per day and 6 or

7 days a week. Shots must be delivered on time in order to keep the show on schedule. There is definitely increased pressure associated with this type of situation, not to mention the physical toll from sitting in front of a machine for 12 hours.

Repetitive Stress Injury is a very real concern for digital artists. It's caused by overuse of tendons in your wrist, arms, hands, or shoulders. It might sound negligible, but I know several artists who can't continue to work as a result of this condition. Imagine working through years of school to land your dream job and then having to take long-term disability because you can't operate a mouse anymore. It happens. Fortunately, most studios take a proactive approach to avoid this problem.

Whichever studio or situation you land in, be sure to take full advantage of that time. Working with the industry's most talented artists in an entertaining and creative environment will be like nothing you've ever experienced, and the benefits will continue to pay off throughout your career.

The material presented in this chapter has been compiled over several years at many of the industry's top studios and with input from many of the top animation talent. It's intended to provide the reader with a general understanding of what to expect when entering the field. Although each facility and production has its individual characteristics, the majority of issues discussed are applicable to the entire industry. Now that you have an idea of the various facets of production, it's time to get specific to the animation process. Chapter 2 takes a look at a variety of methods for creating believable motions.

chapter 2
So You Want to Be an Animator?

This chapter focuses on different aspects of animation training and provides various hints and techniques for getting into the industry. Different disciplines require different tracks of study. Focusing your attention on a particular craft ensures ample time is spent honing those skills. This text is assuming you're interested in working specifically as a character animator.

Choosing a School

Deciding on the right institution can be a pivotal point in your pursuit of a career in animation. The knowledge required to work as a professional animator is extremely particular. Whether you're attending an undergraduate, graduate, or technical school, finding a facility that can supply you with the proper training, equipment, materials, and personnel is critical. Fortunately, you have many choices. The boom in animation has spawned numerous new degree programs and institutions to assist in your pursuit. Taking the time to research some of the more important aspects of these facilities will greatly increase your likelihood of obtaining a solid education.

The Teaching Staff

One of the most influential aspects of your student life will be your professors or instructors. These individuals will be responsible for molding your artistic vision. Their guidance can provide unique insight into the craft of animation that is invaluable. Your teachers can and will have a tremendous impact on your career. Proper training can make or break your pursuit of becoming an animator, and if you are taught fundamentals that are incorrect or outdated, you will probably have a difficult time overcoming those habits.

Look for facilities that have working professionals or veteran animators on staff. (See Figure 2.1.) You'd think teaching animation would require having experience working as an animator; however, this is hardly the case. It's difficult to find schools, universities, or technical colleges that have strong animation faculty members. Many of the professors are individuals who graduated from that particular school and stepped directly into the role of teacher or professor. This doesn't necessarily indicate that the instructors don't know anything about animation; they might have been the most talented artists in the class. However, most higher learning facilities aren't cheap; for the money, I want to hear instructions from someone who's been in the trenches. There's nothing that can replace on-the-job experience. Processes, techniques, and problems are much more evident in a work environment. Instructors who've spent even minimal time working in a production setting should have a tremendous amount of information to pass along. Do everything you can to tap into it.

I directly attribute this insight to my ability to land a job at a feature film facility. Fortunately, I had several veteran animators working at the university I was attending. Their sensibilities about the animation process were incredible. Long gone were the days of wondering whether a shot was going in the right direction. I presented them with a section of work and received instant feedback about the success or failure of a shot. The direction provided was precise and based on a knowledge backed by years of professional credit. Their experience provided an excellent forum for critiques and suggestions. These professionals developed classes that were designed specifically for people interested in practicing the art of animation.

Degree Plans

The courses required for a degree are equally important. Having a plan centered around the art of animation will provide you with the optimum amount of learning opportunities. The plan should include classes that focus on animation techniques and processes. When researching a school, look for courses that are specific to characters and how they move. In addition, make sure the institute has some

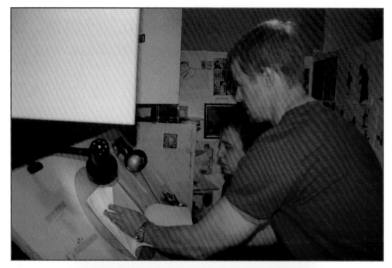

Figure 2.2
This lab supports traditional techniques, as well as computing facilities.

Figure 2.1
Kevin Johnson teaching a class at Cal-Arts. He has worked more than 10 years as a professional animator and is currently employed at Sony Pictures Imageworks.

options for acting. Students should expect to walk away from their studies with a sound foundation of fundamentals and the ability to clearly create emotion in a fictional character.

In addition, courses such as life drawing, screen writing, character design, story development, and traditional filmmaking can provide insight into the world of animation production. They're tried and tested and are the foundations for what computer animators do every day. Polishing traditional drawing skills and better understanding story can help artists more effectively communicate their ideas. Better acquainting yourself with these concepts will enhance your ability as an animator. Make sure the school is tailoring its curriculums toward this goal by providing you with a balanced set of courses.

Alumni

An informative issue when considering a school is the quality and success of its alumni. Strong schools will produce very talented individuals who excel at the craft of animation. These are often the artists who inhabit successful feature, commercial, and game studios. These alumni not only provide a measuring stick for the quality of the institution, but often provide additional insight into the industry. Many schools have routine seminars and events that include these artists. These proceedings can be a great way to meet professionals and an excellent forum for getting some of your questions answered. They can also provide excellent contacts for future job possibilities.

Do the homework and you'll find a place that meets your learning needs. Finding a facility that meets your specific needs will increase your chances of a successful profession. Remember, these institutions are providing the launch pad for your animation career. Don't put that responsibility in just anyone's hands. Take the time to make sure you're getting the most bang for your buck.

Getting the Most Out of Your Education

After you've settled on a place to study, there are a few things you need to remember to ensure that you take full advantage of the time you spend learning animation. Going to the best school isn't going to guarantee you anything except student loans. A good school will most certainly place you in a position to get the best training; however, you'll have a whole new level of responsibility on your shoulders.

Self-Motivation

The mention of self-motivation might seem a bit remedial. However, this is what will eventually get you a job. I may sound like a high school football coach trying to rally his players in the final minutes of a big game, but the truth is, many of the students pursuing a career in animation don't display the initiative to achieve the success they potentially have the talent for. Don't assume that going to a school to learn animation guarantees you a six-figure job. Utilize the resources the institution has to offer and don't waste several years creating mediocre work. I've witnessed this happen firsthand as a teacher, mentor, and fellow student.

If you're going to spend the money on learning the craft of animation, you might as well use that time wisely. Squeeze every bit of information and equipment use out of the school you are attending. Push for purchases of reference materials, better equipment, and ask for guest speakers. (See Figure 2.3.) You're not going to get every request you ask for; however, any extra bit helps.

Utilizing Your Peers

One of the most important resources you'll have while studying animation is the people sitting around you. You'll be spending most of your waking hours with and around them. Your fellow students and peers can be an invaluable resource when learning the craft. Use them for a fresh eye or to spawn an idea that's hidden deep inside you. Just discussing a scene can generate some great ideas about how to better approach the animation. If your peers suggest one thing that will help the scene, you're that much closer to a better shot.

Animation can be a tricky craft to learn. Looking at a motion 100 times taints your opinion about how successful it might be. It can become difficult to see the bigger picture after staring at a character repeating the same action numerous times. This

Figure 2.3
Students at UCLA requested some industry help and were treated to a day with Todd Wilderman and Sean Mullens, animators from Sony Imageworks.

concept doesn't end when you get a job. It's an every day reality. Getting a paycheck for creating animation doesn't mean you have all the answers. I routinely ask a roommate or fellow animator to take a look at my work. Many times they take a quick glance at the motion and make comments about a particular aspect of the animation. It's usually something I haven't noticed and something that needs immediate attention.

I recommend that you find the top animators in your class or studio and befriend them. Routinely showing your work to those folks will dramatically increase your skills. Don't be shy about a little criticism. It's part of being an animator and will become an integral part of your career. Your work will consistently be shown to your peers and evaluated based on the needs of the project. Listening and embracing these critiques will make your work much stronger.

Industry Mentors

Another tremendous resource for those learning animation is industry mentors. As I stated previously, learning from someone who's actively working in production can be the ultimate experience. Mentors are a direct connection to this knowledge and can often provide students with up-to-date technology and technique information. The right mentor can offer direct and accurate information on how to make your work stronger.

I was fortunate enough to find such a mentor while studying at the University of Southern California. He was a talented animator working at a large studio, and he was gracious enough to spend a few hours every other week helping me learn the craft of stop motion animation. I would work for two weeks at a time, and then mail a tape of the shots that were completed. He would call or e-mail comments after reviewing the work. The conversations ranged from the intricacies of armature design to posing, acting, and staging. It was an amazing experience.

These types of mentors don't come easily. Production requirements often keep interested people from actually engaging in this type of relationship. The time constraints of working on a project can limit their availability. If you are unable to find a mentor, I suggest trying the Internet. Searching for animation-related sites will turn up a variety of resources. Look for discussion forums related to animation. These forums are inhabited by a number of working professionals who routinely answer questions and offer advice. These artists are dedicated to the craft and are usually willing to provide assistance to those interested in entering the field.

If you are lucky enough to find an animator who wants to get involved, use that time wisely. Don't waste his efforts commenting on your latest texture map or number of polygons in a model. Be specific about the aspects of production you want him to critique. Ask him for help with timing, poses, and staging of your shots. Focusing his efforts will help focus your efforts.

Narrowing the Field

As you might imagine, I'm partial to character animation and those who pursue and practice the craft. Take the following advice with that in mind. When I decided to enter the world of special effects and film, I knew exactly what I wanted to do. I wanted to place a part of myself on the screen by acting through a digital character. My efforts were concentrated directly toward that goal. Directing the majority of my attention to developing a skill set for character animation helped me produce higher-quality work. I had a tremendous jump on other students trying to enter the same field. Many of them opted for a balanced portfolio that showed decent skills at various disciplines. My projects were centered on the craft of character animation and I attempted to show an understanding of fundamentals and acting. I didn't spend a tremendous amount of time modeling complex environments or painting textures. I used simple characters in simple settings. (See Figure 2.4.)

The moral of this story is to devote your attention to one primary skill set. To produce content at a professional level you must perform at an extremely high degree. It's very rare for an individual to possess all the skills to produce models, textures, and animation at a feature film quality level. Are there people who've done it?

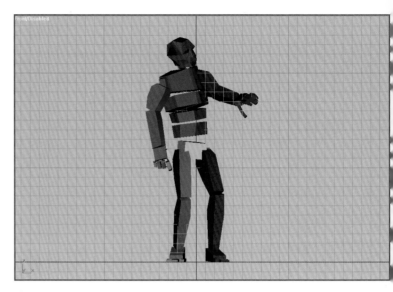

Figure 2.4
A simple character can effectively demonstrate your animation skills. The biped from Character Studio is a simple biped with basic geometry.

Definitely. However, if you look at the major studios producing the strongest work, the majority of those artists are focusing on one discipline. The standards are just too high for the companies not to direct their employee's attention to one craft. If you're working 40 hours per week as an animator, your development in that specialty will be much faster and more intense than a person who's splitting that time as a modeler.

This doesn't mean you can't learn additional traits or specialties while honing your skills as an animator. You'll inherently pick up skills while learning a particular 3D package. Setup, basic modeling, lighting, and a general sense of digital technology are all disciplines you'll dabble in. I recommend a mix that balances your efforts around 70% animation and 30% other craft. This will put the majority of your emphasis on working toward that goal as an animator while allowing you to experience some alternative technology.

After giving this advice, students often comment about this scenario. They question the notion by suggesting that school is a great time to experience every aspect of production. I partially agree. Artists eager to tinker in various disciplines should use this time to find the area they are most interested in. However, a person with mediocre work in many disciplines is going to have a much tougher time finding a job than someone who's absolutely certain where she wants to be. The reel will show it and her attitude will back it up.

Dos and Don'ts of Demo Reels

Businessmen need resumès; animators need demo reels. This short presentation is an employer's best means of assessing your skill. It's also the presentation you'll spend your entire animation career working for. Demo reels don't end when you leave school. They continue to be an integral part of the job application process with each new facility. The right combination of imagery can land you that perfect job.

When presenting your work, it's important to make a good first impression. Studios look at thousands of reels each year. They don't have time to sit through seven minutes of every applicant's work. They make a quick assessment of the contents and decided to continue watching or pass on your work. I've witnessed the eject button being pushed before the 30-second mark on a tape many times. Putting the strongest work you have at the front of your tape puts you in a much better position to make that cut.

The number one mistake you can make when submitting a demo reel is making your tape too long. You can spend countless hours working on that perfect piece of animation. After such an investment, it can become very hard for you to part with that effort. Taking select pieces of animation and using those to present your skill set will have a much greater payoff. Think quality versus quantity. Viewers don't want to wade through subpar animation. A nice short presentation offers plenty of time to sell your wares. (See Figure 2.5.)

One of my animation instructors at the University of Southern California told the class an interesting story. He was a seasoned veteran who'd worked on some of the biggest animation films of all time. He'd worked in the business for 25 years and seen the best and worst tapes. A demo reel came through the studio that created a serious buzz. The tape was a whopping 12 seconds long and caught the attention of some of the top animators in the facility. Those 12 seconds resulted in the applicant being placed in a bidding war between two of the top animation studios. The reel clearly showed the applicant had a strong understanding of animation fundamentals. Needless to say, more doesn't always mean better.

So how long should a reel be? Obviously, those 12 seconds were extraordinary. It would be ridiculous for me to suggest that you try to compact your work into that short of a time frame. However, that example proves that studios aren't looking for animators who work in bulk. I recommend a tape that runs between 30 seconds and 2 minutes. Condensing your samples into a short segment provides an efficient and effective method for showcasing your skills.

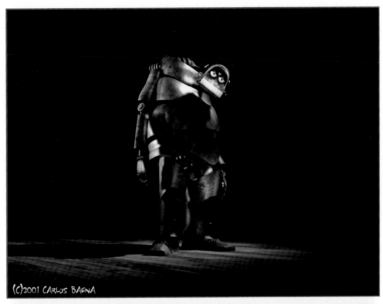

Figure 2.5
Two stills from Carlos Baena. His short films landed him a position at ILM and then at Pixar.

Make sure your reel has work that's geared toward a specific position. Companies are usually looking for a particular skill set when they are trying to fill a position. Most calls for applications clearly state the discipline required for that production. Hopefully you decided what career path you were interested in pursuing. Your reel should reflect that decision. This will send a clear message to the prospective company that you are interested in a specific position. There's nothing worse than an ambiguous reel filled with a variety of mediocre skills. I've seen working professionals submit tapes with this sort of ambiguity; I couldn't tell you what job they were looking for. Naturally, they didn't get hired. Be clear and be specific and you'll be in a much better position to get the job.

Now that I've stepped down from the soapbox, let me contradict myself once again. Do I believe that reels should be catered to one specific job? Absolutely. Based on the preceding paragraph, I hope you trust that I truly believe this. However, there are occasions when an artist trying to enter the field of visual effects, games, or feature animation might want to alter this approach. Over the years, I've taught many students who've displayed talents in a number of digital disciplines. They really aspired to be character animators, but showed an ability to rig characters, model environments, or storyboard sequences. I routinely encouraged them to continue their pursuit of a character animation job, but not to discount the ability to land a position working in a production setting. There are two reasons for this: Some experience is better than no experience, and working professionally can create a variety of facets to pursue your goal. I know several artists who entered a facility as a matchmover and worked their way into a character animator position. Getting in the door can be the tough part. If that dream job isn't available, find the next best thing and start working on your real objective. An artist in this position should take a slightly different approach when creating a reel.

The following two lists give sample breakdowns of how an artist might organize his reel. The first list is ideal if you're applying only as a character animator. The information presented will be completely directed toward showcasing the fundamentals of animation. The second list is ideal if you display a variety of skills. You might be interested in any production position or you might be gearing your presentation to finding work at a smaller studio doing a multitude of tasks.

Animator's Reel

1. **Reel Roll:** Lay down about 12 seconds of black on your tape before the imagery starts. This gives the player time to lock down the tracking. You can also include a tone so that the volume on the television can be set.

2. **Title Card:** Open with a simple graphic that contains your name, phone number, and e-mail address. Fade from black and hold on the card for 3 seconds. Fade back to black.

3. **Animation Examples Section:** This section should contain the best shots from your animation career. Start with the best and most recent work and move chronologically backward.

4. **Traditional Works:** Many animators like to include samples of figure drawings on their reel. This section provides an excellent place to showcase any traditional drawing or painting skills.

5. **Completed Works:** This section is a great place to include a short film. Overlap from the Animation Examples Section should be expected. Viewers have seen your best efforts as an animator, but can now be entertained with your storytelling capabilities.

6. **Title Card Closing:** Close with the same opening graphic. It's a nice moment to refresh the viewer of your name and contact info.

Digital Artist's Reel

1. **Reel Roll:** Lay down about 12 seconds of black on your tape before the imagery starts. This gives the player time to lock down the tracking. You can also include a tone so that the volume on the television can be set.

2. **Title Card:** Open with a simple graphic that contains your name, phone number, and e-mail address. Fade from black and hold on the card for 3 seconds. Fade back to black.

3. **Animation Examples Section:** This section should contain the best shots from your animation career. Start with the best and most recent work and move chronologically backward.

4. **Modeling Examples Section:** Digital models of characters or environments can be showcased in this section. In addition, include samples of texture or matte paintings.

5. **Lighting Examples Section:** Examples of lighting and rendering should inhabit this portion of the reel. The examples could be still images or short moving sequences.

6. **Traditional Works:** Many animators like to include samples of figure drawings on their reel. This section provides an excellent place to showcase any traditional drawing or painting skills.

7. **Completed Works:** This section is a great place to include a short film. Overlap from the Animation Examples Section should be expected. Viewers have seen your best efforts as an animator, but can now be entertained with your storytelling capabilities.

8. **Title Card Closing:** Close with the same opening graphic. It's a nice moment to refresh the viewer of your name and contact info.

Now you have the perfect reel and the person viewing it knows exactly where your talents lie. What else should you include with your submission? Two things come to mind: A resumè and demo reel breakdown. Yes, I know that this is another contradiction. I realize my opening statement suggested resumès weren't important for digital artists. In reality, they aren't that critical. The major emphasis of your submission will definitely be the demo reel. However, it is necessary to include a brief history of your education and work experience. It also provides the company with a quick reference sheet for contact information.

The other important document is the demo reel breakdown. This gives the viewer an exact understanding of what you did and didn't do on a demo reel. A reel can often contain work created by co-workers or fellow students. Artists are often involved in a group effort and are only responsible for a portion of the work. If an animator submits a shot with three main characters interacting, it's important to note exactly what motion the artist created. These notes give the viewer an accurate sense of how to judge the candidate's skills. A simple list that provides a description of the shot and the duties performed is all that's necessary.

Choosing a Studio

In ideal animation society, you'd learn the basics of animation, pick a studio, and begin the long road to learning the craft while enjoying a corner office with the fastest machine. Jobs would be plentiful, salaries high, and digital characters

would have a place in the majority of films you saw. This is obviously not the case. The industry mimics a roller coaster when it comes to the prosperity of its artists. However, if given the chance, here are a few things to consider when looking at a studio. Hopefully, you'll find yourself in a position to choose a studio that matches your needs and desires.

Animation is a subjective medium. Some like it cartoony, some like photo-real, and some prefer an experimental approach. These various styles appear in many different platforms and presentation formats, such as games, television, film, commercials, and the Web. One of the first steps when entering the field is making a decision about the animation style you prefer. As simple as it may seem, it's important to choose a studio producing the work you most enjoy. An artist who prefers the exaggerated motions of a traditional animated show might not enjoy creating the photo-realistic character for *The Mummy*. (See Figure 2.6.) Obviously, you'll be happier working on films that interest you. In addition, animators often find that they perform better in a specific style. Many artists can only perform at their peak working on a particular type of animation. This type of discovery can take time. You might not realize that your talents are better suited to creature work until you've animated on several shows of that variety. However, being conscious of your strengths and weaknesses will eventually help you land in a facility that directly corresponds with your skill set.

Figure 2.6
Style should be a consideration when selecting a studio. *The Mummy* image Copyright © 2002 by Universal Studios. Courtesy of Universal Studios Publishing Rights, a Division of Universal Studios Licensing, Inc. All rights reserved.

Just as a prospective animator needs to research the talent at a university or trade school, having a strong understanding of the talent of a particular studio is a must. Working with and around the best animators has a serious impact on your animation career. These are the individuals who assess your professional work on a daily basis. They'll provide guidance, suggestions, software, and insight on how to animate faster and better. The more sophisticated and accurate their comments are, the faster you progress as an artist. It's important to know the depth of a studio's talent; however, it's not something you can research at the library.

First, take a hard look at the work the company has produced in the past. You can't make *Toy Story* with a crew of B-team animators. Second, research the supervisors. Their information should be readily available. These are the folks who'll be leading the charge. You can't win a battle with a weak general. Third, ask questions when interviewing. Questions about how the employees got started in animation, what facilities they've worked at, and where they studied animation are all key indicators to the artists' talent. Find the right combination of talent to work with and you'll learn more in six weeks than you ever have. (See Figure 2.7.)

What Are Studios Looking For?

Gone are the days when companies would fill a seat with any warm body that would sit still for more than 10 minutes. Production demands for personnel have dramatically changed over the past few years. Companies are refining their standards on a daily basis. They are looking for the brightest and best to fill their

Figure 2.7
Studios like ILM offer artists an environment rich with talent. Copyright © 2002 by Universal Studios. Courtesy of Universal Studios Publishing Rights, a Division of Universal Studios Licensing, Inc. All rights reserved.

production requirements. Candidates must possess some key ingredients to stand above the increasing competition.

Having a complete understanding of animation fundamentals is the first step in turning the head of a potential employer. At this stage in the industry, companies require it. Many facilities are beginning to bypass the training period when they bring inexperienced artists up to speed on the finer points of animation. They're looking for talented individuals who comprehend the basic requirements to create believable characters. In addition to a solid display of animation principles, production experience is becoming increasingly important.

"Looking for character animators with minimum 2 years' experience." "Wanted senior animators with 5 years of professional experience." Any of these ring a bell? How then do you get a job that requires experience if you can't get a job to gain experience? If I had a nickel for every time I heard that question, I'd be retired by now (and then there'd be another opening for a senior animator). Experience is invaluable when studios are assessing your worth. It proves that you have been in a production setting and have some degree of knowledge about what it takes to work in a digital environment. In addition, your skills have potentially been honed in a professional setting among talented and skilled personal. A seasoned Disney veteran is probably not going to have much problem finding work.

How then do you obtain that animation job you so desire? Experience is great, but it's not necessary. However, the alternative takes time, dedication, and a bit of raw talent. I've known several artists who had excellent student work and walked directly into an animation studio and started working on major productions. The work they created and presented to the studios was strong enough to land that coveted job. The time spent during school or after hours was dedicated toward animation and their talent showed through. They also possessed a key ingredient: the ability to get better.

Growth potential is a key element when studios look for new talent. Studios invest a tremendous amount of time and resources into hiring a new employee. As with all investments, it's important to have a good rate of return. They're looking for talent that takes that training and grows at an above average rate. If a potential employee has a strong understanding of the fundamentals of animation, the studio can mold and develop that person into a highly skilled artist. This reinforces the importance of demonstrating your raw talent when submitting a reel.

Complementing this growth potential, and equally important, is the attitude a candidate possesses. I know—that statement sounds like a human resources lecture. However, when looking at potential co-workers, I rate this one near the top. Artists in general are a fickle bunch. (I can say that because I'm an artist as well.) Personalities, work ethic, and the ability to work with others run the entire spectrum. I've the seen the best of the best and the worst of the worst. Believe me, it's not fun working with a pretentious animator who thinks his skills can't get any better. As a famous animator once said, "the day you stop learning animation is the day you quit animating." This is an art form that never stops developing. Like fine wine, animators get better with age. The best artists routinely look for resources to refine their knowledge. They understand the immense amount of knowledge required to master their craft, and add to their understanding of animation on a daily basis. These are the type of people studios look to hire.

As the demands increase, you must continue to develop your skills and be prepared to meet the expectations of the people writing the checks. This industry is like many others; in the end, it's the talented and hard working individuals who get and retain the best jobs.

chapter 3
An Interview with Josh Scherr

Josh is currently an animator at Naughty Dog, Inc. He's had the opportunity to work professionally in almost every animation style and medium. In addition, he has worked at facilities ranging from the industry giants to small boutique shops. The following is an interview about some of those experiences and Josh's thoughts about surviving and thriving in the animation profession.

KYLE: *Give us a little idea of your background.*

JOSH: I got into this field with a combination of relevant hobbies (animation, special effects, and computers) and some really good timing. I had just graduated from Oberlin College with an English/Film Studies degree when the first *Jurassic Park* film hit the theaters. All of a sudden Hollywood got very interested in the potential of digital effects and animation. That same summer, I learned that USC's Cinema-TV school was starting a master's program in animation. Figuring I had nothing to lose, I applied, and much to my surprise, I was accepted. I was there for two years and worked on two films: *The Sentinel* and *Junkyard*. (See Figure 3.1.) *The Sentinel* was my first stab at 3D character animation, and as such, it's a little embarrassing to watch now. *Junkyard*, which was a collaborative effort with my friend Shawn Nelson, turned out much better. I was better at the technical stuff, and he was better with the animation, so our skills complimented each other and helped both of us grow. On both of those films, I did a little bit of everything: modeling, texturing, setup, animation, lighting, you name it. I also had the good fortune to intern with this group of guys who called themselves Propellerhead Design. They were making a proof-of-concept animation test for a computer generated television show, and working with them really brought me up to speed quickly. Since I graduated in 1995, I've worked for numerous companies doing all manner of work. I started at Digital Domain's New Media division as an animator on *Ted Shred*, a game that never saw the light of day. From there I moved on to DreamWorks Feature Animation, where I worked with the Propellerhead guys again on an early animation test for *Shrek*. I did some animation and compositing while I was there, and although it was a great learning experience, the entire crew was laid off upon completion of the test (long story). My next stop was Disney Feature Animation where I was an assistant animator on *Dinosaur*. This mostly entailed doing cleanup work on other people's shots, and while it wasn't always exciting—I animated a *lot* of lemur tails—I worked with some amazing leads like Larry White, Trey Thomas, and Bill Fletcher. Hell, I learned a ton just watching co-director Eric Leighton critique work during dailies. After *Dinosaur* wrapped up, a unique opportunity presented itself. Some folks I worked with at DreamWorks were putting together a CG short film about a cowboy and a samurai called *Los Gringos*. They were hoping to use it as a movie pitch and start a studio called Bonk Pictures. While the risks were great—I would be working on this full-time, no pay, for about six months— I figured the rewards could be great as well. I did a lot of character animation and compositing for the film and pulled many all-nighters along with the rest of the crew. Reaction to the finished project was phenomenal. Unfortunately, for reasons too complicated to explain here, Bonk Pictures fizzled out soon afterward. I freelanced for about a year after that, working on things like the music video *Californication* for the Red Hot Chili Peppers over at Pixel Envy, a few commercials back at Digital Domain, and most bizarre, a movie about a killer piñata. I also re-joined some of the Bonk Pictures crew briefly for an animation test at Nickelodeon, but that was over almost before it started. I'm now working for a video game company called Naughty Dog, the people responsible for the *Crash Bandicoot* series on Sony PlayStation. We released *Jak and Daxter*, our first PlayStation 2 title, back in December of 2001. I've been doing nothing but character animation since I got here, and it's been fantastic. They have a really talented crew of artists and programmers.

KYLE: *You've seen many different facets of production. What's been your favorite and why?*

JOSH: Character animation, definitely. While I enjoy doing things like lighting and compositing (I'm a terrible modeler, though), I find animation to be the most rewarding. Most of that has to do with my love of storytelling, and that's really what character animation is all about: conveying a story through your acting, your poses, and your timing. While the other aspects of production require a great deal of

Figure 3.1
Junkyard was Josh's second effort in 3D animation. The film was produced at the University of Southern California.

artistry, they also involve a lot more technical noodling. I found that with lighting and compositing I was spending a lot of time making minor adjustments and fighting the computer, whereas with the animation, as long as I had a good setup, I could focus on being creative. It's kind of funny—I spent the first part of my career trying to be the jack-of-all-trades, and I'm now trying to avoid that so I can focus on the animation side of things.

KYLE: *It's interesting that you've had a chance to work in almost every style of animation. Do you feel one particular medium stands out as your favorite?*

JOSH: Not especially. For me, what's important is the work that I'm doing and not the medium I'm doing it in. During my job searches, I always tried to work on a project that looked interesting and would help me improve as an animator. Whether it was film, commercials, music videos, or games didn't really matter to me. There

are even times when the subject matter isn't important—I worked on a film about a killer piñata, for goodness' sake—it's the experience that counts.

KYLE: *Which situation presented the best opportunity for learning and advancing your animation skill set?*

JOSH: Hard question. If I had to choose just one job, it would have to be my present position at Naughty Dog. I'm part of a small team of animators who worked exclusively on the cut-scenes (non-interactive movies) for *Jak and Daxter*. (See Figure 3.2.) We have a fairly unique way of working here—there are no "lead" animators and our scenes are entirely self-directed. So for a given scene, I would pick out the takes of dialogue I wanted, do the scene layout, and animate all of the characters. Naturally, we show our work to one another for feedback and suggestions, and Jason Rubin (Naughty Dog's co-founder) has the final say on the scenes, but I

Figure 3.3
Animating lemurs for the Walt Disney Pictures' animated film *Dinosaur* presented Josh with an excellent learning opportunity. © DISNEY ENTERPRISES, INC.

performance." Getting the mechanics right—the weight, the overlap, etc.—comes with lots and lots of practice, and early on I spent a lot of time bogged down in this area. I'd always have to stand up and shift my weight to remind myself which way the hip rotates during a walk, or consult my notes regarding the timing of blinks, spacing of walks, and so on. I've gotten better with the mechanics over the years, and while there's always room for improvement, I spend much less time worrying about the basics, leaving more time to make my animation better.

KYLE: *Getting out of your chair is EXTREMELY important. Too many animators try to work through their mechanics from a chair. What devices do you use in your planning?*

JOSH: Sock puppets. When those aren't available, I find the most useful tools to be a pad of paper, a pencil, a mirror, and a video camera. There might be some animators who can visualize everything in their head, but I'm not one of them. I always do some thumbnail sketches of my various poses and keys, usually nothing more complicated than a stick figure with googly eyes. (Figures 3.4 and 3.5 show the results of that effort.) We also have a full-length mirror near our desks at work, so I'll often stand in front of that and try out some poses. When there's some really complex motion or acting involved, it's a good idea to have someone videotape you acting out the scene. For example, one of the cut-scenes I animated for *Jak and Daxter's* intro movie involved a canister that was picked up, shaken, and tossed to another character; videotaping this helped immensely with the staging. Also, when you're doing lip-sync, nothing beats having a little mirror on your desk.

KYLE: *How does your specific blocking process work?*

JOSH: It really depends on the shot, but it's usually a combination of pose-to-pose blocking and straight-ahead animation. When a character is just "acting" and not really moving around too much, I'll do things pose-to-pose. If they're going to be walking and talking, I'll usually block out where their footfalls are going to be and then start figuring out my poses. If it's going to be a complex motion, such as a character flying through the air and bouncing on the ground, I'll often just animate that straight-ahead in a rough manner, then go back and tweak the timing later. Getting more specific, I used to start by blocking out the torso and waist since everything else is attached to them, and once that looked good, I'd do the legs and arms and head. The problem with that method—in my case, at least—is that my poses would sometimes get a little mushy and indistinct. More recently, I switched to blocking the whole body out at once, and I think my poses have improved as a result.

Figure 3.4
Thumbnail drawings from a scene in *Jak and Daxter*.

Figure 3.5
The resulting rendered frames from Josh's thumbnail drawings.

3. An Interview with Josh Scherr

KYLE: *I think a lot of the CG-born animators have a difficult time creating strong poses. What advice would you give to someone wanting to develop that skill?*

JOSH: I agree with you completely—in fact, I'm a textbook example. I think my initial trouble with poses arose from two things—my lack of formal art training and my technical computer background. I would build a character, know its limitations and problems, and I'd end up with timid poses before I was afraid to break all my careful setup and skinning work. Ideally, you should simply try to pose the model the way you want without knowing or caring about its limitations. I've still got room for improvement in regard to my poses, but there are a number of things that can help anyone. First and foremost, if you don't have formal art training, then get some! Take life-drawing classes. The more you know about human construction and anatomy, the easier it becomes to exaggerate the attitudes and get really strong poses. One of the great things about working for Disney was they offered a life drawing workshop nearly every day of the week; I took advantage of this as often as I could. In between Disney and *Los Gringos*, I took a class with Glen Vilppu that met three days a week for six hours a day. My poses got much better after this class, not to mention my drawing skills. Another thing that can help your poses, not to mention your animation, is to study other people's work. Thanks to the availability of animation on DVD, this has gotten much easier. Watch Disney films, watch Pixar films, watch the classic Chuck Jones and Tex Avery cartoons, let their work inspire and inform your own. Finally, you can improve your poses if you seek guidance from people who are better than you! Disney was great in this regard, and the animators at Naughty Dog have helped me a lot as well.

KYLE: *Yeah, I'm a textbook example as well. Although I agree with your thoughts about life drawing, I don't know that it ever helped me that much. I found studying stills from movies and print much more beneficial. Maybe I just needed a better instructor.*

JOSH: The important thing is to find classes that are geared toward the animator and not the "fine" artist. Drawing the same pose for two hours will help you with your body construction and anatomy, which is important, but my increased proficiency with poses came from faster sittings. With the Disney and Vilppu classes, we were usually doing very quick poses, starting at thirty seconds, generally hovering around three to ten minutes, the longest ones being fifteen minutes. It taught me how to find the lines of action and center of gravity quickly, not to mention where I could exaggerate for effect and where I had to keep the proportions to maintain proper weight and balance. Regardless of whether it helps your poses or not, taking life drawing classes is a good idea.

KYLE: Los Gringos *and* Jak and Daxter *both had an exaggerated style of facial animation. How did you guys achieve that look?*

JOSH: Unfortunately, I can't get too specific, but you should follow a couple of basic principles. First of all, when making your character, try to make your facial shapes as extreme as possible; in other words, make your open mouth shape unnaturally wide, make your smile shape stretch the skin to its breaking point, and so on. You might never need to go to those extremes, but at least you'll have the option. Second, make shapes specifically for squashing and stretching the face and jaw area. The mouth and face should follow the same rules of overlap and squash and stretch as the rest of the body. So, if your character is going to scream "WHAT?!", the "wooooo" sound at the beginning should be combined with a squash, then stretch into the "aaaaaaa" part. (See Figure 3.6.) The more cartoony Disney films such as *The Emperor's New Groove* and *Aladdin* are good references for this style of facial animation.

KYLE: *Give us your three favorite exercises to show off your animation skills.*

JOSH: Exercises and tests are good for keeping your skills fresh—bouncing balls for squash, stretch, and spacing; ropes and whips for overlap, walks, runs, and so on. However, if you really want to show off your animation skills, you need to be a little more ambitious. Back when I started in CG—wait, does that make me sound old? Anyway, back when the CG animation boom was starting up, there were a lot more seats to fill than talented animators to fill them, so studios were hiring anyone who could copy Preston Blair's walk cycle in 3D. Things have changed a lot. There are a lot more programs like USC's and CalArts, a lot more traditional animators transitioning to 3D, and a lot more competition in general. Just having a bunch of walk cycles on your reel won't really cut it anymore. Companies want to see that you are good with the mechanics *and* that you can make your characters act. My ideal exercise involves a single character that undergoes a few emotional changes throughout the scene. Here's an example: Your guy is waiting for a phone call. He's pacing because he's either nervous or excited. The phone rings. He dashes across the room and answers, happy. There's a pause. It's a wrong number or a solicitor. He slams the phone down, angry. In that scene I just described, you've got running and pacing for your mechanics and two emotional changes, and you don't even need dialogue if you pull it off well. If you want to try doing an animation to some dialogue, nothing beats using old radio shows. You could also use a sound clip from a movie, but your audience has most likely seen the movie and might have a preconceived notion of how the scene plays, which could work against you. Using radio clips forces you to come up with your own staging and performances. Some old radio shows are really corny and melodramatic, but that can be really fun to animate!

Figure 3.6
The "w" shape squashes the face and the "a" shape stretches it. The sequence of images from squash, to stretch, to relaxed.

KYLE: *Any last words for the readers?*

JOSH: Some of the best advice I ever received came from Tom Sito, a 20-year animation veteran and one of my teachers at USC. In between animation lessons and historical anecdotes, he told us when looking for a job, we should weigh our options in this order of priority: experience first, prestige second, and salary a distant third. In other words, try to find the jobs that will help you improve your skills, and if the job is for a big-name company that looks good on a resume, so much the better. The hours in this industry can get insane, so if you're going to be sacrificing your social life and your health for a project, it's in your best interest if you get something out of it besides money. Another important tip: don't be an ass. This is a very small industry, and stories regarding people with attitudes and bad personal skills spread quickly. Finally, the tip I always give people just starting out: save your money. Two reasons for this: the animation industry goes through boom and bust cycles, and you want to start a nest egg during a boom so you can ride out the bust. Second, the majority of animation studios now hire on a project-by-project basis, rather than hiring permanent staff, so layoffs at the end of a project are happening more often than not.

> He told us when looking for a job, we should weigh our options in this order of priority: experience first, prestige second, and salary a distant third.

Having a nest egg also allows you to take more risks. I wouldn't have been able to work without salary for six months on *Los Gringos* if I hadn't saved all my overtime pay from Disney. Oh, wait, one last thing, and then I'll shut up. The long hours you work in this business can easily lead to burn out, no matter how much you love your job. Whenever possible, take *long* vacations after you finish a project. Travel. See your friends and family that you neglected for months. Go to animation screenings and get yourself inspired again. Most importantly, *get away from the computer*.

3. An Interview with Josh Scherr

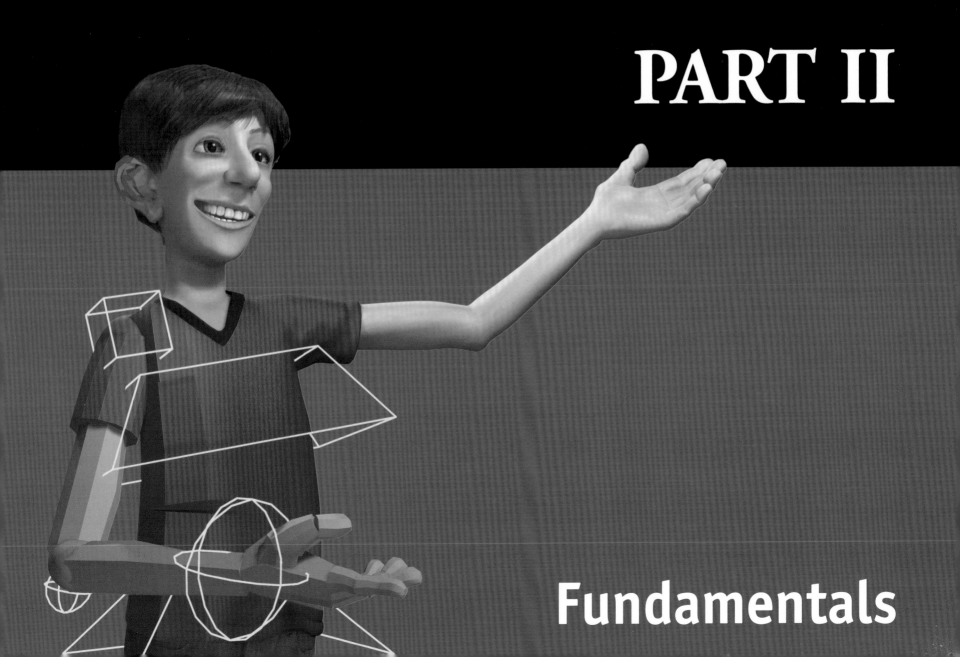

inspired
3D CHARACTER ANIMATION

PART II

Fundamentals

chapter 4
Tools of the Trade

Computer graphic software packages offer many tools and techniques for creating animation. The list of devices to edit and create motions can be daunting to say the least. I often find animators spending more time learning all the bells and whistles of a piece of software instead of working on their animation skill set. However, to be an effective animator, it's important to learn the tools that will assist you in mastering the craft of character animation. This chapter takes a look at some of the major digital tools that I use on a day-to-day basis and a few others that I feel are important.

I've included this chapter toward the front of this book to better prepare you for discussions in the following chapters. I'll use many of the tools and procedures from this chapter when dissecting various aspects of animation. I've also included an explanation of the character rig that I use for the entire text. I'll reference it on a regular basis.

The Character Rig

When characters are created in the computing environment, they need a system that enables the animators to move and pose the model. This system is referred to as a character rig or character setup. This rig is a set of bones, locators, and objects that mimics that of a real-life skeleton. Figure 4.1 shows one of these skeleton systems. As you can see, the inner workings of a human animation setup can be extremely complex. The majority of those objects, however, don't pertain to animators. Fortunately, you only need to deal with certain aspects of these models.

Figure 4.2 is a diagram of the rig this text will be using. It's much less complicated than Figure 4.1 and shows the two things that animators need to be concerned with: low-resolution geometry and control objects. The control objects are the animator's main interaction with a character. If I want to move the wrist, I grab the controller located at the wrist and translate it on the screen. The movement of this

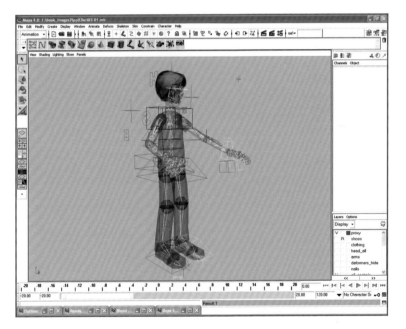

Figure 4.1
The skeletal system in a character setup.

controller drives the rigging of the character and positions the arm appropriately. (See Figure 4.3.) The low-res geometry (or cut geometry) is provided purely for speed. It's a simple representation of the more complicated geometry final character, and allows the animator to work much more quickly.

This particular rig was built by Mike Ford and Alan Lehman. They specialize in character rigging. Their book, *Inspired 3D Character Setup*, provides an in-depth

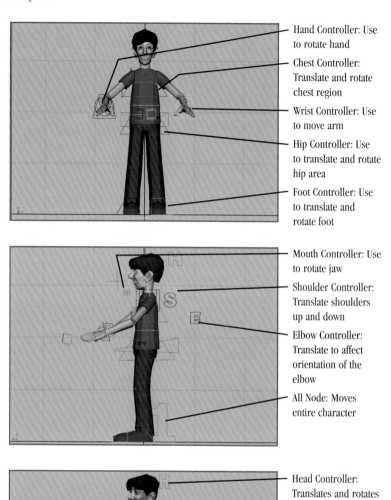

Hand Controller: Use to rotate hand

Chest Controller: Translate and rotate chest region

Wrist Controller: Use to move arm

Hip Controller: Use to translate and rotate hip area

Foot Controller: Use to translate and rotate foot

Mouth Controller: Use to rotate jaw

Shoulder Controller: Translate shoulders up and down

Elbow Controller: Translate to affect orientation of the elbow

All Node: Moves entire character

Head Controller: Translates and rotates the head

COG Controller: Translates and rotates the entire body with the exception of the legs

Knee Controller: Use to affect orientation of knee

Figure 4.2
The yellow control boxes alter the underlying skeleton.

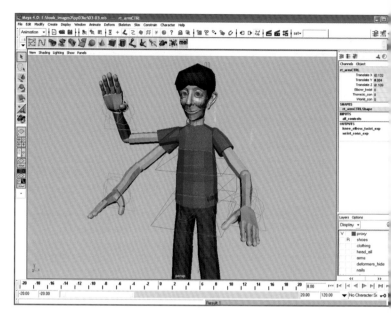

Figure 4.3
Moving the wrist controller updates the arm position.

look at the entire process of creating a human skeletal system. If you are interested in learning the craft of character setup, I highly recommend reading their book.

Dope Sheet

The dope sheet is one of the most powerful tools in computer animation. It's also one of the least used and usually takes second seat to the ever-popular curve editor (discussed later). The dope sheet is the ultimate way to edit timing. It's particularly important during those first days or hours of a scene when you're trying to get the timing just right. By using this tool, modifications to the timings of a motion can be altered quickly and effectively.

Functionality

The dope sheet is basically a graphical representation of the key frames that have been set on a character or object. When a key frame is set, the dope sheet creates a bar or dot that is representative of the transforms for the selected object. The transforms are animatable attributes of an object and include items such as rotation, translations, and scaling. This graphic is paired with a timeline and packaged in an easy-to-understand interface. Figure 4.4 shows a diagram of this tool.

Name of object selected   Scene summary shows keys for entire file   Frame numbers   Unselected keys   Key frames selected turn yellow

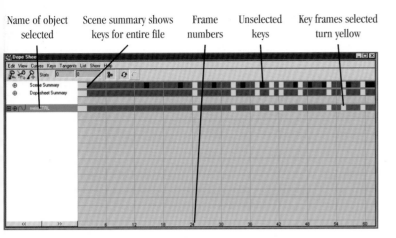

Figure 4.4
Diagram of a dope sheet.

In addition to the single bar, dope sheets are usually expandable to reveal an additional graphic. By expanding the levels, I can see that a particular object has both translation and rotation, or possibly just scaling. (See Figure 4.5.)

Expanding the selected object reveals the individual transforms

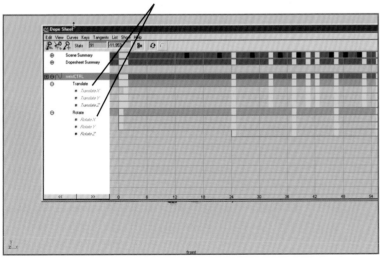

Figure 4.5
An expanded dope sheet revealing translation and rotation.

The bars within a dope sheet can be grabbed and moved, successfully altering the timing of your character or object. You can move selected keys without affecting other key frames around them, have the keys retain their original relationship, or have the entire animation move when you insert additional keys. If expanded, these various transforms can be edited separately. I can alter the translation of an object without affecting the rotation. (See Figure 4.6.) This provides excellent control when altering timings.

Rotation keys are shifted one frame from the translation ones

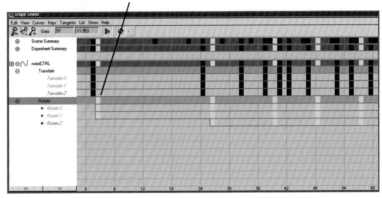

Figure 4.6
Altering the rotation keys. The translation keys remain in the same location.

I get the most mileage from editing the timings with the character's top node selected. By selecting the top of the hierarchy, I can globally adjust the timings of my entire character without having to select each individual controller. I can add three frames in the middle of an action and it will affect all parts of the body. This is especially true when I first begin a scene. After preplanning the scene, I make an initial pass on the poses and alter the timings as necessary.

For example, let's say I created an animation of a character looking to the right and then back to the left. I show the scene to my supervisor or director and he asks for an additional eight-frame pause on screen right. No problem. My character hits the pose at frame 40 and holds that position until frame 48 and then returns back to the right at frame 80. Based on the feedback from the director, I need to have the character pause until frame 54. This is going to add six more frames to the motion and result in the last frame being 86. First, I'll select the character's top node and open the dope sheet. The ALL node is displayed on the left side. This is the top level of my character's hierarchy and includes all objects and keys for the entire character. Next, I select all the keys from frame 48 to the end of the scene and move them down to frame 56. (See Figure 4.7.) This creates the eight-frame pause my director requested.

Original timings   Modified timings   Sliding the keys to frame 54 makes the character pause an additional 6 frames

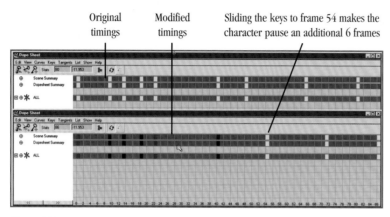

Figure 4.7
The dope sheet pre- and post-move.

This is the big advantage over the curve editor. With one selection, I effectively changed the timing for a character's entire animation. There's no need to select all the transform keys within the curve editor merely to add a few frames. It's a rare occasion that your initial timing decisions will be absolutely correct. The need to shift, add, or delete a few keys is almost inevitable. Using the dope sheet makes this a simple task.

There's also plenty of opportunity to edit the timing on individual controllers of a rig. The functionality is exactly the same as modifying the entire character's timing. It just affects a specific part of the skeleton. A prime example is the opening of a hand. I created poses for the closed hand and the opened hand. (See Figure 4.8.) However, when playing the animation, the fingers are hitting the open pose at the exact same time. Having each finger open at different timings will give the motion a more natural feel.

The closed pose for the hand is currently set on frame 24, and the open pose has a key on frame 32. For this particular example, I want the pointer finger to finish opening at frame 32. This is going to require moving the other fingers back a couple of frames. I've determined that a difference of 2 frames for each finger is going to work best for this situation. That means the ring middle will finish opening at frame 30, the ring finger at frame 28, and the pinky at frame 26. I select the pinky

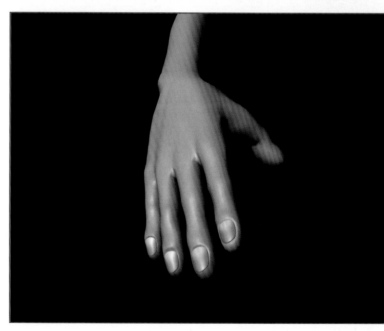

Figure 4.8
The closed and opened pose for the hand.

finger, open the dope sheet, and select the keys at frame 24 and frame 32. I then move those back 6 frames to 18 and 26, respectively. Next, I select the ring finger keys and frames 24 and 32 and move them back to frames 20 and 28, respectively. The middle finger keys get moved to 22 and 30 and the index finger remains at the same keys. The result of this adjustment is a hand with fingers that open at different times. (See Figure 4.9.)

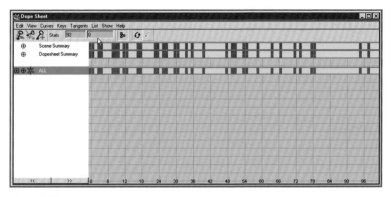

Figure 4.10
The dope sheet of a completed scene. The ALL node is selected and shows the keys for every controller on the character.

Hopefully, you can see the advantages of the dope sheet and will begin using it in your process of animation. It's the fastest way to affect the timing of a scene and provides an easy-to-use interface. Many of the dope sheet functions can be performed using other digital functions; however, they are more laborious and the results are exactly the same. As you'll soon see, those tools have a place in the production process.

Function Curves and the Curve Editor

Based on the preceding section, you might feel that I've discounted the power of the curve editor. That's not the case; I fully respect the power of this utility and routinely use it in my day-to-day process. It has some remarkable capabilities. It's a tool that must be fully understood and routinely used in order to obtain a refined level of animation.

Notice that I said "refined" animation. That's exactly where I place the importance of the curve editor. Its true power is shown when the refinement process begins. After the initial poses and timing have been decided, you must begin to refine the way the software is moving between those poses. The computer has generated a set of interpolations (or in-betweens) between the keys that have been created. The curve editor provides an excellent place to adjust those in-betweens. Understanding how those keys are connected is the first step to controlling them.

So what is interpolation? *Interpolation* is the computer's attempt to fill in the blanks between two key frames. If I select an object and place a key at frame 1 and another at frame 20, the animation software will produce a curve that dictates how the object moves between these two points. (See Figure 4.11.) The computer is essentially filling in the blanks. This is one of the most appealing concepts of computer animation. You no longer need to draw or move a puppet for every single frame. The software, in a sense, produces free motion.

Figure 4.9
The result of the altered timing is a hand that has fingers hitting their open position at different times. This is frame 26. The pinky has fully opened.

This tool is most powerful before the refining of the animation takes over. While in the process of altering the timings of a scene, it's important to keep your key frames in a workable state. By workable state I'm referring to the fact that most keys for all portions of the body are on the same frame. The keys for the entire scene are neatly contained on a small number of frames. Keeping your keys in order helps make the process of retiming much easier. Remember, this is only during the early stages of a scene.

Most scenes will become extremely key intensive before they're finished. Different parts of the body will move at different times. The dope sheet of a complete scene will eventually look like a solid bar of key frames. (See Figure 4.10.) The editing capabilities are still in existence; however, pushing around keys on a scene this complex is going to be pretty confusing.

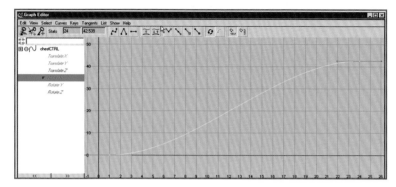

Figure 4.11
The generic ease in/ease out created between two keys.

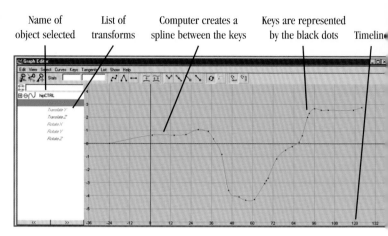

Name of object selected | List of transforms | Computer creates a spline between the keys | Keys are represented by the black dots | Timeline

Figure 4.12
The breakdown of a curve editor.

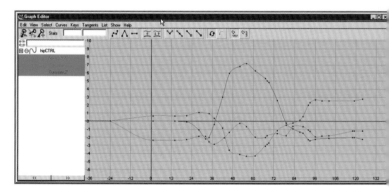

Figure 4.13
Three different curves generated for the X, Y, and Z translations of an object.

This notion sounds great. I can set a few keys, press the render button, and go home, right? I don't think so. That "free" motion is usually the downfall of a 3D animator. Not paying proper attention to the in-betweens of a scene will result in less than stellar animation. This is where the function curve editor becomes an integral part of the work process. Editing the curves will have a tremendous impact on how the software interpolates your poses. If you are looking for the computer to do most of the work, it's very important for you to massage the curves to generate a motion that you really like.

Functionality

Although they often look a bit different, curve editors in various 3D packages are basically the same. They are a graphical representation of the value and location of keys with respect to time. This sounds similar to the dope sheet. However, the major addition of the interpolation curve that links the keys together makes this tool unique.

The editor is composed of several elements, most importantly key frames and curves. Key frames are represented as a dot and the curves as lines. The dot is a representation of an object's location in the scene at a given time. The left side of the graph shows the integer value for the object that has been selected, and the bottom of the graph shows its location along the timeline. When multiple keys are set, a curve is created and connects the keys together. Figure 4.12 shows a diagram of this tool.

Curves are generated when you set a specific transform on an object. For example, I alter my character's head controller at frames 1 and 20. I set a rotation key frame at both locations a curve is generated for each axis of rotation. The standard X, Y, and Z axes will have a specific value at both key frames. (See Figure 4.13.) I could have also generated curves for translation or scaling if desired.

Each key or dot along the curve represents a place to modify your animation. These keys can be adjusted individually or edited as a group. Moving the editor's dots in a vertical fashion alters the relative value of an object. Moving the keys in a horizontal direction modifies the timing of an object.

Make sense? It's fairly straightforward. Understanding the components and how they work is the easy part. Most people can pick up the nuts and bolts of this tool in a short period of time. The real challenge comes in understanding how to use it Knowing how to decipher a function curve takes some practice.

To look at how this tool works, let's take the simple example of a bouncing ball. I created two bouncing balls and opened the Y translation for both bounces. The Y translation corresponds with the up and down motion of the balls. Figure 4.14

Pattern A

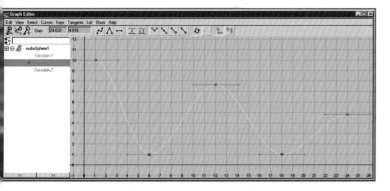

Pattern B

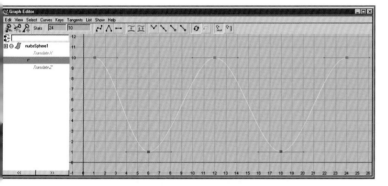

Figure 4.14
The graph for Pattern A is shown above. Pattern B is shown below. The red keys indicate the top of a bounce, and the blue keys occur at the bottom of a bounce.

shows the graphical representation of the two different bounces. Study the two images and see whether you can decipher what the two balls are doing.

Pattern A's curve is representative of a ball that bounces lower and lower as time goes by. By looking at the keys located at the top of the curve, you can see the values decreasing over the course of the action. The height of the ball gets lower each time it leaves the ground. Image B shows a continuous bounce. Its peak returns to the same height after leaving the ground. I can look at these curves and easily decipher what the spheres are doing. I don't even need to glance at the numbers on the left side. It's important not to get bogged down studying the individual value of your keys. The actual value isn't important; it's the relationship that counts.

It's also important to understand what direction the object is moving. If you're having trouble with the relationship between object and curve, look for the translation

that's easiest to decipher. For this example, it is the Y translation of the curve. It is the simplest to comprehend because the graph is showing exactly what the object is doing in the scene. Up is up and down is down. It can become a bit more complicated when looking at other transforms. Our previous example had the y-axis moving in the up and down directions. That places the x-axis from left to right, and the z-axis front to back. Trying to make sense of a curve for the X translation is fairly difficult. The curve suggests the object is moving up or down when in actuality it's moving side to side.

To illustrate this awkward relationship, I'm going to use a sphere with translation set on one axis. I've created a ball moving from screen left to screen right and then back again. This action happens along the x-axis. The ball begins at the extreme left, moves to the extreme right, and then returns to its original position. I set the keys and opened the curve that represents that motion. (See Figure 4.15.) By looking at the curve, you can see the three keys that were set. Notice the relationship between these keys. The first frame is an extreme, the second key is an extreme, and the third key is somewhere in the middle. The curve clearly shows that relationship.

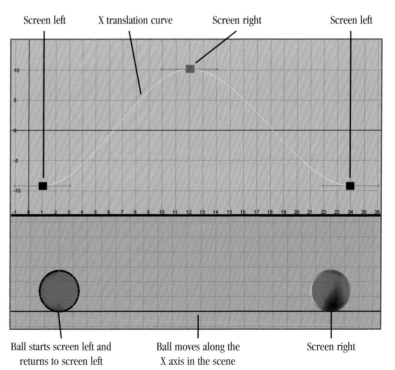

Figure 4.15
The X translation curve for the left to right motion of the sphere.

4. Tools of the Trade

One of the curve editor's most important attributes is the ability to change the amplitude or intensity of an object. Many situations call for pushing or dampening the amount an object moves. As Figure 4.15 shows, the graphic representations created by the curve editor give us a clear picture of the magnitude of an object. By selecting the specific keys, an animator can easily adjust these values.

For example, let's say you are animating a walk. You've begun by setting an up/down value for the hips. After reviewing the animation, it's apparent that the up and down motions are entirely too big; the character looks too bouncy. No problem. Select the hip controller, open the Y translation curve (or whatever axis corresponds with your scene), and select all the keys for the extreme up position in the walk. You can now easily pull those keys down and reduce the amount of up and down in the character. (See Figure 4.16.) As a note, the curve that's shown in this example is only intended to display the editing capabilities of this tool. I'll discuss this area of animation in greater detail in Chapter 14, "Walks."

Original curve   Modified curve

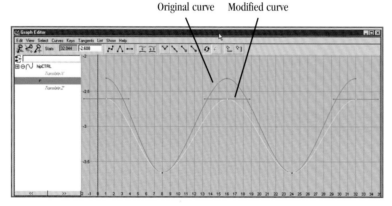

Figure 4.16
The up position of the character's walk is altered by moving the Y translation keys.

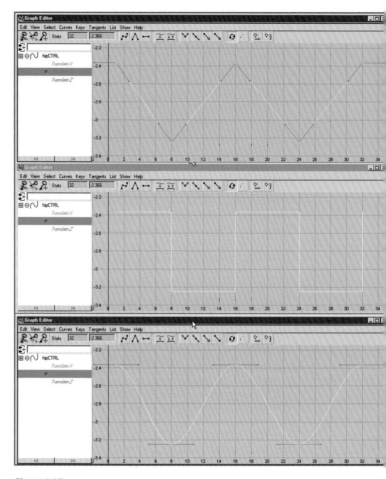

Figure 4.17
A linear curve, a step curve, and a standard (spline) curve.

Up to this point we've been looking at a default curve that the software package Maya creates when two keys are set. It has a general ease in and ease out from each key. Ease in and ease out refers to the gentle transition the curve makes as it leaves a key frame. As I'll discuss in Chapter 6, "Force: Lead and Follow," objects need longer to start and stop moving. A car, for example, builds its speed from a resting state. The theory was built into the generic way computer graphics software interpolates between keys. There are, however, other options.

Most packages have various options for the style of curves they can create. Among the choices are curves with linear interpolation, step interpolation, or the standard or spline version. (See Figure 4.17.) As with most computer graphics tools, these

names change between packages, but the functionality remains the same. These additional settings provide some alternate settings to control how the computer transitions between selected keys.

It's important to understand how to control the various types of curves. The main control point lies in the handles or tangents of the editor. (See Figure 4.18.) These handles appear at every key frame and have a great impact on what the curve between keys actually looks like and how the motion of your object behaves. Most packages allow the handles to be modified in multiple ways. For example, an animator can often affect one tangent while leaving the other at its current position. Or both handles can be altered, keeping their tangency constant.

Handles are the control
points for f curves

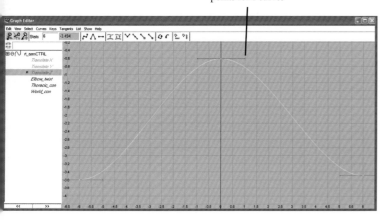

Figure 4.18
The handles have tremendous control on the interpolations between keys.

Here are a few examples of how different tangent settings affect their corresponding curves.

1. **Spline Tangent:** *Ease in, ease out the same amount.* The object begins to slow down as it approaches the key and then eases out as it leaves that key frame. This produces a "soft" action. (See Figure 4.19.)

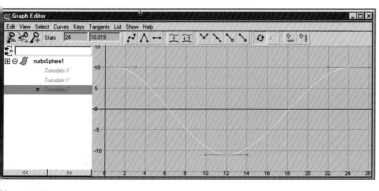

Figure 4.19
The spline tangent or standard curve.

2. **Broken Tangent:** *Fast in, fast out.* The object maintains a constant speed as it approaches the key and then quickly changes speed in the opposite direction. This produces a much sharper action. You might see a curve like this in

a bouncing ball animation. As the ball begins to fall, it accelerates, hits the ground, and quickly rebounds. (See Figure 4.20.)

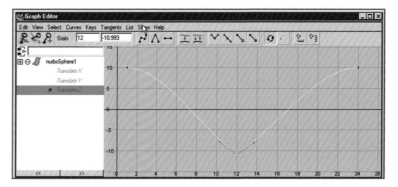

Figure 4.20
The broken tangent curve.

3. **Different Tangent:** *Slow in, fast out.* This tangent has been broken on one side and remains flat on the other. The result is an object moving slowly into a key and then accelerating from it. (See Figure 4.21.)

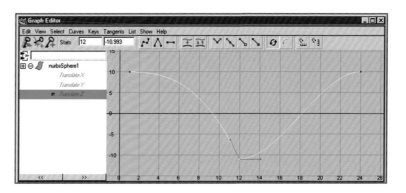

Figure 4.21
Alternate tangents on each side of a key.

Beyond the various editing control the editor provides for adjusting key frame values and altering handle tangency, the editor is a great place to "clean" your animation. The curve that's generated can often have some impurities that are less than desirable. The computer tends to create interpolations that just need a little refinement. It's important to take the time to edit these impurities to obtain a clean motion between keys. The following examples illustrate a few scenarios when this wackiness occurs.

4. Tools of the Trade

1. **The curve bubbles between two keys.** (See Figure 4.22—Image A.) In this example, I've set two keys at the same value. The computer has tried to in-between these keys and produced a bubble in the animation. This can happen when trying to lock a foot to the floor. By selecting the keys on both sides, I can flatten the tangents and produce the straight interpolation as desired. (See Figure 4.22—Image B.)

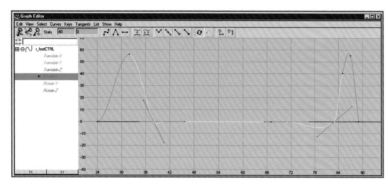

Figure 4.22a
Image A shows the bubble between two keys.

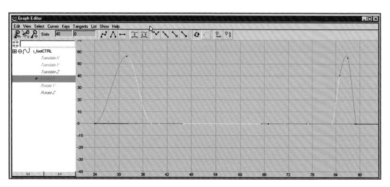

Figure 4.22b
Image B shows the flattened curve.

2. **Spike in the curve.** On many occasions, two key frames have a relationship that the curve editor simply cannot calculate. The computer is trying to interpolate between two points and the result is a spike in the curve. These spikes can cause very strange pops in your animation and often need to be cleaned up. There are, of course, certain occasions when you might actually want this type of spike. You can either break a tangent and adjust the handle accordingly or consider removing the key altogether. (See Figure 4.23.)

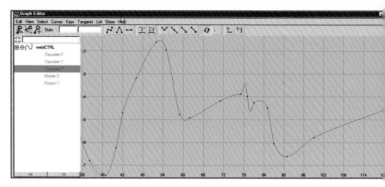

Figure 4.23
The spike in a curve is fixed by breaking the tangents on one side.

3. **Curve overshoot.** This oddity occurs when the computer can't effectively make the spline interpolation between two keys. The curve bends out in an effort to make the transition between two keys. Flattening the tangents easily fixes this problem. (See Figure 4.24.)

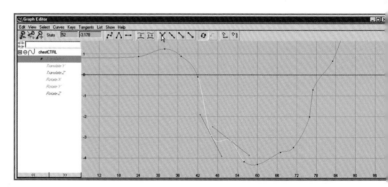

Figure 4.24
An unwanted bend in the curve between two keys.

The concept of a curve editor is straightforward. Actually understanding the computer's chicken scratch is another story. The curves carry a tremendous amount of information, but require some thought when trying to decipher them. It took me awhile to get the optimum benefit from these charts. As I said, your style of animation is going to dictate how integral the curve editor is to your day-to-day function. However, I've yet to see an animator who didn't use this tool to some degree.

Copying and Pasting Keys

Copying and pasting keys are useful techniques that make a routine appearance in my animation process. They provide simple yet effective ways to reuse animation that you've already created. These techniques take an existing key frame and place it in a desired location. You can easily re-create a pose or gesture with a few quick clicks of the mouse. Copying and pasting keys work very similarly to cutting a piece of test and placing it in a new location. The functions can be performed in several places within the interface, thus giving you plenty of flexibility. With animation being such a time-intensive medium, any help in speeding up the process is greeted with open arms.

Copying and pasting the pose of a character has advantages in several situations. You might want a character to look left, then right, and then return to his original position. By selecting that initial pose and copying its values, you can quickly reposition the character by pasting the pose in its new location. In addition, you might want to copy the intricate gesture of a hand pose from one scene to the next. Why spend the time repositioning all five fingers if it's been done before? I use these fairly regularly, but rely on this technique often for one particular task.

This process is most useful when creating a moving hold. A moving hold allows the character to hit an extreme and remain in that position for a number of frames. Those extra frames allow the viewer to gain full understanding of that moment in a scene. It also provides time for secondary items on the character to settle into place. The trick is to not let the digital actor feel lifeless. Copying and pasting keys can give you an excellent foundation to build such an action.

For example, my character needs to hit an extreme pose at frame 40 and hold it for 12 frames. I first set the character's pose at frame 40 and then select the top node of my character and open the dope sheet. By selecting the top node, I can copy the keys for the entire character. I select the bar at frame 40, copy the key, and then paste the same pose at frame 52. The character is now holding the same position for 12 frames.

I'm not done yet. I don't want the animation to remain completely static. I need the character to have a slight drift in order to keep him alive. Why, then, did I copy the pose from frame 40? The pose at frame 40 provides a great foundation for what I need at frame 52. The difference between the poses is fairly minimal, and I can reuse much of the information that's already been created. By tweaking several of the controllers, frame 52 will provide the right amount of drift for the scene.

I use a similar technique to the dope sheet version of the copying and pasting process that doesn't actually involve copying a key but results in something that's very similar. Most 3D packages allow you to scroll through the scene without updating any

keys. In Maya, for example, holding down the right mouse key allows you to move the time slider back and forth while the character remains in the same position.

I can produce the same results in the moving hold example by using the right mouse key function. I'll move the time slider to frame 40 and select all the objects that I'd like to copy keys from. I hold the right mouse key down, and move the time slider to frame 52. The scene has not been updated and my character remains in the same position as frame 40. I can then set keys on the selected objects at frame 52 and start the process of tweaking the pose.

Multiple Views Are a Must

One of the most important things to remember when working on a shot is to utilize the multiple view ports that CG software provides. The top, side, front, perspective, and camera views all provide different angles to view your character's motion. (See Figure 4.25.) Becoming familiar with these different views and routinely looking through them will ensure your character's poses and actions are actually working from both a technical and an artistic standpoint.

The top, side, and front modes provide static views of a character or object along a specific axis. These are great if you're working on action that's particular to one direction. If I'm setting the side-to-side motion of the hips in a walk, I'll use the front view to isolate the z-axis movement. (See Figure 4.26.) If I'm working on the translation forward of that walk, I'll use the side view to isolate the x-axis motion of the character. (See Figure 4.27.) Granted, the axis/view port relationship will

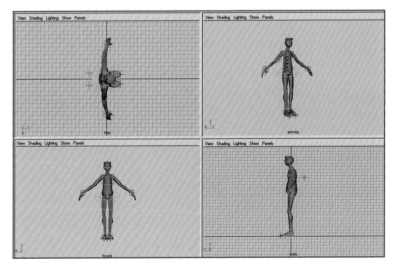

Figure 4.25
The front, side, top, and perspective views of a scene.

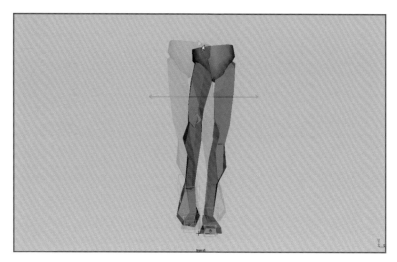

Figure 4.26
The side-to-side motion is easily viewed in the front port.

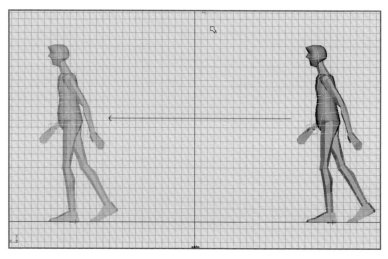

Figure 4.27
The side view works best when modifying the forward translation of a character.

change depending on your software and character setup. The concept, however, remains the same.

In my opinion, the most useful view port is the perspective, camera, or user state. This mode allows you to tumble around the scene and view it from multiple angles. (See Figure 4.28.) This becomes an integral part of setting poses on a character. It allows you to see all parts of the body working in harmony and

Figure 4.28
The perspective window shows the dimensionality of a 3D character and allows you to see the action from many angles.

provides easy access to manipulating all sections of the character. This is necessary for both artistic and technical reasons.

The environment within 3D animation packages is just that: three-dimensional. The parts of the body must be working together in a real-world structural fashion in order to appear and render correctly. This is not only important for a single pose, but also extremely important for the translations between multiple poses.

When animating a scene for features or a commercial, you are usually working toward a specified camera. (Chapter 16, "Getting Started: The Animated Short," provides more detail on this topic.) The end result will be a rendered image from this particular view. That requires the animation poses and staging play directly toward that view; however, the final view can be deceiving.

Look at the two following images. (See Figure 4.29.) Both shots are taken from the camera window and appear to be similar. However, if you view these poses from a different view, it's apparent that they are not the same. (See Figure 4.30.) This becomes crucial when you begin the process of interpolating between poses. The animation from the first pose is going to be much less successful than that of the second pose. I've observed several veteran 2D animators struggle over this notion. The character isn't always in the pose that you think.

Figure 4.29
Two poses that appear identical.

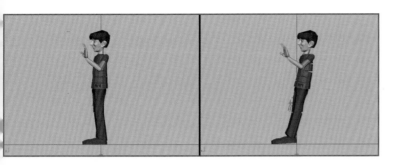

Figure 4.30
The same two poses from a different angle.

As I said, this has technical implications as well. The lights and shadows won't respond correctly to the pose shown in Figure 4.30. In addition, the skinning and cloth of the model could potentially break. These types of mistakes will ultimately be unacceptable when the final renders begin.

Selection Menus

Don't confuse my use of the name selection menus with another function that might bear a similar nomenclature. The concept I'm referring to works the same in the majority of animation software, but often has a completely different name. The tool I'm describing allows you to create a set of levels or menus. Objects are selected and assigned to those layers. The contents can be hidden or unhidden with the click of a button.

The main purpose for using selection menus is to isolate various parts of a character from the other sections of a scene. Working with a complex character in a complex scene can result in an overwhelming amount of information. A common practice would include placing the props of a scene on their own layer. The animator could turn these objects on and off whenever desired. This might increase efficiency for renders or make an animator focus entirely on the character's actions. These layers could also include specific sections of the body. I routinely hide various appendages. Isolating a section of the body can be beneficial in identifying its success or failure.

As I'm progressing through a scene, there inevitably comes a time when I need to focus on one or two parts of the body. For example, I might be working on a character's jump and just can't nail the intricate rotations and translations involved in the hips. In addition, my legs pushing from the ground and landing back again are just not reading that well. I have some general poses created for the upper body, but because the hips are driving the scene, it's important to make sure they are working first.

The solution is to create a layer with all the contents of the upper body. I simply select all portions of the upper body and assign them to a layer. I can then hide and unhide this section whenever needed. This allows me to concentrate on the motion of the lower body. I render, adjust, and then re-render many times looking at the lower body. I can take this an additional step and assign the arms to their own layer. I might work out the kinks in the lower body and then add the torso and head to the scene and see how they are working. You can essentially create layers for any section that you'd like to isolate. I even create one for the head when working on facial. This allows me to quickly hide the other portions of the character and concentrate only on the face.

It's important to remember that you must continue to look at all parts of the body. The scene cannot be successful without all poses and gestures working together. I generally use the preceding methods when trying to work out a physical problem within my animation, and I apply the utility much less when working on an acting problem. However, when I do use layers, I constantly turn them on and off. I want to make absolutely sure that any pose changes still work with the overall feeling of my animation.

The technique of selection menus is a breeze. Setting them is fast and simple and can greatly increase the speed at which you work. It's one of the first steps I take when starting a scene. They are a staple of my workday and provide a clarity that's absolutely necessary to completing a scene.

Overlaying Animation

Imagine spending five days on a piece of animation getting the motion just right. You're extremely happy with the performance and ready for a nice, relaxing weekend. The director walks in around 4:00 p.m. on Friday and takes a look. He thinks it's great, but would like one change. "How about delivering the same actions with a 90-degree turn in the waist, and, oh yeah, let's get that done before you leave tonight." Welcome to the world of animation and your new best friend: the overlaying technique.

Layering animation is becoming increasingly popular. The ability to make a major change in an action without destroying the intricacies of the motion can be quite refreshing. It's particularly useful when an animation is key-frame intensive and editing function curves or readjusting poses is too laborious. It provides a quick remedy to an otherwise time-intensive situation. As with many of the utilities I'll discuss, this technique has multiple names. Don't confuse this technique with the "layering approach to animation." I'll discuss that, along with other approaches to animation in Chapter 5, "Approaches to Animation."

Take the example of a character waving his hand. A request is made to have the wave occur higher above the character's head. The process is quite simple: With the wave created, a new layer is built to accept adjustments to the original action. I can modify the character's position on the new layer and preview the results. If satisfactory, those actions can be merged with the original action.

Trajectories of Objects

As an object moves through space, it travels in a specific path. The parts of a character's body, the motion of a space ship, or the tip of a dinosaur's tail all have a trajectory associated with them. As you'll see in Chapter 11, "Arcs and In-Betweens," these paths have a great deal to do with the success or failure of your animation. Fortunately, many of the popular CG packages provide you with ways to visualize and edit those paths.

If you're lucky enough to be working with a piece of software that has a trajectory function already built into the interface, this process is easy. 3ds max, for example, has a dedicated button that's used to display the trajectory of an object. You can select any part of an object or a character and click the display trajectory option to display the curve of the object. It is visible in all views and conveniently displays the key frames associated with that object. (See Figure 4.31.)

Editing this type of trajectory is easy. By selecting the keys that appear along the curve, you can affect the path of the object. You can sculpt and mold the curve to obtain the desired motion. In addition, physically moving the character will result in the trajectory updating.

Path Animation

At some point during your animation career, you will need to use path animation. Although this process isn't on the top of my daily user list, at times it can be extremely powerful. The simplicity of affecting a motion by editing a curve can be a welcome change. Path animation inherently has a visual nature to it and allows you to easily modify an object's course of travel by adjusting select points along the path. Be careful, however, and use this method in instances when it makes the most sense. That patch can take control of a scene; therefore, it's important to keep the control in your hands.

The process of path animation involves the assigning of an object to travel along a designated path. (See Figure 4.32.) This path is a curve that's been created by you and can take on just about any form desired. Choose an object to travel on that path and you're ready to go. The object and path are selected in succession and constraints are set. The object is now restricted to follow the designated curve.

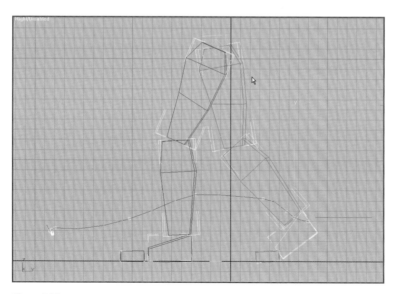

Figure 4.31
The curve represents the object's path of action and the tick marks represent the key frames for that object.

Figure 4.32
Rocky used path animation to travel in a circle around the room in the shot from *The Adventures of Rocky and Bullwinkle*. I found path animation to be extremely valuable in this situation. Copyright © 2002 by Universal Studios. Courtesy of Universal Studios Publishing Rights, a Division of Universal Studios Licensing, Inc. All rights reserved.

The path provides a distinct orientation, distance, and direction for the object to travel. The options associated with the tool let you dictate which transforms and axes stay on the curve. The path can be adjusted at any time resulting in the object changing its line of action. In addition, start times, end times, and duration can all be adjusted, thus affecting the speed and velocity at which the object moves down the path.

I find this process to be useful when dealing with flying objects. Creating a ship traveling through space, a bird banking across the sky, or a character flying on a broom all lend themselves to situations that might involve path animation. (See Figure 4.33.) It provides a unique method to roughing in this type of motion and usually has enough freedom to layer in the additional details of a character's or an object's motion.

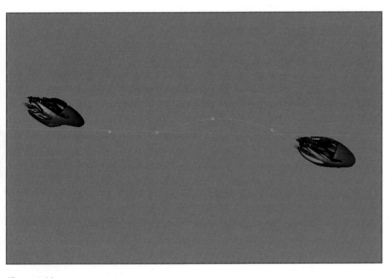

Figure 4.33
A ship traveling across the sky and the path it's attached to.

Notice that I mentioned the "freedom" of adding details. When using the process, it's important to make sure you aren't limiting the editing capabilities of a motion. Don't let the path take over. It's similar to the computer's process of in-betweening. You can get a lot of motion for free when using paths, but free isn't always good. Just because it's moving, doesn't mean it's good. Make sure to keep the creative ability in your hands.

Counter Animation

Counter animation is less of a tool and more of a technique. However, I'm including this concept within this chapter because it fits into the overall picture of computer-specific procedures. It doesn't fall into the fundamentals category due to its inception in the digital era. Traditional animators never had to consider this when working on a scene; digital animators aren't that lucky.

The notion of counter animation involves moving portions of the body in the opposite direction of other sections. Confused? I understand; it's a little tricky. Let's take a simple example. I want the character to turn toward the right. However, I don't want the hips, shoulders, and head to all turn at the same time. As you'll see in Chapter 6, "Force: Lead and Follow," everything in the human body moves at different rates. If I select the hip node of my character and rotate it to the right, the shoulders and head follow accordingly. (See Figure 4.34.) This results in a stiff motion because all parts would be hitting the pose at exactly the same time.

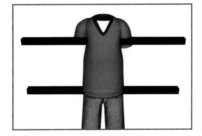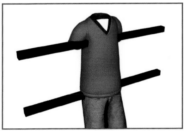

Figure 4.34
The character facing forward and turning to the right. All sections are moving at the same time.

To create a more believable turn, I need the shoulders and head to follow behind. For this example, the hips are going to lead the action. I set the starting pose at frame 1 and the second pose at frame 30. I move the cursor to frame 15 and counter animate the shoulders and head back toward the first pose. (See Figure 4.35.) This simply involves rotating the shoulders and head in the opposite direction from the hips. I actually move the head farther back so that it follows behind the shoulders. This will be a good start, but the motion will definitely require some more tweaking.

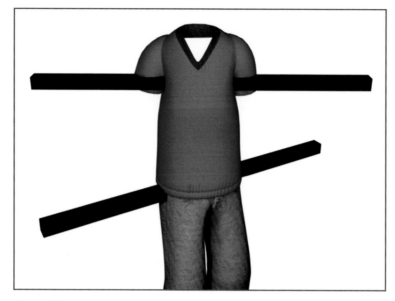

Figure 4.35
The hips are rotated to the right while the shoulders and head get rotated back toward the initial pose.

The idea of counter moving an object is directly associated with the style of character setup you have the opportunity to work with. Some setups are counter-animation intensive. Personally, I don't care for this style of skeleton; I'd rather have a character with independent control over sections of the body. However, different facilities have varying opinions about which method is the correct one. Needless to say, most skeletal systems require some form of countering to correctly solve a scene.

This set of tools provides you with a solid foundation in which to animate creatures, characters, and objects. It by no means represents the complete set of utilities and techniques available to you. That list is extremely expansive. However, these tools have made their way into my production process during the years of working on features, commercials, and games. They're integral to controlling the complex environment that digital animation creates. Understand the tools and you'll be much closer to obtaining the motions you desire.

chapter 5
Approaches to Animation

Artists' approaches to animation are about as varied as the personalities of the artists themselves. Ask an animator how he works, and you'll probably get a jumbled response full of comments like, "it just works" or "I'm not sure how that part goes." Every person who takes on this craft uses his knowledge to produce animation in a unique and special way. However, most of these methods stem from popular approaches and are built on foundations that can be explained.

The following sections take a look at the popular digital procedures. You'll probably find that your final method of working will involve various parts of one or more of the defined methods. Most animators work in a Frankenstein-like manner that takes small parts from several of the animation approaches. In addition, two scenes might require a different path to get the desired motion. I routinely alter my approach to better fit the required action.

As the author and a working animator, I obviously have a specific approach toward creating my scenes. This doesn't mean that I don't see the benefit of other methods of working. My intent is to provide a well-rounded chapter that provides positive and negative aspects to each approach. However, don't be surprised if my opinion slips in now and then; I've spent too many days discussing these approaches not to chime in from time to time.

Layering

The layering approach is popular among many animators in the CG industry. It dates back to the early days of Pixar and the groundbreaking short film *Luxo Jr.* (See Figure 5.1.) John Lasseter and company devised a procedure to make the digital animation more efficient, effective, and easy to edit. His paper titled "Principles of Traditional Animation Applied to 3D Computer Animation" opened the door for other artists to see how a traditionally trained artist applied his knowledge to the new set of tools. The approach gathered much support and spawned a

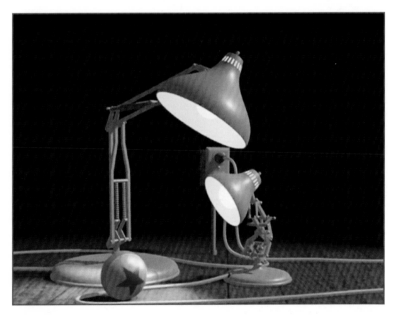

Figure 5.1
The forward motion was the first layer set in *Luxo Jr.* © Pixar.

whole new way of thinking about a shot. Artists have taken this procedure and molded and modified its foundation to suit their individual style of working.

Layering works best in a hierarchical-based model. Most character models are built using this form of bones system. The skeleton has a root node that controls the entire body and a number of subcontrollers that govern the various sections of the body. (A more formal explanation of this system is explained in Chapter 4,

"Tools of the Trade.") This form of organization enables you to control the parts of the character that need to be moved without disturbing the other parts of the body. By taking advantage of this order, you can isolate important parts of an animation without being distracted by the minute details. (See Figure 5.2.)

Process Specifics

The key to working in the layering method is working the parts of the body from generic to specific. Many of the decisions about timing, staging, and emotion can be displayed with a few keys in the proper locations. When using this approach, you should approach the scene by working from the broad actions before moving on to the detailed motions. There's no sense in working out the intricacies of a wrist motion if the timing of the hips is going to change. Let's look at an example.

This scene involves a simple character jumping over a box that's moving from screen left to screen right. The timing that's chosen will have a great deal to do with the attitude and personality of the character. If he's a large, lazy man, the jump will be much more labored. If he's a young, athletic type, the jump will come very easily. I can capture the essence of either type of character by working with the root level and setting some basic keys on that layer or level of the character.

For this example, the box timing has been set, and the character needs to correspond with those timings. Start with the root node of your character to set the general timing of the jump. Most models have a hip or center of gravity control that will affect the entire character when moved. I set several keys on the hip controller. They will control the anticipation before the jump, the high point in the jump, the landing, and the recovery. At this point, I'm only concerned with this level of the character. (See Figure 5.3.)

Figure 5.2
The keys are being set on the main controller of the character. Details such as the fingers will be addressed at a later stage of the animation.

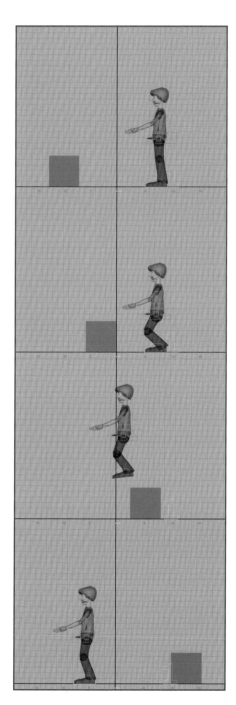

When I'm happy with the timing of this hip node, I begin to work outward from the body. In this example, the hip is driving the action. I move on to the shoulders and refinement of the feet. When that level is complete, it is time to address the wrists and head. I work my way from general to specific making sure the previous level or layer is satisfactory.

Pros

Layering works great with digital animation. It offers the greatest editing capabilities of all the processes. You don't have to wade through massive amounts of curves and key frames to alter a particular portion of their motion. Key frames are set only where they're needed and not for the entire character as the pose-to-pose method suggests. They can isolate that particular layer and address the individual controller for that part of the body. You might need a tremendous amount of keys on the hand, but only need a few on the hips. In addition, you are building a strong foundation before addressing the specific details. If the hip motion is successful, you can set keys on the shoulders and hips and be confident that the underlying action won't change. You wouldn't build a skyscraper and start with the top story. Creating that strong foundation is essential in making this approach successful.

Cons

The only negative to this approach is that an animator, a director, or a supervisor must be able to visualize the action you are trying to create. Those reviewing the motions must be able to see the direction you are going without seeing a complete set of poses. You're not going to deliver a piece of motion with fully fleshed out details. Directors sometimes have trouble viewing this style of animation and commenting on whether they like the action. On many occasions I've heard a director comment that he just can't tell if the animation is working. "Keep going" usually follows, and two days later a more refined animation is presented for comment. If the motion isn't suitable at that point, you have wasted two days going down the wrong path. It takes the trained eye of an experienced animator to decipher the rough stages of this approach.

Pose-to-Pose

The pose-to-pose methodology dates back to the early Disney days. Animators at that renowned facility generally chose this as one of the two approaches they took toward completing a motion. Animators concentrated on the main poses or keys in a shot. These key poses created the foundation of a scene. They carefully considered which drawings best told the action or emotion of a character. Those drawings were given a timing breakdown and handed to another artist to fill in the gaps. His job was to connect the animator's drawing and give the character a sense of fluidity as he moved across the screen. This method proved to be extremely beneficial and still remains a staple in the 2D community. (See Figure 5.4.)

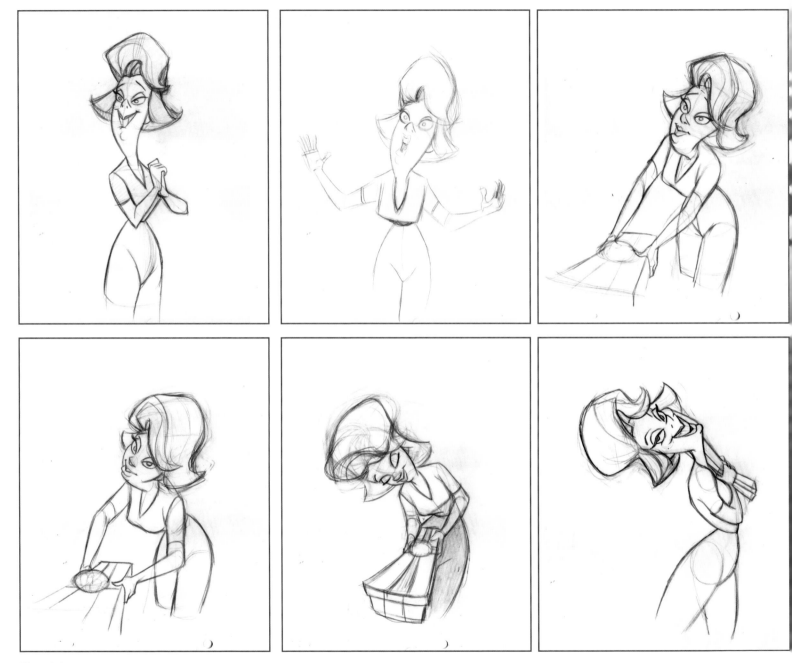

Figure 5.4
The key poses from a scene by Jim van der Keyl.

Along with many other proven techniques, this process has made its way into the 3D world. As with most things relating to animation, artists draw on the experiences of seasoned veterans. Many of those artists are now working as 3D animators and have brought their methods to the digital workplace. These techniques translate fairly well. The main difference is the absence of the in-betweener. The computer has now taken that role.

Process Specifics

As the title of this method suggests, the main thing to consider when working with this method is the individual poses or keys. These keys are going to provide the framework for your animation. By choosing this approach it's imperative that you are absolutely sure where the scene is going. A significant amount of time will be spent creating the right poses for a scene. Without the proper planning, you can spend a great deal of time going down the wrong path. It's very important to have a strong idea of the action and timing of the scene before you begin. Taking the time to pre-think the animation will ensure its clarity and can save you headaches. (See Figure 5.5.)

Although generating thumbnails for a scene isn't required, it can definitely be beneficial. Remember, these drawings are simply to generate ideas for the artist actually animating the shot. They don't have to be seen by anyone else. As long as you can decipher which direction he is headed, a successful thumbnail has been generated. I've drawn many thumbnails that resemble a kindergartener's work. However, I was able to follow the scratches and pose my scene accordingly. (See Chapter 16, "Getting Started: The Animated Short," for more info on preparing to animate a scene.)

> Wayne Gilbert offers an excellent book, *Simplified Drawing for Planning Animation*, for learning some basic planning skills. It's available through his Web site at http://www.anamie.com. (See Figure 5.6.)

Figure 5.5
The animators planning sketches on the top and the resulting poses on the bottom.

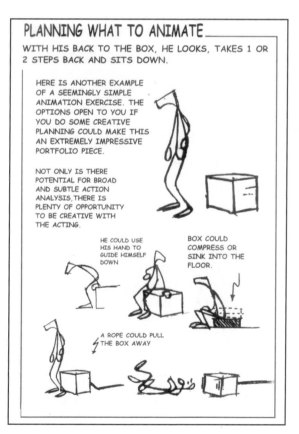

Figure 5.6
A page from Wayne's book, *Simplified Drawing for Planning Animation*.

The next step in this process is creating the first set of keys. These should be the most important poses in the shot. One pose per emotional state should be able to convey the entire idea of the scene. If your character is going from happy to sad, you need a happy pose and a sad pose. Look at any single Norman Rockwell painting or drawing and you'll be able to visualize an entire story from each character's single pose. If you can achieve that with a pose or two, then you're way ahead with your scene already. You should also be conscious of both staging and silhouette at this state. Poses should read as clearly as possible, and the character should be performing in a manner that best solves the scene.

When a pose is set, it's important to create keys for everything related to the character at that particular frame. The theory here is that each pose is the same as a single drawing in traditional animation. The idea is to place everything where you mean for it to be placed at that frame in the scene. This means incorporating overlap, follow-through, and all the other animation principles as you're setting the initial poses. Part of learning the art of animating is learning how to incorporate all the principles as you go. You can't add overlap to a drawing, and you shouldn't add it to a CG pose later either. Even when setting the initial extremes, your poses should imply the overlap and motion that you will be flushing out later.

Using step curves during this part of the process can make viewing your poses much easier. The scene should have only a few key frames created. The computer's generic in-betweening can be a huge distraction. Setting the curves to pop between poses allows you to clearly focus on the main storytelling points. A rendered version would show a pose holding for a designated number of frames and then popping to the next pose in a matter of one frame.

There's an entire stage of the scene that needs to be addressed at this point: breakdowns. After the key poses are worked out and you feel you've achieved a clear representation of the performance you're going for, it's time to focus on the movement to back it up. Breakdowns serve that purpose. These additional poses begin to indicate arcs, slow ins and outs, squash and stretch, timing, and overlap. The motion really begins to take shape during this phase.

After the scene is broken down, it's time to switch to a spline-based curve and begin to interpolate between keys. For traditional animators, this would be the point equivalent to when you hand the scene off to an in-betweener. There will obviously be some clean-up at this stage. The computer won't always generate the desired motion between poses and some altering of the curves or additional keys will need to be taken care of.

Pros

One of the main benefits of this approach is the strength of poses you can display. Other methods can place the emphasis of a motion on other aspects of animation and let the level of poses slide a bit. However, with this approach, it's hard to make that mistake. You should be taking ample time to ensure each part of the body is correctly positioned. He is looking at that frame as though it might be the cover art for the latest issue of the popular CG magazine. If done correctly, the important beats of a scene are clearly defined. The animation is well thought out and the key positions work well as whole.

This approach definitely lends itself to adjusting the timing of a shot. Just as the veteran 2D animators can shoot their drawings with a different number of frames between keys, the digital environment makes it extremely easy to move the timings of poses around. The character's poses are neatly contained at intervals along the shot and altering their location in time is effortless. Let's say you have set keys on frames 1, 5, 10, and 20. You find the pause between frames 10 and 20 is a bit too long. Making the change only involves moving entire key sets at frame 20 back 4 frames. Obviously, you would have made your best guess at the timing before starting the scene. However, minor changes should be expected. Having this flexibility is a great convenience. (See Figure 5.7.)

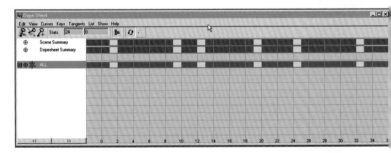

Figure 5.7
The keys are neatly arranged during the early stages of the pose-to-pose file. Here's a snapshot of the dope sheet from an animation file.

Cons

The most unappealing thing about this approach is the editing capabilities. I spent several days debating this notion with a co-worker at Sony. He was a diehard proponent of the pose-to-pose approach. His days as a 2D animator had greatly influenced his approach, and had helped him develop into a superb animator. My argument toward his award-winning approach was the ability to change his scene at the drop of a hat. As is customary with many animation and effects productions, directors routinely ask for scenes to be completely reworked. Not just a nip and tuck but a complete redo.

5. Approaches to Animation

This is never a pleasant task. However, it becomes much more painful after you have spent blood, sweat, and tears making a series of the finest poses the industry has ever seen. Keys have been set on the majority of controllers and body parts. The scene is littered with keys that will need re-posing given one of those drastic changes. You might be forced into a situation of removing complete poses and rethinking the scene. That initial investment of creating a beautiful pose is wasted.

The amount of in-between action you must create adds to the time-intensive nature of this process. Setting a complex pose at the designated frames to accurately portray an action can result in the computer's interpolations being less than stellar. As I'll discuss in Chapter 11, "Arcs and In-Betweens," the computer looks for the fastest means of translating between keys. A series of very different poses can cre-

ate havoc for a software package to correctly decipher the intended arcs and paths of action for the character. You will need to spend significant time working on the motions between your main keys.

As with most of these methods, there are both positive and negative aspects about approaching a scene in this manner. Its roots are obviously traced to the people who revolutionized the art of animation. It's a time-tested technique in the traditional animation world and has made a significant mark for many artists now working in the digital world. Several of the most talented animators I've worked with live and die by this approach. They've been successful thus far and have created some memorable scenes. (See Figure 5.8.) Spend the proper time planning your shot, and you too can take advantage of this popular approach.

Figure 5.8
Stuart meets his new parents. Animated by Todd Wilderman. "STUART LITTLE" © 2002 Columbia Pictures Industries, Inc. All Rights Reserved. Courtesy of Columbia Pictures.

5. Approaches to Animation

Straight-Ahead

The straight-ahead approach was the second of the Disney methodologies used for animating a scene. Its title is an excellent indication of what you do. You start with the first drawing in a scene and move straight-ahead with the next drawing until the motion is complete. You know what action is needed to create a successful scene and you push forward until that motion is completed. The results are often pleasant. Motions have a sense of spontaneity that the pose-to-pose approach can't produce.

Process Specifics

This approach works best with physical actions. Put a character through a series of steps, stumbles, and crashes and you'll probably want to consider this method of animating your scene. It's extremely difficult to plan this sort of motion. If you are successful at planning it, there's a great chance that you'll change your course of action while creating the scene. A physical motion of this sort will inevitably call for the motion to slightly change. Working straight-ahead enables you to take advantage of these alterations and work them into the scene.

I encountered a situation while working on a series of shots in *Episode 1* where the sequence involved Jar Jar getting his foot caught in the entrails of a broken droid. The director was looking for a panicked action that put Jar Jar in a very awkward state. The action had a series of stumbles and an overall tone of unbalance as he desperately tried to free his tangled foot from the mass of wires. (See Figure 5.9.)

When the shot was assigned to me, I spent several hours thinking and planning what the character might do. I even rigged up a dummy droid and tied a small piece of rope to my ankle. (See Figure 5.10.) It was a simple configuration, but it gave me an idea of what it feels like to have something stuck on your foot. Video reference ensued as I began to work out the various motions. It was difficult to choreograph the entire shot. It ran about 300 frames and I found it difficult to re-create the motion on a consistent basis. The straight-ahead approach lent itself toward making various adjustments while I was setting keys.

Figure 5.9
Jar Jar tries to free himself from the captive reins of a fallen droid. COURTESY OF LUCASFILM LTD. Star Wars: Episode I – The Phantom Menace © Lucasfilm Ltd. & ™. All rights reserved. Used under authorization. Unauthorized duplication is a violation of applicable law.

Figure 5.10
The rough model I built to help my reference efforts.

This method is similar to animating in the stop-motion medium. You are setting extensive amounts of keys to work the character through the scene. Details such as overlap and secondary action are built into each pose. You work through the scene and must continually reassess where the character is going. As I stated earlier, this method is geared toward physical actions and requires a heightened physical effort from you. That reassessment involves and requires you to get out of your chair on a regular basis.

In Figure 5.9, I used the physical approach on a daily basis. I animated for a few minutes and then stood up and began acting and assessing the next action in the scene. Routinely, I worked the character into a pose or position that was not planned. I left the character in its awkward pose and jumped out of my seat to figure out what came next. The video camera was always on standby to provide reference if needed.

Pros

This method has some great advantages. The spontaneity it generates can create some extremely successful results. You can feel your way through a scene and alter the conclusion if you desire. In addition, complex motions can be pared down to mini-actions that are easier to resolve. I don't need to determine the entire logistics of having a character spin on one leg and then roll backward before standing

up. After an initial investment of time to pre-think the action, I can work out the details in smaller chunks. I'm fully aware of where I want the character to be during any portion of the scene. In addition, I've taken the time to ensure the direction of animation is going to solve the scene in an interesting way. I can take these ideas to a scene file and begin putting the character through its paces making minor adjustments as I work through the shot.

Cons

The most difficult part about working in this method is the inability to quickly edit your scene. This approach will inevitably involve many key frames. The keys from the scene above looked like a United States roadmap when everything was said and done. (See Figure 5.11.) I remember getting very close to finishing the shot. I worked several weeks on the series of four shots and was waiting for the final approval from the director. That's when the roof caved in. The editor wanted ten frames taken from the middle of the scene. He altered the timing of the cuts on his digital editing system and decided this change would make the scene play a little faster. Those ten frames nearly put me in a pine box. Removing them wasn't a matter of just sliding a few poses around in the dope sheet. I had a mountain of things to alter and the straight-ahead approach I'd taken was now paying an unwanted visit.

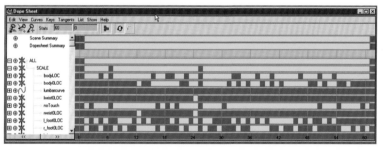

Figure 5.11
A scene can be very key-intensive when using the straight-ahead approach. The dope sheet shown here is a complete mess compared to the pose-to-pose one from above.

In the end, the shot turned out close to what I'd envisioned. With the exception of the difficult nature of changing the motion, the scene progressed nicely. The straight-ahead approach generated a host of ideas that never would have seen the light of day. The process lends itself toward this type of action and proved to be a worthy companion.

5. Approaches to Animation

Give Me the Combo

Like most animators, I developed my own style of animating a scene over the years. Some of the decisions about my approach were made out of necessity. Others arose from my particular skill set. The following paragraphs are a brief explanation about how I choose to animate a scene. I'm not insinuating that it's the right way to work. However, I think it's important that you understand you aren't limited to the previously mentioned theories. Take your skill set and your production situation and develop a method that works for your scenario.

My animation experience began as a stop-motion artist. I primarily practiced that technique while studying at The University of Southern California. I enjoyed the

hands-on approach of crafting models and sets and loved cutting together actual film stock. (See Figure 5.12.) As you might expect, stop-motion works in the straight-ahead approach. There's a certain amount of prep time involved with this approach to ensure that the camera and the character are in sync. I acted out my scene, broke down the timings, and then roughly moved the puppet through the scene checking camera, lights, and props. This production cycle continued for two years until I made the switch to CG.

When I was first given a 3D model, I was a bit uncertain about how to handle it. Everything prior to that time had involved grabbing the puppet and painstakingly moving it frame by frame. I began animating in CG just as I had done with the

Figure 5.12
One of the characters from the stop-motion film *Switchback*.

armature and foam latex. It seemed like a great plan. I didn't have to worry about bumping the set and ruining my animation, and the thought of a light blowing out during a shoot never crossed my mind. CG was going to solve all my production problems.

It was good until I had to edit one of my animations. Stop-motion didn't have any editing capabilities. If a shot didn't work, you redid it. This was obviously my thought pattern as I proceeded to set entirely too many key frames on my first few 3D tests. It was similar to editing motion capture. I had to rethink my method without compromising the skills I'd learned. One of my classmates took a class

from Pixar animators and heard about the layering approach. He gave me a few pointers and I went off to develop a hybrid technique that's been part of my process ever since. (See Figure 5.13.)

Process Specifics

As I stated earlier, the layering approach lends itself very well to digital technology. It cuts down on excessive keys and provides you with an easier means to edit a scene. I began to work this method into my scenes. I first planned the shot with some video reference or quick thumbnail drawings. I had a good sense about the timings that were needed and made a note of those on my simple drawings. Then,

Figure 5.13
A shot I animated from *Rocky and Bullwinkle* that used the combo approach to animation. Copyright © 2002 by Universal Studios. Courtesy of Universal Studios Publishing Rights, a Division of Universal Studios Licensing, Inc. All rights reserved.

as the layering approach states, I began with the hip node and worked the basic blocking of the shot out. The character either remained in a fairly generic pose or took on a few rough poses. This provided the framework for the next step of my process.

After hitting those generic beats, I like to make a second pass that starts to work in a more refined set of poses and build in some of the lead and follow portions of the character's actions. This is where the stop-motion and straight-ahead influence comes in. It was important for me to show some of the physical aspects of lead and follow in the shot during the early stages. Many animators set a few main poses as if the character is a rigid doll. They then rethink the actions of the body and begin the process of breaking up the timings. I don't recommend setting a bunch of poses and then offsetting the various parts of the body to break up the actions. I'd rather think about the actions as they occur and vary the amount of lead and follow based on that particular motion. I'll hit those poses when I feel it's necessary to explain my intentions of the scene and present it for review.

Pros

At this stage, my keys are fairly light and editing or changing the scene can happen with the smallest of efforts. I tried to get the most information into the scene with the fewest number of keys. My character is hitting all the necessary beats and has a decent sense of timing. A viewer should be able to look at the scene and tell exactly what the character is doing. However, a few things are still missing.

Cons

Although the scene may have the general beats and timing, my first pass usually doesn't have the most refined poses. I'm definitely conscious of the staging of the character, but I often give the scene a set of generic poses. As I said earlier,

approaches often develop out of necessity and personal skills. When working in visual effects, necessity often calls for a host of changes. By not spending a tremendous amount of time working a specific pose to completion, I can push through the scene and show my intentions to the director. If he likes the general direction, I can go back and spice up the poses. I'd rather spend the time refining something I'm fairly certain will make it into the shot. Additionally, my 2D skills aren't as refined as many traditionally trained artists. I need to work and refine my poses in a 3D setting to make them really stand out.

This approach isn't intended to discount the need for strong poses. Giving a character interesting and strong poses is one of the main qualifications of generating a successful scene. That quality separates the great animators from the mediocre ones. It's still very important to my process, but it happens at a different time than other approaches. Having spent the majority of my career animating for special effects, the overwhelming need to change a scene pushed me in this direction. Had I been trained in a facility that was mainly composed of animators, my method might have taken a different turn. In any case, the important thing to remember is to develop your approach based on the situation.

One of the most confusing aspects of animating on the computer is how to approach your animation. Deciding on a methodology is crucial. It sets the tone for every shot an animator tackles. Whether you favor a traditional approach or prefer a technique that was developed primarily for a computer graphics situation, find a method that fits you and continually work to improve it.

chapter 6
Force: Lead and Follow

> **Force (n)**
> The power, strength, or energy that somebody or something possesses.

Forces exist in every aspect of nature. From the blowing of the wind to the internal workings of a living creature, force plays an integral part in the behavior of every object that interacts with it. The construction, material, and emotion determine how varying forces respond to an object. A good animator will always evaluate these forces and take the time to clearly show their influence within a scene. I have stated several times the importance of creating believable characters. A big portion of that believability lies in giving characters a true sense of physicality. The viewer must believe that the character has a sense of weight and is responding in accordance to the laws of the surrounding environment.

I'm not suggesting that characters need to be photo-real at every moment. The ability to break rules is one of the unique and appealing aspects of animation. You've seen a character hang in mid-air, free from the laws of gravity, and then suddenly shoot down to the canyon floor. (See Figure 6.1.) The audience suspends its expectations about real-world physics due to the cartoon style. The viewer will forgive the extra beat as the character suspends, because it knows the situation is a fictional one. Although these occurrences are a part of the make-believe world of animation, they should not be overused. The rules cannot be repeatedly broken or the audience will lose perspective about what objects actually are. A fat character, in most situations, needs to move in a manner that the audience expects.

The bottom line is that physics are important to the success of animation. Liberties can be taken, but the animator must understand how to give a character real-world sensibilities. Force is at the foundation of this principle. Understanding its

Figure 6.1
Physics are being temporarily suspended as the character steps off a cliff's edge.

presence in both characters and inanimate objects is essential in producing successful animation.

I was introduced to the concept of forces in animation when I first began working, and a paper was circulating between some colleagues of mine. This short text outlined a new way of thinking with regard to how and why characters move, and suggested that animators not concentrate so much on form; rather, consider the forces that were involved in a particular action. An animator who just draws forms gets a series of lifeless images, whereas the animator who pays attention to thrust will have a figure with vitality. Although much of this argument originally pertained to the hand-drawn method of animation, its concept can still have a dramatic effect on the quality of animation in any medium.

If you are anything like I was early in my career, this concept probably seems a bit obscure. It actually took me several weeks of really thinking about this notion before it actually sunk in. Visualizing the forces was key in the understanding process. By studying a few motions, I was able to make a clear connection between specific forces and the effect they had on a character.

Take, for example, the force of a driving wind and its impact on a small tree. Wind, for the most part, blows horizontally. As the wind travels along that axis, it applies a certain amount of force to the tree. That tree reacts accordingly. The lower section is much more stiff and has less of a bend while the upper branches have a much greater range of motion. This particular force is one-directional and fairly easy to visualize.

Another example is that of a ball being kicked, in which we can see a more directional and specific force. The amount of inertia generated from the swinging foot will have an immediate impact on the distance the ball travels. In addition, the angle at which the foot contacts the ball is related to the trajectory that object will travel.

These examples are only a small sample of how forces are at work in everyday life. Understanding their origin and affect on surrounding objects is critical to fully realizing the performance of your character. Keep in mind that an artist cannot be successful by merely understanding physics in animated characters. Creating a believable character from a physical standpoint is just one of the pieces of the puzzle. It is, however, an important piece. As soon as an artist can get the physical aspects under control, he can begin the long road to creating emotion and feelings within his characters.

Initiating versus Reactionary

It is important not to lump all forces into a single category. For this discussion, I will divide types of forces into two categories: reactionary and initiating. These two groups comprise the entire set of motions from both a physical and an emotional standpoint. Animators who incorporate these forces into their scene will give the viewer a much clearer picture of *why* characters are performing a specific action, and the characters will perform that action in a believable manner.

Understanding and controlling both types of forces is critical to the success of a scene. An animator must spend the time to make accurate assessments of what

Figure 6.2
Bullwinkle gets violently shaken from the plane crash. Copyright © 2002 by Universal Studios. Courtesy of Universal Studios Publishing Rights, a Division of Universal Studios Licensing, Inc. All rights reserved.

forces are at work before attempting to re-create them. Making these decisions will result in a more efficient implementation of a shot. The guesswork of where a character is going will be completely removed.

Reactionary

As the name suggests, reactionary forces occur in response to a specific energy. An object remains dormant until something acts upon it. This external force produces an action. The resulting motions are physically-based and have a direct correlation to the force from the object that has affected them. A football player sprinting for the end zone who gets leveled by an opposing player is an example. The running back's trajectory and speed of movement sideways is directly related to the force of the tackle.

In an animated shot for the feature film *Rocky and Bullwinkle* where the character's action relied completely on reactionary forces, Bullwinkle was seated in the

cockpit of an airplane that crashed headfirst into the ground; the impact forced the character's body to thrust violently forward. Every key frame set on his body was in direct relation to the motion of the plane. (See Figure 6.2.)

When working through a scene, I find the reactionary portions of an action to be the least difficult to solve. They are scientific in nature and can easily be visualized. After the forces have been identified, it's just a matter of making the body parts react accordingly. It is much more about physical behavior than an emotion or a thought process. The difficult task of developing a thinking character falls on the shoulders of the second type of force.

Initiating

As defined by *Webster's Dictionary*, *initiation* is an action that causes something, especially an important process or event, to begin. This comprises the second category of forces that an animator must pay attention to. Initiating forces are the basis for the multitude of actions and decisions that encompass a character. They can be both an internal decision and a force that is reacting to one thing but instigating the motion of another. Sorting through the distinction takes some practice, but will result in a better understanding of the intricacies involved in putting something in motion. Figure 6.3 shows an initiating force coming from the troll in *Harry Potter and the Sorcerer's Stone*. His actions are initiating the digital Harry on his shoulders.

In the previous few paragraphs, the idea of reactionary forces was discussed. The examples illustrated various objects being affected by a driving energy. The forearm in a character, for example, moves in

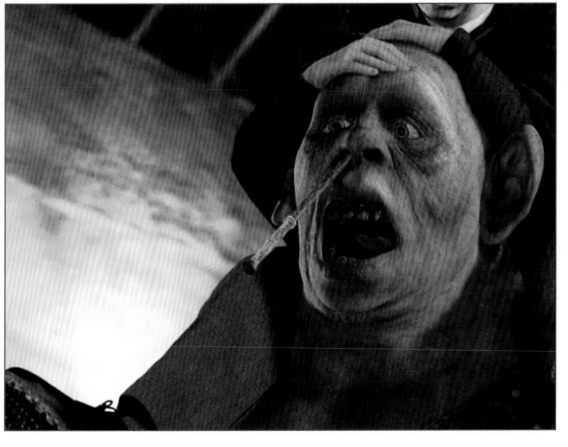

Figure 6.3
The troll is initiating Harry's body movements. HARRY POTTER AND THE SORCERER'S STONE © 2001 Warner Bros., a division of Time Warner Entertainment Company, L.P. All Rights Reserved.

reaction to the elbow. The elbow is the initiating force for the forearm and wrist. However, the elbow is reacting to the motion of the shoulder. The shoulder starts the motion for the elbow; the elbow reacts, and in turn drives the forearm and wrist. The bendable joint is playing two roles. In one moment it follows the lead from the shoulder and in the next moment the elbow is driving the lower sections of the arm. (See Figure 6.4.) This chain of events covers physical aspects of initiating forces. An animator must also be concerned with the mental facets.

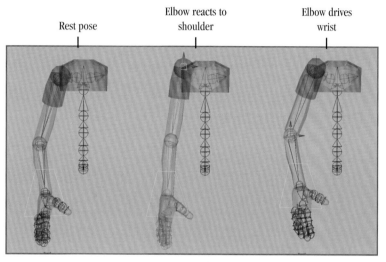

Rest pose · Elbow reacts to shoulder · Elbow drives wrist

Figure 6.4
The elbow is involved in both a reactionary and an initiating force.

Initiating forces are often internal. They originate from the brain and are the foundation for creating character emotion. Unlike the reactionary force, an initiating force determines the tone of a scene. It is the basis for every action a character performs, and defines the physical degree and attitude at which the character performs it. When someone is going to express an emotion or make a decision, that person's body will position itself in order to properly communicate these gestures. This sets in motion a series of responding forces that shape how the body will react. For example, a character thinks about changing the channel, picks up the remote, and clicks to a different station. The forces at work through the shoulder, arm, and hand began with the character's thought or desire to watch something different. The animator must replicate this thought process to successfully complete a scene.

This type of force stems from a decision made in the brain. The animator must take into consideration the mental state of the character and use that as a motivation for the action. The performance of a bored character will differ from one who is upbeat. One emotional state will result in slower movements while another might contain very fast actions with direct forces. A tired person haplessly searching for a television program will have a lethargic set of forces as his mind is altered from a long day at the office. Conversely, a person trying to watch two major sporting events will excitedly switch back and forth between stations and have a much more intent set of motions. (See Figure 6.5.)

Essentially, you must act it out yourself so that you can decipher and understand the correct sequence of movements to animate. As in acting, you are attempting to

Figure 6.5
The emotional state of the character has a direct relation to the posture and actions of his motions. The character on the left is bored with the flickering television, while the character on the right is keeping track of two programs.

recall an emotional state. This is often difficult to do, and as a result, emotions and the internal forces behind them are considered some of the most difficult to successfully animate. The mind is driving the motion and does not provide a straightforward approach that a purely physical action might present.

Dissecting a Shot—The Boxing Match

Now that I've discussed the various types of forces that are at work in any given action, let me dissect a short series of actions to find out exactly how the forces originate in the mind and are implemented by the body. I chose a boxing match to illustrate the point. It has an excellent balance of both internal and external decisions.

Two men are in a ring—Boxer A on the left and Boxer B on the right. As the two fighters square off, both have a mental state of wanting to win the match. Intensity is high on both sides of the ring. They are constantly updating their opponent's position while maintaining a back-and-forth movement. When the opponent is vulnerable, a punch will be delivered.

Boxer B drops his right glove and Boxer A makes the decision to strike him on that side. This decision is the initiating force. Boxer A's brain takes his current emotional state and connects that with an opening in Boxer B's stance. This internal force will dictate the next few motions and trigger a series of forces to deliver a blow to Boxer B. (See Figure 6.6.)

First, the shoulder draws the elbow and wrist back in anticipation of the hit. This is a combination of both initiating and reactionary actions. The shoulder initiates the raising of the elbow and the elbow reacts appropriately. The elbow initiates the raising of the fist and puts the arm in striking pose. (See Figure 6.7.)

Figure 6.6
Boxer A sees an opening and makes a conscious decision to deliver a blow.

Figure 6.7
The series of forces, instigated by the mental decision to swing, cause the boxer to ready his arm for a punch.

The hips then drive forward and create the catalyst for the shoulder, elbow, and wrist to stretch toward the opponent. (See Figure 6.8.) The next section, "Follow the Leader," will shed some light on this concept.

Boxer A's thrust toward his opponent's face causes a reactionary force to be triggered. Boxer B does not see the punch coming and takes the direct blow without defense. The reaction snaps his head backward. The magnitude of this reaction is proportional to the speed at which Boxer A delivered the blow. Boxer B's head movement is void of any mental or internal decision-making process. (See Figure 6.9.)

This exchange of initiating and reactionary forces continues as the two boxers exchange punches. Boxer B makes decisions and exerts forces that Boxer A reacts to. These exchanges occur in fractions of a second. However, they can be easily broken down and examined.

Follow the Leader

A good way to approach forces in animation is to use a method from traditional hand-drawn animation, known as lead and follow. *Lead and follow* essentially refers to the order in which sections of the body move. A portion of the body "leads" a motion as others "follow." This notion serves as a road map for the physical aspects of a character's movement. After the initiating force is determined, it is easy to determine the motion of the remaining body parts. The result is a motion that is true to the mass and makeup of the character.

To illustrate this concept, I will use the simple motion of a character standing from a crouched position. Figure 6.10 shows the progression of the motion. The character begins in a crouched pose (Position A). As the feet drive the hips upward, the shoulders and head stay relatively stable (Position B). The upper body is yet to

Figure 6.8
Boxer A extends his arm toward Boxer B.

Figure 6.9
The head snaps back from the direct force applied. The shoulders will follow along with the hips.

A   B   C   D   E   F   G   H

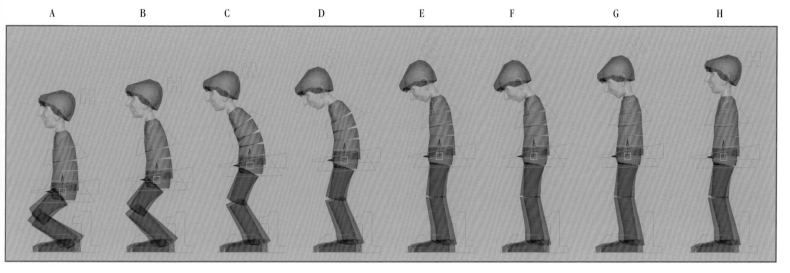

Figure 6.10
The progression of poses as the character stands up.

be affected by the driving lower body. Position C shows the first affects of the upward motion in the chest. It begins to roll forward as the head stays static. Position D shows the hips finishing their driving motion. The shoulders continue to follow behind and the head is starting to feel the effects of the shoulder rotation. The hips have stopped moving at Position E. The shoulders have started rolling backward and the head is still dipping forward. Positions F, G, and H have the shoulders settling in to a relaxed position with the head finally reaching its stopping point in the final pose. The initiating force must travel through the body in the proper succession.

The order in which a character changes his body posture has a tremendous influence on the outcome of a shot. This motion is a visual description for what emotional state the character is in. It's important to remember that the leading and following actions change from scene to scene. Unfortunately, there isn't a magic manual that tells you exactly how characters move. The situation dictates the order of events.

The bulk of human, animal, and creature motion begins with the hips. You can, for example, base the majority of action in a walk on the translation and rotations in a character's midsection. The hips drive the shoulders and chest region, which in turn drive the arms and head. The arms drive the wrists, which drive the fingers. Every motion down to the fingertips is emanating from the initial movement generated by the pelvic region. Chapter 14, "Walks," discusses this sequence of events in greater detail.

There are, however, many times when an alternate portion of the body is actually leading the action. For example, say a character has his head down and is reading a book. The character hears a loud noise and looks up to see what has happened. This motion actually begins with the lifting of the head. The chest follows with a possible rise in the hips. The chest is responding to the turn of the head, and the hips are responding to the change in the shoulders and chest region. Remember, individual sections of the body are relying on the leading force to affect them. If the head is leading, it will make an initial move before the chest can respond. A breakdown of this animation is illustrated in Figure 6.11.

It is important to first determine the emotional state of a character and let that dictate which part of the body is leading and the order of sections that follow. Consider two examples that involve the same situation but have completely different emotional states: A young man sits on the couch watching television. The doorbell rings. His reaction follows two paths, depending on his emotional reaction to the doorbell.

In the first example, our character is feeling depressed. His girlfriend has recently left him and he is hoping she will change her mind and take him back. He is excited at the possibility that she is at the door. He immediately looks over, quickly stands up, and then moves in that direction. His head leads the action toward the door, and his chest and hips follow. Getting to the door as quickly as possible dictates his movement.

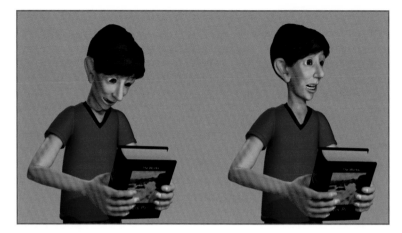

Figure 6.11
The character begins the action by lifting his head toward the startling noise.

In our second example, the same character is watching his favorite team in an important game. The score is close and his concentration is focused on the screen. The doorbell rings and he does not even look in the direction of the sound. The importance of not missing the next play has him moving toward the door while keeping his attention on the television. His hips are leading the movement, with his shoulders and head following. The movement toward the door is much slower because he is not as interested in the visitor as he is in the game.

As you can see, different emotional environments and circumstances will impact the speed and mechanics of a character's movements. By using a follow and lead approach, an animator can quickly determine the following: what kind of emotional tone the scene has, where the motion in the object/character originates, and the sequence of the other moving parts in the action. This road map becomes especially helpful in complex movements, but should be applied to any scene that requires emotional impact and believable body language.

Exercise: The Tail Whip

A great way to practice lead and follow is to animate a tail. The initiating force is easy to locate and the sections of the tail routinely follow its lead. You do not need to be concerned with additional forces altering the action created by the backside of the character. Animators can easily visualize the forces as they travel through the sections of the tail.

This exercise will be executed entirely in the top view port. Isolating the view helps to minimize the number of directions an animator needs to worry about. This

motion will primarily occur along the x-axis. However, to fully realize the actual motion of a tail swing, multiple views need to be addressed.

The setup for this example uses the standards created for the biped character in Chapter 4, "Tools of the Trade." Five bones make up the length of tail constrained to five boxes for controlling the movements. Keys are being set exclusively on these control points to limit the number of joints you need to manage. For visual clarity, the boxes are scaled down as they move away from the body to simulate the narrowing of the mesh. (See Figure 6.12.) In addition, controllers are labeled 1 through 5 for easier identification.

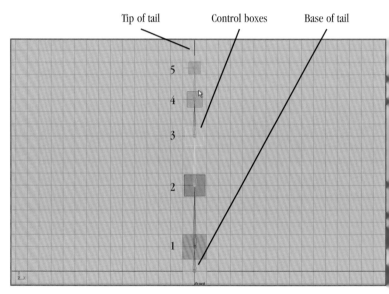

Figure 6.12
The basic tail setup from the top view.

The driving force in the tail motion is the hips. The side-to-side motion occurs when the body shifts its weight over a supporting leg. This rear-end section will determine how the remaining divisions of the tail behave. However, to make things simple, I've removed the hip node and am just concentrating on the tail controllers.

> The tail exercise is animated using the straight-ahead approach discussed in Chapter 5, "Approaches to Animation." Keys are being set on every third frame in order to capture an accurate description of the action that is occurring.

Figure 6.13 shows the initial move. The first step is moving the base of the tail in the direction of the initial hip motion. Controller 1, the red shaded square, slightly shifts to the left as the hips drive over the leg. It travels slightly behind the hip movement, but moves before any of the remaining controllers are affected. I set the timeline to frame 3 and move controller 1 over a small amount. All controllers get a key frame at this location.

As you can see in Figure 6.14, at frame 6 controller 1 has traveled farther along the x-axis. Controller 2 begins to be affected and follows the lead from controller 1. Controller 3 is actually getting some influence, but only moves slightly. Controllers 4 and 5 remain stagnant because the thrust from the hips has not reached them at this stage in the motion. Keys are set on all controllers.

By frame 9 (see Figure 6.15), the hips have reached their extreme position. Controller 1 is doing the same and only slightly moves. The remaining sections, however, are still pushing toward their limit. Controllers 2 and 3 continue to move to the left. Controllers 4 and 5 are finally moving because the force has reached their location.

Figure 6.16 shows that frame number 12 brings a new pattern. Controller 1 is moving the other direction following the lead from the hips. It is actually going the

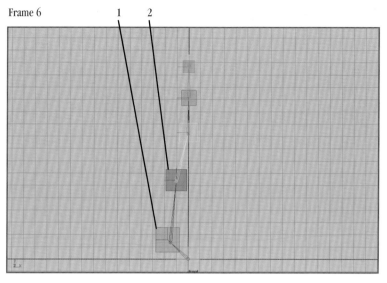

Figure 6.14
Frame 6 in the timeline shows the first two sections having the majority of influence.

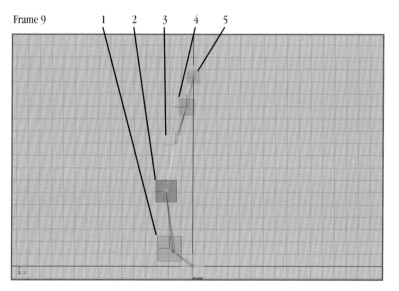

Figure 6.15
Controller 1 is reaching its limit as the other controllers follow along.

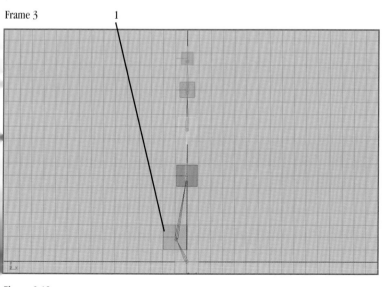

Figure 6.13
The base of the tail moves first.

Frame 12   Controller 1 moves to the right   5   4   3   2

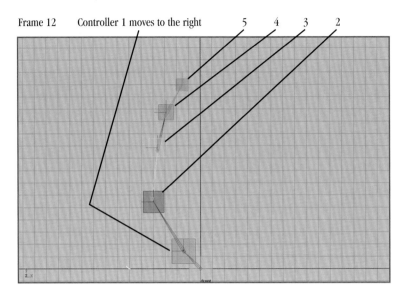

Figure 6.16
Controller 1 starts back to the right as the remaining controllers push toward the left.

Frame 15   Controllers 1 and 2 move to the right   5   4   3

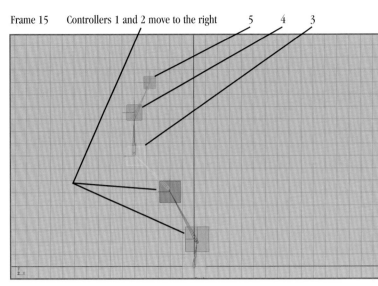

Figure 6.17
The tail makes a nice "s" shape as the base travels one direction and the end travels another.

opposite direction of the remaining controllers, because they've not reached the extreme position on screen left. Controllers 2, 3, 4, and 5 continue in that direction, each one following the motion of its predecessor.

At frame 15 (see Figure 6.17), controllers 1 and 2 are headed to the right; controller 3 is reaching its extreme to the left with controllers 4 and 5 following behind. The sections of the tail are actually moving in opposite directions at this point. This is largely due to the fact that the force is being delayed in its delivery to the end joints. In addition, controller 5 has much farther to travel than controller 1.

In Figure 6.18, you can see that by frame 18 controller 4 has hit its extreme to the left with controller 5 close behind. Controller 1 is approaching its extreme position at the right as the remaining joints follow behind.

The tail continues in the pattern until the hips stop moving or alter their motion. Just as the shoulder had to raise the elbow, which raised the arm, section 1 of the tail will always drive section 2, and so on down the tail.

Once again you see that after you have found the major initiating force, everything else falls into place. The tail sections will always follow the hip movement of the creature. The force of the hips can certainly change direction, amplitude, or pace. Simply adjust the tail accordingly.

Frame 18

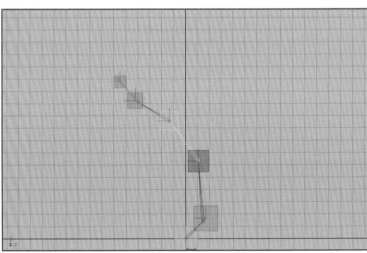

Figure 6.18
The tail is close to completing its motion to the left.

chapter 7
An Interview with Richie Baneham

Richie Baneham is an accomplished animator. He's had tremendous success as both a traditional and a CG artist. He brings a unique perspective to animation by combining his 2D skills with current digital techniques. These skills have been honed on a number of productions and facilities. Richie understands the importance of fundamentals and teaches those principles in schools and colleges around the world.

KYLE: *Give me a brief bio of your career.*

RICHIE: I started studying in Ballyfermot College in Ireland way back in the late '80s and early '90s. From there I went to Don Bluth's, which was in Dublin at the time. I was an in-betweener. Bluth went rocky a couple of times due to budgetary issues and I went back to finish the course in Ballyfermot and just came straight to the United States. I went to work for Rich Animation and did one picture with them, *The Swan Princess*, and after that they promoted me to animator, which was grand. After that I did a couple of things in the CD-ROM area; the whole "edutainment" thing was starting to pick up. There was a guy called Don Canter and he was the head of animation on the *The Land Before Time*. I had an opportunity to work with that guy. That was an interesting couple of months. It was a small facility, but he was cool and he was a good animator. I then went to Warner Brothers and have pretty much been here ever since.

KYLE: *Which projects have you been involved with?*

RICHIE: The first one out of the gates was *Quest for Camelot*. I originally came onto *Quest* when Bill Kroyer was the director. It was at the very beginning. We did a lot of R&D. A lot of the good stuff was trashed and we changed directors and all that. The movie didn't do much, but it was a good training ground for me. It was nice to get my first feature-animated film under my belt. I switched over to *The Iron Giant* after that. That was the big changeup for me career wise. They offered all of the 2D guys a chance to switch over to 3D.

KYLE: *Was that a difficult transition?*

RICHIE: I took about 3 or 4 weeks to switch over. Part of the problem with a lot of 2D guys trying to switch over is the intimidation factor. People tend to think of it as a completely different skill. In actuality it's exactly the same principals if you get your head around the fact that this is basically a huge expensive pencil. Learn what you need to learn to make the character move around, and don't kill yourself trying to learn the technical side. Just step back and learn the basics and apply the fundamentals from 2D into 3D and you'll do fine.

KYLE: *Did you animate on the computer during* Giant?

RICHIE: I kind of got a lucky break. I did a couple of scenes of the giant's hand and Hogarth.

KYLE: *Are you referring to the bathroom sequence?*

RICHIE: Yeah. I did one or two scenes, and then Brad Bird really liked what was going on and gave me the whole sequence. I was the only 2D animator that switched over quickly to 3D and I basically found a little niche. Anytime they needed 2D and 3D in the same scene I would do both of them. So I did Hogarth and the hand whenever they interacted and also a lot of Hogarth and the giant. If there was any choreography that needed to be done between those two characters or two animators, they'd hand it off to me. It was really grand. It got me ahead of the game. (See Figure 7.1.)

KYLE: *What was next?*

RICHIE: Actually, I switched over and did six months' development on *The Amazing Mr. Limpet*. It was pretty weird as it kept dying and coming back.

KYLE: *That thing is probably still floating around at some studio.*

RICHIE: Yeah. It was the project that would never die. Next, I did *Osmosis Jones* and worked more or less in the same role as *Giant*. I did Drix and Osmosis. (See Figure 7.2.) Both were lead characters. That made for some good fun. After that I was the animation director on *Cats and Dogs*, and then moved over to my current position as animation supervisor on *Scooby-Doo*.

KYLE: *I understand you've done some teaching.*

RICHIE: I had a good foundation in both 2D and 3D, and it sort of led to my teaching. I was teaching 2D for Warner Brothers at a lot of schools around the country. When everything started to switch over to 3D, I found that there were a lot of CG animators that wanted to know about 2D animation and really improve their fundamentals. Even if they didn't have great drawing skills, they still seemed to have the interest. I was amazed at how many guys I came across that went to technical schools and were never taught the principles of animation. It wasn't that they didn't understand the fundamentals, they were just never taught. I started teaching basic animation at the Associates of Art College. We had a large number of 3D animators in the class. Concepts such as bouncing ball, squash and stretch, and overlapping action were simple principles that were missing.

KYLE: *So these were people that had learned a great deal of technical skills, but were missing the basic fundamentals of animation?*

RICHIE: They had done a lot, probably more with sheer will than anything. There are a couple of schools that are decent, but most of them don't concentrate on character animation. They tend to teach the technical basics of using the computer.

Figure 7.1
The Iron Giant offered Richie an opportunity to animate both traditionally and digitally. The giant was CG whereas Hogarth was hand-drawn. THE IRON GIANT © 1999 Warner Bros., a division of Time Warner Entertainment Company, L.P. All Rights Reserved.

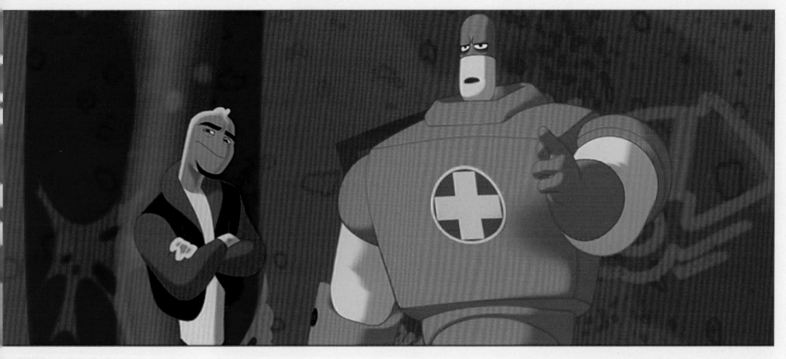

Figure 7.2
Osmosis Jones features both 2D and 3D characters. OSMOSIS JONES © 2001 Warner Bros., a division of Time Warner Entertainment Company, L.P. All Rights Reserved.

KYLE: *What are some of the exercises that you had those students do to learn those fundamentals?*

RICHIE: This goes back to the very basics of animation. The one I always start a class with is the bouncing ball. You apply two of the strongest principles. Timing issues must be taken into account and then the idea of squash and stretch or displacement of volume. Once you actually understand what's exactly happening, and how you replicate real life by displacing masses, and the effects achieved by adjusting your timing, a lot can be accomplished. The funny thing is a lot of people will look down on that. I'd say, "All right, let's do the bouncing ball," and they'd say, "I've done it before." Everybody has done it before. However, can you absolutely state before you start what that ball is going to look like at the end? Anybody can do a bouncing ball, but can you do the bouncing ball that you want? It's about intent. Actually starting with the intention of doing something and getting those results, and not just haphazardly going through the motions and achieving a result that's just a happy mistake. You can do the bouncing ball for your whole life and get a different result and energy from it each time.

KYLE: *What would you build on from there?*

RICHIE: I'd then move into overlapping action and breaking of the joints. I'd use a whip action for the exercise. Then you put them together and use one to drive the other. You take a bouncing ball and apply a tail. You have a bouncing ball with squash and stretch and timing issues and a tail with secondary motion. One leads the other and you can see where the forces come from. Understanding that just because a hand is moving, it doesn't make it the motivational force. Quite often it's the body below it. It's very important to understand what drives what.

KYLE: *I think that notion of force and lead and follow is one of the most misunderstood aspects of animation. People have a very difficult time grasping this concept.*

RICHIE: I think people didn't quite grasp some of the animation methods of the old guys like Milt Kahl and Frank Thomas and Ollie Johnson. They taught young animators to work in a pose-to-pose method. Many generations of animators have adopted this method of working. What tends to get left out, however, is that those guys were already taking into account the driving forces when they created drawings. They were THAT good. They could anticipate what was leading and following and the poses already reflected what forces were at work. (See Figure 7.3.)

77

Figure 7.3
The Disney greats already factored in the lead and follow when animating a shot. Milt Kahl animates King Louie in Disney's *Jungle Book*. © DISNEY ENTERPRISES, INC.

However, when many young animators work toward that pose-to-pose method, they get two nice drawings but miss the fundamental step of the breakdown. This is the transitional drawing or pose between two major poses. That's where you would apply most of the leading and motivational forces within the body. It's also the point where arcs are defined. Getting the in-between right is probably the most important thing about animation. Great poses are nice, but it's actually how you get from one pose to another that's important. Animation isn't about nice drawings or nice-looking characters. It's great if those attributes are there, but it's not important. It's about fluidity of movement and whether or not you achieve what you started out to achieve. Does something move the way you wanted? Does it say something about the character? That's probably what's missing most in the

> **Great poses are nice, but it's actually how you get from one pose to another that's important.**

3D industry. Pixar is probably the only one really nailing it right now. I think that's one of the fundamentals that isn't taught. There is a great deal of importance in transitional poses and how they create the fluidity and timing of movement.

KYLE: *As you said, what's leading and following doesn't just have an impact on the physical presence of the character, but actually has a big impact on the personality of the character.*

RICHIE: It's also what you are telling your audience about the character. The way a character moves has a great deal to do with his emotion. If he moves slowly, he'll feel heavy and depressed, but if his actions are fast, he'll appear light and happy. This goes back to the simplicity of the bouncing ball. If you weight your curves and arcs toward the top, it will bounce with a light and airy feel. If you weight them toward the bottom, it will appear sad and depressed. People don't see that connection and don't teach that connection.

KYLE: *You've mentioned squash and stretch several times. How do you think that principle applies in the 3D world? Digital character setups don't always have the convenience of displacing masses.*

RICHIE: It really depends on how you build the model and who is overseeing the model at the time it's built. It can be as easy as a few simple blend shapes. The same mass and shape can be changed, and by keeping the same volume you essentially create squash and stretch.

KYLE: *Yeah, it's not that difficult from a technical standpoint. However, I don't think the majority of 3D models place the same emphasis on displacing masses as traditional animators might.*

RICHIE: You're talking about the same principles, but just applied differently.

KYLE: *Exactly.*

RICHIE: In a case such as the T-Rex, you are dealing with much more of a physical matter than a character issue. You are trying to sell the audience that this is a real creature with real mass. You have to find another way to make that work. People don't necessarily look like they have squash and stretch, but if you slow down film you'll actually see the displacement. It's very subtle, but it's there. You have to find a different way to achieve the same principle. If you have a T-Rex, when the foot hits the ground you have to create a secondary action that runs through the body. (See Figure 7.4.)

Figure 7.4
Squash and stretch is also applicable in photo-real characters. Copyright © 2002 by Universal Studios. Courtesy of Universal Studios Publishing Rights, a Division of Universal Studios Licensing, Inc. All rights reserved.

KYLE: *Sure, like muscle jiggle.*

RICHIE: Yeah. You can also do things like curving the spine a slightly different way to do the same thing. Opposing the curve of the spine against the ground plane will make the character seem taller and slimmer or lower and flatter. That's the same two principles as the bouncing ball. The same displacement of a ball approaching the ground and then squashing can be achieved by manipulating the posture of the character. It may not be as obvious, but it is still there.

KYLE: *Another thing you commented on was the intent of a scene. Do you think people jump into animation too quickly and don't spend the time really thinking about the intent of their scene?*

RICHIE: Part of that is the pressure of production. The sheer pressures of turning around scenes doesn't always allow for that thought process to happen. Personally, I like to take the time to do some thumbnails. It just takes creating small sketches on the page. Even if you don't draw very well, I'd advise everybody to thumbnail his or her ideas. Just create small poses to get an idea of what your intention is.

KYLE: *Yeah, no one has to see the drawings except you, so it doesn't matter what your skill level is.*

RICHIE: Who cares? All you are doing is putting yourself through the paces.

Another thing is empathy. That's one of the things that you see more in 2D, but less in 3D. In a 2D studio environment, you see people get up and act things out. You'd see people in the halls working on their scenes. (See Figure 7.5.) Again, this goes back to empathy and intent. You don't see that much in CG. It's probably because the manner people are taught. You have to get up and act it out and feel where the weight is. Through this process before animation begins, you are setting some goals. How is the character going to act? How is he going to walk?

KYLE: *I think that production pressure is a huge trap. I've personally fallen into it many times. I know one particular case where I was assigned a shot that was due the next morning. I jumped right in and started setting keys. Eight hours later, I had nothing. I came back the next morning, thumbnailed the shot, and was done in 45 minutes. That small investment of time can often pay off very big.*

RICHIE: That ability to step back is often hindsight. Quite often people do just jump in. There is a certain amount of serendipity to this process. You have to be lucky. Sometimes you don't always know exactly what you are looking for, and sometimes it's the little happy accidents that really make the character show through, and you've just stumbled on them. You can't depend on that, though. I agree with you. I personally have fallen into the same trap of getting busy on a production and jumping straight in. Occasionally it works, but 9 times out of 10 it just kills you. It's that one shot that keeps bouncing back.

KYLE: *As a supervisor, do you try to promote those types of things?*

RICHIE: Of course. That is a very important thing.

KYLE: *Do you mind talking a bit about facial animation?*

RICHIE: Facial is a very similar process. People get caught up too much in the dialogue, particularly in a speaking character. They feel it's extremely necessary to nail the mouth just right. In reality, the dialogue comes second. If you can act out a scene in the mirror and apply those same basic poses and timings in the computer, you can leave out the dialogue. If a scene is executed well, you should be able to turn down the volume and still be able to tell what is going on.

KYLE: *Sure, the eyes tell 90% of what's going on. The mouth movement is just icing on the cake.*

Figure 7.5
An artist practicing his moves in front of a wall of mirrors.

RICHIE: Exactly. It's secondary. It's literally a mechanical process.

KYLE: *I agree. However, there is definitely a craft to making the eyes, brows, and lids tell an emotion. In a close-up shot, animators often have to rely on those facets of the character to really sell the emotion.*

RICHIE: You absolute do. You can think of it as the Bermuda Triangle. Take the two eyes and the end of the nose and that's where the audience is looking. (See Figure 7.6.) Regardless of what's going on in the mouth, that's where people are looking. As soon as a character shows up onscreen, the audience's natural reaction is to look at the eyes. You can use that to your advantage when composing a scene; you can invite the audience to look in that direction. Performance is often about the timing. Finding the right time to spend on a pose is very important.

> **As soon as a character shows up onscreen, the audience's natural reaction is to look at the eyes.**

KYLE: *This is true of both face and body.*

RICHIE: One of the things that I think is different about how 2D and 3D character animated characters act is the time spent on poses. When you have an emotion or expression that you want to read, give it some time. Give it a beat. One thing that happens in CG is you can hit poses and the computer will automatically flow between them. You tend not to actually ever hit a pose. Sometimes you have to make a conscious effort to make sure it stays the same. That's the difference from 2D. It's easy to reproduce the same expression. It means you don't have to do an in-between. In CG you have to make time for that. You have to hit a pose, like it, and then give it a beat. Literally flatten out your curves, don't let it flow through, and give the audience some time to read the pose. Going back to the facial stuff: Pick your emotions. Be clear about what they are. Plan it and give them space and time to read, and you'll be in good shape.

KYLE: *That's a very common mistake. Everyone wants to do some acting; however, they tend to jam 8 poses into a 3-second shot.*

RICHIE: Animation is about making choices—especially the ones you make at the beginning. It's those choices you make when standing up and acting it out. You go through it 30 or 40 iterations and invariably you'll end up back at the same thing you did the first time. The reason you do that is because that's probably the most natural way to solve the line. Your gut feeling is usually the right one.

Figure 7.6
The audience will primarily focus on the eyes of the face. Animators should focus their attention in this area.

KYLE: *Can you walk us through your personal steps of animating a shot?*

RICHIE: The first step, and one that I have to consciously make myself do, is look at a scene in context. Look at the storyboard and see what emotional beats flow before and after. This is quite often a problem in animation. Things can become very disjointed when handed out to different animators. I make a conscious effort to look at what's going on around my scene. As a supervisor, I can try to fix this by handing shot sequences to the same artist. That helps add continuity straightaway.

So back to my personal approach—it's looking at the boards and looking at them in place with the dialogue. I check it out on the avid and get a sense of how my scene needs to work. Usually, I'll thumbnail and act out what it is that I want to do. Acting it out is so important. It's really where you get a sense of the timing and where the weight is. It's not even about looking in the mirror; it's about feeling it. I start with the basic model and do a rough first pass. I won't do any facial, but rather concentrate on the body action only. I'll go right through and leave out any overlapping action like fingers or ears. I like to leave out anything that gets fussy. I try to get the timing right, and then go back and add the extra bits. I don't even worry too much about things like footsteps. I'll just get a general placement of where your character is in the scene. How is he interacting with the props? How much screen is being used?

> **If at any point you think you've learned everything, you might as well give up.**

Are you giving space to other characters in the scene? This has a terrible tendency to happen in animation. You really have to look at who else is on the screen. You have to give them space and time to act. Look for the spaces between their performances. The quiet moments and busy moments tell you when and when not to move. At that point you can start blocking. I like to work from the body out.

KYLE: *You leave the extremities until the last?*

RICHIE: Yeah. Things like hands will come last. Hands actually tell a lot about the character. When you talk to people, you tend to express yourself with the hands. It's really nice if you can reinforce a character by acting with the hands. It's pretty simple, and quite often missed.

KYLE: *When you block out your first pass are you setting key poses and working on the majority of the body?*

RICHIE: It really depends on the scene. It's a case-by-case basis. Action scenes I tend to do straight-ahead. Action tends to flow easier that way. If it's an acting scene, I'll work more from a pose method. If it's a combination of both, I'll literally go from poses to straight-ahead and try to meld the two together. I don't ever tie into poses too early. It's nice to set them up, but don't marry yourself to a pose or a drawing. You can quite often feel that. I've fallen victim to it so often—particularly in my early career doing 2D. You do a drawing, like the drawing, and do everything you can to force it in. Sometimes it just doesn't belong. It's a nice pose and as a single statement says a lot about the scene, but when push comes to shove and the motion begins to happen, it really doesn't belong in there. You need to do it again.

KYLE: *Sometimes making that change can add some spontaneity.*

RICHIE: Exactly. When you marry into poses sometimes it can kill you. Some people work like that all the time. Animation that is strictly pose-to-pose tends to be stiff. I usually block the major motions in the body and go back and do a pass at the secondary on every fourth frame. That way, you tend to be able to follow the larger movements in the body and let everything that's secondary be reactionary to the body.

KYLE: *Plus, you are making the decision about how the character interpolates between poses as opposed to letting the generic f-curve translation take over.*

RICHIE: You can't depend on what the computer gives you. You really have to go in and make choices about manipulating those curves. It will work and it might look okay, but you'll never get a real feeling of weight, and the spark will never be there. You have to make choices.

KYLE: *Any last words for the readers?*

RICHIE: There is one thing I would encourage everybody to do. No matter how high you are on the ladder or how you good you are as an animator, bounce your ideas off of other people. Be open to people's responses. You can actually learn quite a lot from other people. People's reactions can tell you a great deal. Even if you don't agree with one person, getting the same reaction over and over you have to consider that the scene is not reading.

KYLE: *The people that are open to comments and want to share their work with others are the animators who end up on top. Then there is a large faction of people who don't want to listen to anyone. They tend to get very stale.*

> **You can't depend on what the computer gives you. You really have to go in and make choices about manipulating those curves.**

RICHIE: If at any point you think you've learned everything, you might as well give up. You can keep picking up tidbits of information everywhere. And that goes for everybody. Milt Kahl and those guys were still learning at the end and they were brilliant. Keep that in mind.

chapter 8
Timing

Timing is one of the most important elements of animation and one of the hardest to master. It is the foundation for the emotional and physical state of everything moving on the screen. I consider it to be the backbone of animation and have devoted countless hours developing my "inner clock." Spending the proper amount of time on an action will be a key factor in the success or failure of every scene an animator touches.

In its simplest form, timing is the number of seconds or frames that an object or a character requires to complete a particular movement. For example, the four seconds it takes a bowling ball to roll down the lane is that object's timing for that action. This measurement is the framework for all animation. In other words, animators use timing to determine the duration of a specific motion. The scale is based on the number of frames that are projected in a given second.

Animation began in the early days of cinema. Film projector standards required that 24 frames of celluloid pass through the projector's lens over the duration of one second. That equates to 1,440 images in one minute. This continues to be the standard for modern film. An additional format was created with the advent of the television. American video broadcasts run at the rate of 30 frames per second while European standards run around 25 frames per second. This requires a small adjustment for the animator who moves between television and film formats, but the concept remains the same.

For the animator to properly time the movements in a performance or action, it is important that he grasp the notion of thinking of time in terms of frames. Most animated actions don't occur in even and simple segments, such as one or two seconds. In fact, the majority happens over a fraction of a second and requires the artist to dissect his actions into smaller ticks of the clock. Thinking of a door clos-ing in 24 frames or a finger snapping in 3 frames is something an animator must learn to ensure proper timing.

How Much Time?

Inexperienced animators often have a difficult time putting frame numbers to motions they are trying to create. The number one question routinely asked from people studying animation is "how long does it take?". Answering this question requires experience, trial and error, significant studying, and observation. Once this question can be answered accurately, however, it will unlock an enormous piece of the animation puzzle.

As a general note, heavy things tend to move slower than lighter objects. An object with a large mass requires more time to begin moving than its lightweight counter-part. (See Figure 8.1.) The heavy item requires a stronger force to project it, whereas the object with less size and weight can be moved with even a slight impact.

Take, for example, the moving of a wheelbarrow. If the bin is empty, it is easy to lift the wheelbarrow and propel it forward. The mass is fairly small and requires mini-mal effort to reposition. From a complete rest, the wheelbarrow can be lifted and put into motion in about 24 frames. See Figure 8.2 for the series of frames and corresponding frame counts.

Now let's take that same wheelbarrow and load it down with heavy items. The mass has been drastically increased. The weight of the load is approaching the 150-pound mark and will require a serious effort to even budge. A much larger force is required to shift the holder, and as a result, more frames will be needed. See Figure 8.3 for a timing breakdown.

Figure 8.1
A dinosaur's mass requires some time to get moving. Copyright © 2002 by Universal Studios. Courtesy of Universal Studios Publishing Rights, a Division of Universal Studios Licensing, Inc. All rights reserved.

The concept of heavy versus light is pretty simple to comprehend, but how does that notion translate into the world of animation? It's imperative that animators understand what controls and affects the timing of an object. In order to better understand this essential aspect, we must introduce another variable to the equation. That variable is distance traveled.

Timing is a factor of speed and distance traveled. An animator can't just rely on a given amount of frames to convey the weight of a character. He or she must also factor in the amount of ground that character covers in a specific amount of time. For example, if two boxes of equal mass begin traveling across the screen from left to right and move for 48 frames, which box is heavier? Given the constant variable of the 48 frames, the object that travels the shorter distance will be the box with

greater weight. Remember, heavier objects take longer to begin moving. The lighter box would begin its journey quicker and thus cover a greater space than the heavier box in the allotted time. (See Figure 8.4.)

Look at Figures 8.2 and 8.3. Notice the marks placed along the lower portion of the walls. Compare the number of marks revealed with the number of frames noted on the picture. The lighter container moved a considerable number of marks more than the heavier bin in the same number of frames.

Unfortunately, there isn't a reference chart for animators to give accurate frame counts for every action imaginable. It really depends on the situation, emotion, physical construction, and style of the scene or shot you are working on.

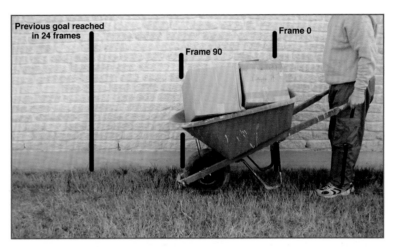

Figure 8.3
The container takes much longer to reposition when loaded to capacity.

Figure 8.2
The various frame counts to moving the unloaded wheelbarrow.

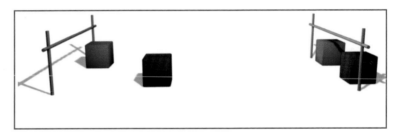

Figure 8.4
The blue box will appear heavier as it travels a smaller distance in the 48 frames.

The previous example might have a completely different set of timings if it occurred in a Warner Brothers' cartoon. These rules are just a starting point. They provide a foundation for understanding the laws of physics and how they are re-created in the animation environment. Animators must rely on their own sensibilities and observation to create characters and objects that move correctly based on their physical and emotional circumstances. It is possible, however, to study various movements in order to expand your awareness of how long things take to move from point A to point B.

Broad Timings First

I prefer to start the process of building a timing library by working from broad to specific. General timings are actually quite easy to accomplish. By "general" I'm referring to the total number of frames a scene takes. A stopwatch is a great tool for calculating how long a shot might last. (See the section "Develop Your Timing" later in this chapter for more information.) Obtaining this measurement is the first step in understanding the process of how many frames an entire action requires. This framework is critical in order to determine how much time the smaller movements "within" the action will take. For example, by deciding on the number of frames that are needed to reach over and grab something, you can then start to determine how many frames your fingers will have to open and grasp the item.

Below are a few general timings of various events. These frame counts were generated using the tools mentioned in this chapter. These are broad measurements to provide a basic idea of how long certain actions take. As you'll soon see, other factors will play a part in determining the time in which a character performs an activity.

◆ The dropping of a soda can. This motion can be accomplished in around half a second or 12 frames. The action begins as the hand releases the can and finishes when the can reaches the ground.

◆ A small woman lifting a heavy box from the floor and setting it on the table takes about 5 seconds or 120 frames. The count starts as the character begins lifting the box and ends after she has released it on the table. (See Figure 8.5.)

◆ The casting of a fishing pole happens in about 3.8 or 92 frames. This includes the character preparing to cast, his wind up, and the finishing pose from the toss. Figure 8.6 shows some of those timings.

> The frame counts listed in this chapter are based on the film standard of 24 frames per second (fps). If you'd like to convert them to the video or game standard of 30 frames per second, multiply the number of seconds by 30. A 2-second shot in the video format would be 60 frames.

Frame 1   Frame 80   Frame 120

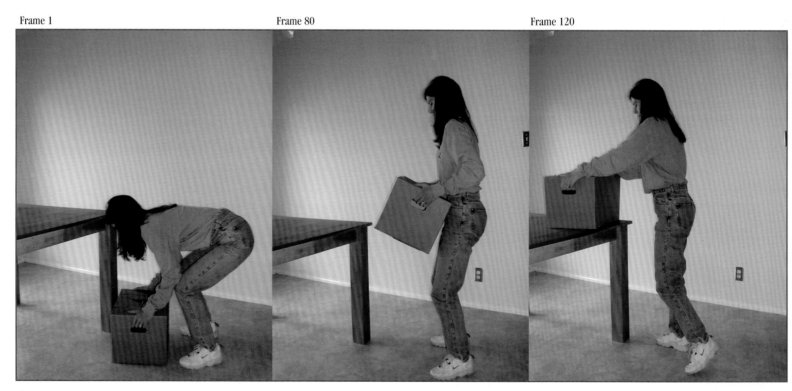

Figure 8.5
The sequence of poses and the frame numbers as the woman picks up the box.

Frame 1   Frame 42   Frame 74   Frame 88   Frame 92

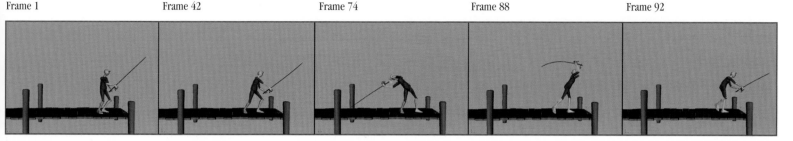

Figure 8.6
The series of casting poses and their corresponding timings.

The preceding frame counts should reveal that very few actions can actually take place in a given amount of time. Beginning animators generally try to pack too many motions or ideas into their shots. Keep it simple and make sure you spend the proper amount of time to fully explain a concept, an emotion, or an idea a character is trying to convey. I'll explain this in more detail in Chapter 16, "Getting Started: The Animated Short."

The proper amount of time is contingent on the circumstances of the scene and the style the animator is trying to achieve. The preceding examples are based on a human performance monitored with a stopwatch. Although these provide an excellent starting point, timings will often need some adjustment and exaggeration in order to play correctly.

Adjusted for Animation

Animation and exaggeration of movement are two very closely tied concepts. (See Chapter 12, "Anticipation and Exaggeration.") Animation lends itself to the portrayal of characters and objects that are fantastic and unique in their movement. This requires animators to take the same liberties with their timings as the art department takes with their designs of characters and creatures. It takes just the right adjustments to retain the natural physics of an object while maintaining cohesion with the animated world it exists in.

Simply put, an animated object will have faster timing than a similar object in the real world. This is obviously a generality. A photo-realistic digital bear will tend to have timings that are almost identical to an actual grizzly. However, when dealing with an object that has even the slightest amount of caricature, the animator will need to alter her internal clock to address it. The audience's perception needs this increased speed to compensate for watching a character that it doesn't see in everyday life. Ignoring this idea will result in soft animation that's lifeless in its delivery and will quickly lose the audience's interest.

Consider the action of throwing a ball. I recently worked with an animator who was replicating this action in an animated environment. We shot several minutes of video reference and digitized the footage. Upon breakdown of the action, it was agreed that the action took around 36 frames to complete. The animator transferred this information to his animated character and previewed the results. The action was mechanically correct, but it felt too slow. The animated version was modified to cover 24 frames. (See Figure 8.7.)

This resulted in an action that played better considering the environment in which it was taking place. The motion matched its stylized surroundings. It had the extra spark required to sell the action. Additionally, it better matched the frantic mental state of the creature. Timing has an affect on the personality of characters as well.

Personality and Emotional Results from Varying Timing

In addition to comprehending time in terms of frames, animators must factor in a few more concepts to correctly portray the character's true nature. We know that timing gives animation an identity from a physical standpoint. It also provides emotional and personality distinctiveness. The difference of a few frames can project an entirely different character to the audience. Various emotional states have timing tendencies associated with them. The character will behave in a manner according to the nature of his inner self. These motions will be fast, slow, or a combination of both depending on the situation in which he has been placed.

In the preceding examples, I provided a physical description of the character lifting the heavy box. The label of "woman" was necessary to decipher how a character might attempt a particular action. However, a physical description isn't enough.

The amount of time a character takes to perform an action has a great impact on what his emotional state is. Take the action of blinking, for example. The character might blink at the sight of a butterfly floating gently near his face. This relaxed state

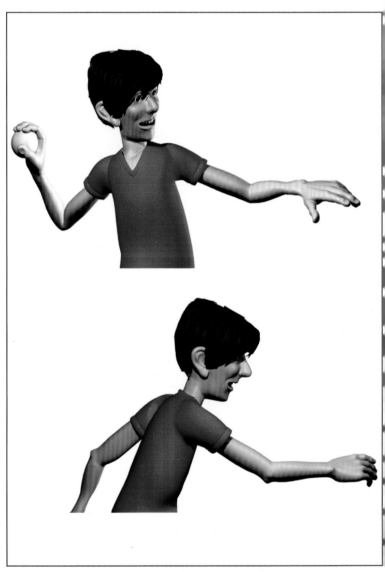

Figure 8.7
The left side frames show the motion of a human throwing. The right side frames show the same action from an animated character.

would require a much slower moving of the eyelids up and down. Figure 8.8 shows this sequence. The character's eyelids would move from an open state to a fully closed blink in 3 frames (Position A to Position B). He would then hold pose closed for 2 frames (Position B), before moving 2 frames to Position C and 1 final frame to Position D. The total blink would encompass 8 frames.

Take that same character and put him in a dark house with a host of spooky sounds and the blinks will have a different timing. The scared state will result in a pair of eyelids quickly moving up and down as he reacts to every creak of a floorboard or footstep. Figure 8.9 shows the three major poses. The character would move from an open eye (Position A) to a closed pose (Position B) in 2 frames. Position B would hold for 2 frames and open to Position C in 2 frames. The total scared blink would encompass 6 frames.

So you can see, timing is the foundation for changing an emotion. By altering a small number of frames, you can have a significant impact on the emotion displayed by a character. A few emotions, as well as some general timings with respect to their emotional states, are listed next.

◆ **Sad:** The character has a strong tendency to ease in and ease out from poses. Motions are soft in nature and tend to be very slow. The simple motion of raising a troubled head could take 60 frames. (See Figure 8.10.)

◆ **Excited:** Actions occur more frequently and faster. The character's energy results in quick transitions between poses. Sixty frames could result in a person jumping up and down three times. (See Figure 8.11.)

A   B   C   D

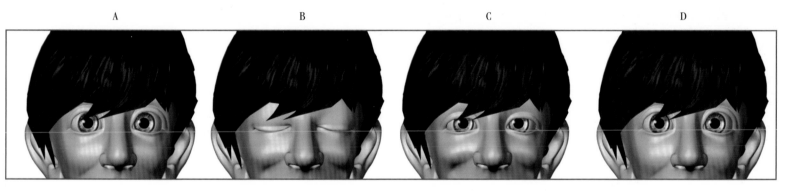

Figure 8.8
The timings of a relaxed blink starting from left and moving right.

A   B   C

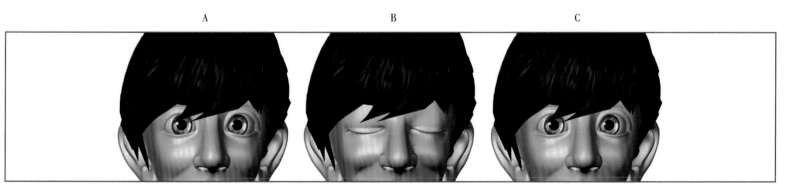

Figure 8.9
The timings of a scared blink.

Figure 8.10
The first and last frame of an unhappy character raising his head.

◆ **Nervous:** The character's motions are quick short bursts with longer pauses between poses. The sections of the body are snapping between poses in just a few frames. Two and a half seconds might result in six head turns. (See Figure 8.12.)

These breakdowns are provided to show the extremes in which various emotions cover specific amounts of time. Animators must begin to think in terms of how timing will affect not only the physical aspects of the scene but also the mental states. This type of knowledge doesn't come easily. It takes experience, trial and error, and a little natural ability. There are, however, steps you can take to accelerate this learning process.

Develop Your Timing

Some people are born with an exceptional sense of how long motions take. Most of us, however, are not. Without that natural ability, it takes a significant amount of effort to understand the complexity of what can happen over an eight-frame period. It can be done, though. I've seen several students evolve their timing sensibilities over a number of months. Just like a long-distance runner becomes accustomed to the many miles she can travel, an animator can develop her sensibilities about timing with the proper training and a little patience.

The first tool recommended to me upon entering animation school was a stopwatch. (See Figure 8.13.) I ran out and purchased one immediately not knowing

Figure 8.11
The character could move from a crouched position to full extension three times over the course of 2.5 seconds.

exactly what to do with it. If it was going to make me a better animator, however, I had to have one.

The key to learning from a stopwatch is using it. Sounds fairly simple, but you would be surprised at the number of animators who carry one in their backpacks

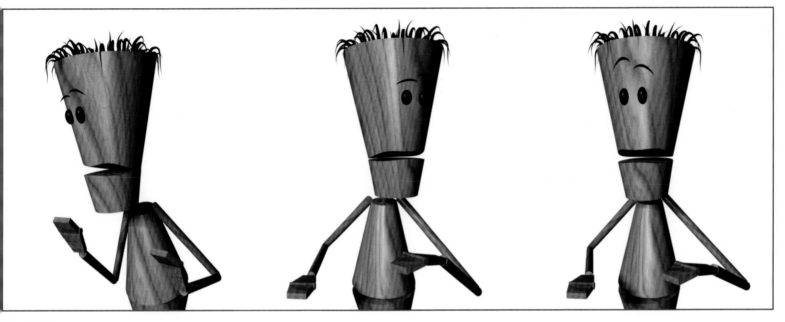

Figure 8.12
The head moves in quick bursts as the character looks around.

Figure 8.13
An analog stopwatch.

and never pull it out. Timing a motion requires that you, the animator, must perform that motion. This requires standing up and acting with your stopwatch. Oftentimes this scenario plays out in the computer lab with other animators. The shy nature of the artist kicks in and the stopwatch lies dormant in the bottom of his bag. Once you've made the decision to actually put that tool to work, you will see your ability to animate with proper timing improve dramatically.

First, time the overall action for your scene. This will give you a good idea of how much information you can pack into a given amount of time. You'll be amazed at how fast two seconds can disappear. Start the clock and act out every action you intend to include in the shot. Stop the watch when the acting is finished and record the results. Try to disregard the ticking hands. You'll get much better results from rehearsing naturally and not worrying about how much or how little is occurring during that moment. As with each of the following steps, I recommend acting out the movement several times and taking an average of the results. You'll find the timings become much more accurate after multiple performances.

Once the scene length has been determined, begin breaking down the complete action into smaller movements. I tend to focus on details during this part of the process. The more precise my measurements, the closer the initial pass of animation will resemble my routine. For example, my character stands up out of his chair and then reacts to a loud noise to the left. I'll break this down into the following parts:

1. Anticipation of getting up.
2. Stand up from the chair.
3. Settle from standing up.
4. Anticipation when noise is heard.
5. Turn toward noise.
6. Settle from turn.

At each of these steps, I'll start and stop the watch and write down the amount of time transpired. Each section gets three or four takes for a better average. Keep in mind that recording a six-frame move can be somewhat difficult. Record the smallest increments you can possibly capture, and make educated guesses for actions you just can't get. Coupled with our next tool, "x-sheets," the stopwatch breakdown can be further refined and laid out.

The use of x-sheets can be a great help during the recording stage. X-sheets were originally developed for traditional 2D animators to provide camera and audio notations. The animators would record their poses and timings on these sheets and hand them off to assistants to aid in the in-between process. These documents provided all the necessary information to animate a scene. Although CG animation doesn't require the same type of information to be passed around, these sheets are valuable assets to an animator's toolbox.

I use the following guidelines to organize my x-sheets. Figure 8.18 shows a completed version of the shot in *Rocky and Bullwinkle* shown in Figure 8.14.

Figure 8.14
Bullwinkle tries to keep his balance on the plane's wing. Copyright © 2002 by Universal Studios. Courtesy of Universal Studios Publishing Rights, a Division of Universal Studios Licensing, Inc. All rights reserved.

1. **Lefthand Column:** I like to draw my thumbnails in this section. It provides ample room for a small drawing and provides a nice visual cue when looking down the page. I'll also mark specific frame numbers if required. The dark lines divide the sheet into eight frame sections. (See Figure 8.15.)

2. **Second Column:** The second section gets all the necessary information for the dialogue of a scene. I mark the phoneme sounds under the "dialogue" column and mark movements in the jaw with an arc and holds with a straight line in the jaw rotation column. (See Figure 8.16.) Chapter 15, "Lip-Sync and Facial Animation," will explain this process in detail.

3. **Long Column on Right:** I use this portion for any notes that will help me get through the scene. I'll document occurrences in the plate such as an actor entering or leaving, or I'll scribble the emotional state of the scene. (See Figure 8.17.)

These specifications were adjusted over the years to meet the various requirements of my animation process. Feel free to customize the format to meet your conditions. After all, the information is being recorded by the individual artist and only intended to assist in his animation efforts. No one is going to critique the "correctness" of an x-sheet.

Another tool that I would suggest is the age-old practice of observation. You can learn a great deal by simply viewing the work of skilled animators. By observing I'm referring to the watching and re-watching of animated films. It makes sense to

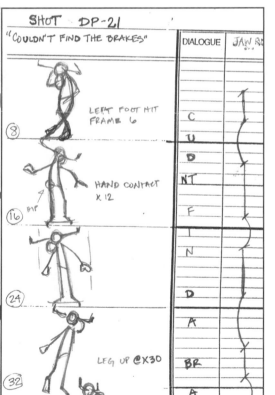

Figure 8.15
Small thumbnails and frame notations provide excellent benchmarks for the animation.

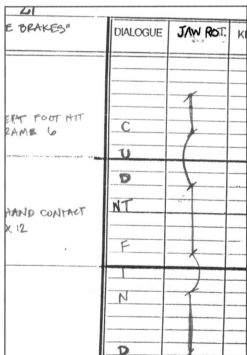

Figure 8.16
The notations for dialogue.

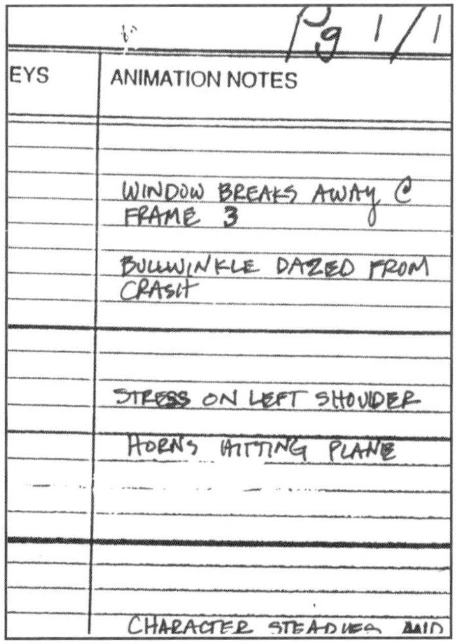

Figure 8.17
The right column is an excellent area for general notes.

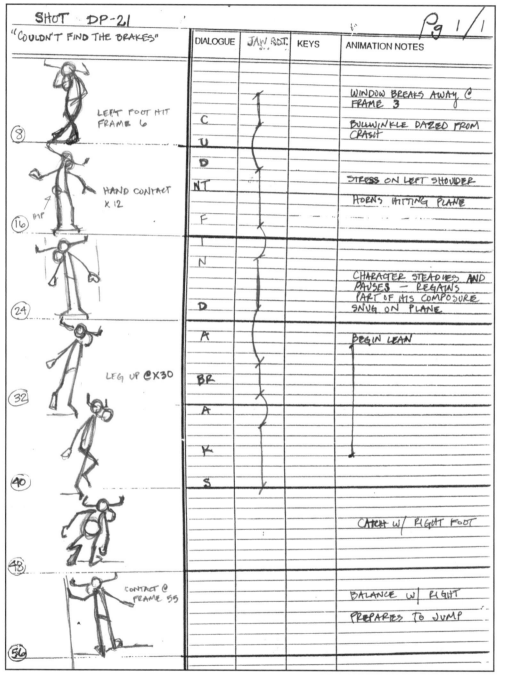

Figure 8.18
The completed x-sheet.

find out how the best animators approach their work and try to replicate their methods in your own.

As a student, I spent hundreds of hours going frame by frame through animated films. I was doing a walk with a stop-motion character, and watched *The Nightmare Before Christmas* countless times. There is an excellent shot of Jack Skellington strolling through the forest, and it had the perfect framing for analyzing the motion. The slow motion and pause settings on the VCR enabled me to carefully watch every frame. I did some drawing and counted frames to find out specifics about how long it took to get the feet up and how long it took them to fall. I obviously had to change the frame counts to meet the needs of my character but this provided a great starting point and gave insights into how my character might move.

Exercise: The Heavy Push

Let's put some of these ideas into practice. I've chosen the action of a character pushing a heavy box. This scenario is an excellent way to visualize the effect that timing has on the weight of an object. The timing chosen will give the object a specific identity as a heavy object. In addition, the manner in which the simple character performs the operation of pushing the block will tell a great deal about his attitude. A strong muscleman will have a much different approach to moving the box than a small, frail character. The scene begins with some simple planning.

The intent of this push is to try to make the box as heavy as possible. Because I don't often push around objects that weigh a lot, a little research is in order. I begin by pushing an empty box and do my best to react as if it were heavy. Using a stopwatch, I'll record the general timings of the action and record them on an x-sheet or in a sketchbook. With the simple planning in check, I can begin the process of roughing in some key frames. (See more info on planning in Chapter 16, "Getting Started: The Animated Short.")

The first step is setting keys at the major points in the push. The first frame, contact moment with the box, the initial thrust, and the finish pose as the box moves across the screen will give me a general feel for the scene. (See Figure 8.19.) Those keys occur at frame 1, frame 30, frame 50, and frame 120, respectively.

The most important portion of the action will occur as the character begins applying pressure to the box. The number of frames required to move the box and the distance traveled during that critical moment will be a good indication of how much it actually weighs. Because I'm hoping to convey a large mass, I set the next

key at frame 70. The outcome is a significant number of frames passing with the box only slightly moving. (See Figure 8.20.)

The next critical section is the momentum the box has as it moves toward the resting position. Even though the box has begun moving, it's still important to have it slowly gain energy. Moving the box too quickly at this point would negate the keys I've already put in place. I set a key at frame 90 in order to maintain the slow thrust that has already been established. (See Figure 8.21.)

Frame 1   Frame 30   Frame 50   Frame 120

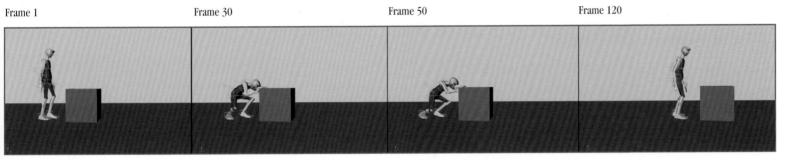

Figure 8.19
The first pass of keys.

Frame 50 ⊢—⊣ Frame 70

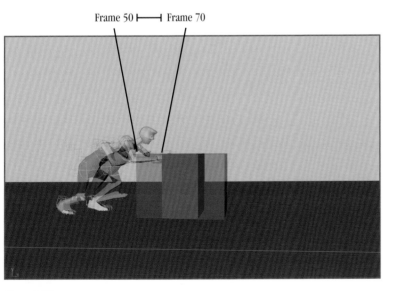

Figure 8.20
The fifth key set gives the box a hefty quality.

Frame 50 ⊢————⊣ Frame 90

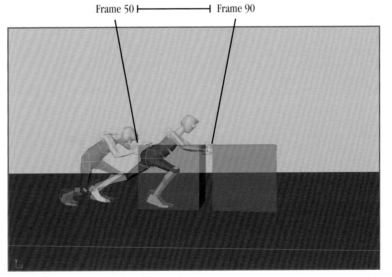

Figure 8.21
The sixth key keeps the box at the desired pace.

8. Timing

The last issue to be resolved is the stopping of the object. Because heavy things take a long time to get moving, they also take some time to settle into a resting pose. I want the box to gently settle into the final position. Setting a key at frame 105 will satisfy this requirement. (See Figure 8.22.)

Frame 90 ⊢——⊣ Frame 105

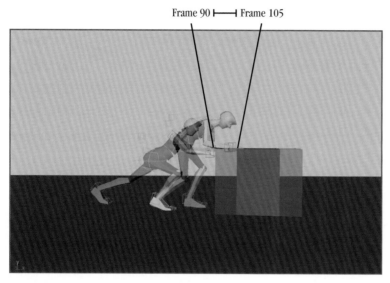

Figure 8.22
The seventh key begins the slowing down of the object.

These keys provide a solid framework for a heavy push. They are the major places to control the timing of the character's efforts. Although additional keys will be required, the impression of a large object has been established. The animator can sense the weight of the item and begin the process of refining the remaining portions of the scene.

As you can see, timing has a great impact on how a character or an object moves. It directly affects the physicality and personality. And although it's elusive in nature, there are tools and procedures to help you learn to polish your timing. They are simple but can be extremely effective. Remember, learning the art of timing can take considerable effort and dedication. Stay with it, however, and you'll be thinking in frames in no time.

chapter 9
Posing and Staging

This chapter describes how to create appealing and effective poses as well as staging for animated characters. By poses and staging I'm referring to the concept of clearly conveying an emotion or idea through the positioning of a character and how that figure is viewed from the perspective of the camera. It's important not to confuse this notion with the form of staging that relates to how the camera moves. It's true that the camera placement will have a significant effect on how the action is perceived. A close-up shot has a different emotional impact than an establishing shot. That concept is extremely important, but it's an entire text in itself. This chapter is more concerned with providing sound fundamentals in regard to individual poses and how the character performs the action in relation to the viewer. (See Figure 9.1.) This is a concept that dates back to the early days of stage performance.

Figure 9.1
A shot of the troll and a digital Harry from the film *Harry Potter and the Sorcerer's Stone*. The director wanted me to clearly present the dangling Harry. HARRY POTTER AND THE SORCERER'S STONE © 2001 Warner Bros., a division of Time Warner Entertainment Company, L.P. All Rights Reserved.

> **pose** v.
> To adopt a particular physical posture for a photograph or painting, or position somebody or something for this purpose.

Animators borrowed from these traditional stage and cinema techniques and began concentrating on stronger presentations of gestures and poses. Clearly defining specific motions and emotions led to stronger audience relationships. Story points were better defined and actions unmistakably presented. This fundamental continues to be an integral part of animated production as audiences continue to sophisticate themselves to moving images; artists must find clever ways to present their ideas.

Presenting Clear Ideas

I'm sure everyone has seen a billboard now and again while driving on the freeway. These signs bombard drivers with products and ideas by using a limited amount of imagery and text. Most of the time, they are effective. Viewers gain a strong understanding even from this limited information. These same principles can be applied to the world of animation when you have very short periods of time to convey complicated emotions and actions. Animators must strive to find the simplest and most effective ways to express the ideas of a shot. The following paragraphs provide a framework for that presentation.

Emotional Punctuation

The most important thing to remember when creating a pose is ensuring that the gesture plainly and definitely conveys the emotion of a scene. Emotion is at the core of creating believable characters and one of the primary vehicles for relaying that emotion is the character's physical posture. If used properly, a gesture can carry an immense amount of information. This information is vital to keeping a connection with the audience, and an animator must take full advantage of her poses to best present the story idea at that moment. Because of the sheer volume of poses required in good character animation, it is imperative that an animator break down the scene into its most simple form—the single pose. In essence, take it one pose at a time.

Sean Mullen emphasizes this point during his interview in Chapter 10. His work method relies on capturing the emotion of a scene with a single pose. That single pose dictates how and when a character moves and sets the foundation for the entire shot. The success of his effort is resting on the emotion created in a single frame gesture. (See Figure 9.2.) By concentrating efforts on one emotion, the exact point of the scene can be clearly emphasized. Many times, this notion is overlooked.

Figure 9.2
The viewer quickly understands the excited nature of the character.

Contrary to what many people expect, a scene doesn't require an extensive number of poses to clearly demonstrate an idea. In fact, many people go to great lengths to jam so many ideas into a shot that the viewer is left confused by the onslaught of too much information. The end result is a jumbled mess of actions and motions that do nothing more than move around the screen. Remember, the animator's job is to maintain clarity of emotion by keeping the viewer seeing one, and only one, idea in a shot. Limiting the amount of information presented is a step in the right direction.

Direct the Eye

Image composition can include a number of objects, characters, colors, and events. These items combine to create a palette that is both informational and emotional. Although necessary, all these items can be a distraction to the idea an animator is trying to convey. The proper use of a pose can minimize these distractions and point the audience in the right direction.

As I said, clarity is the key to illustrating a point. The audience's attention needs to be directed toward the concept being presented. Imagine a soda commercial. If an actor is going to proudly display the product, he'll want the audience to clearly see the label on the can. Any ambiguity would distract the audience and lessen the impact of the advertisement. (See Figure 9.3.)

By directing the audience's eyes to a specific location, the animator is making a direct comment on what needs to be viewed. The essential story beats are given proper screening time and keep the audience connected with the events that are unfolding. Actions are direct in their staging and contain the necessary accents to make them most effective.

During the production of *Episode I*, I was assigned a shot that contained the character Sebulba. The shot required that he sabotage another racer's vehicle. He slowly crept up to a control device, reached up, and broke the piece from the engine. This moment was necessary for future plot developments and critical that the audience clearly see the action. Creating the proper pose would be necessary to unmistakably sell the action.

The end result was Sebulba directing his posture and appendages toward the important engine part. (See Figure 9.4.) As he approached the device, I pointed both arms and head toward the lever, and created a "C" shaped figure with his body. This semicircular composition guided the viewer's eye to the area of interest.

Figure 9.3
The character on the left is ambiguous in his presentation. The character on the right clearly shows the product being displayed.

Silhouette Value

While attempting to maintain clarity, a few additional precautions can be taken in order to make your character's statements as clear as possible. Constructing strong silhouettes in your poses can do this. This will result in actions that occur in the open without interference from other characters or objects.

A silhouette is the outline of an object filled with a solid color. The single line represents the extremities of a figure. The shading represents everything within that boundary. Animators can use that line to determine whether a character's gestures are occurring in a space that's plainly visible to the audience. The shading portion hides additional information that might be useful in reading the gesture. A simple test can illustrate this point.

9. Posing and Staging

Figure 9.4
Sebulba's sabotage is clearly seen and enhanced by the direct nature of the pose. COURTESY OF LUCASFILM LTD. Star Wars: Episode I – The Phantom Menace © Lucasfilm Ltd. & ™. All rights reserved. Used under authorization. Unauthorized duplication is a violation of applicable law.

100

Look at Figure 9.5. This is the silhouette of a simple pose I created. It's void of any specific information and looks like the basic outline of a human being. Now look at Figure 9.6. I've turned the lights on revealing the shaded portions of the figure. It's apparent now that the character was gesturing toward his watch. By comparing the two images, you can see that the silhouette isn't very strong. The viewer should be able to fully understand the intent of the pose with the shading intact. Modifying a few details will result in a much stronger pointing action.

Figure 9.7 shows the newly created pose. The silhouette plainly shows the character motioning toward his wrist. The viewer doesn't gain any additional information by revealing the "inner" portions of the outlined figure. The animator is relying on a strong body gesture to convey the character's action or emotion.

Most 3D packages have settings that will automatically create a silhouetted figure for you. Oftentimes it's accessible within the actual working view port. Other times, it will be necessary to create a quick render to get the results. Regardless of the options available, make every effort to routinely view your work in this mode.

Figure 9.5
A simple, silhouetted pose.

Figure 9.6
The weakness of the gesture is revealed when the lights are turned on.

Figure 9.7
The stronger silhouette exposes the goal of the gesture.

Anatomy of a Pose

Now that the artistic aspects of poses have been discussed, it's time to consider the mechanics that are present in a strong pose. Several fundamentals are needed in creating appealing character gestures, and providing the necessary backbone and technical foundation for your character's expressions and actions. When combined with the artistic elements, the result is a character with both appeal and functionality.

Balance

The most common mistake I've seen is the inability to maintain proper balance. I've witnessed many shots fail to meet their expectations when an animator breaks the balance barrier and places the character in a pose that would not be possible in the physical world. The action or pose breaks the rules of physics and distracts the viewer with sheer defiance of the laws of gravity.

Characters need proper balance from a physical standpoint. This physical state involves anatomy and physics. Animated figures, although make-believe, must maintain some semblance of real-world abilities. Breaking this barrier creates an unwanted separation between audience and character.

So what constitutes proper balance? A friend and colleague, Wayne Gilbert, had an excellent method for explaining this notion. He stated that balance occurs when the character has 50% of his body mass on each side of the center of gravity. The center of gravity is an imaginary straight line that extends perpendicularly upward from the ground plane through the character. A figure must keep an equal distribution of weight on each side of that line in order to be balanced. (See Figure 9.8.)

Center of gravity

Figure 9.8
The black line shows center of gravity on several poses.

Take, for example, the lifting of a leg. I want to place the character in a one-leg standing pose that's going to require that he lift a foot off the ground. Many animators will solve the equation the way shown in Figure 9.9. They simply pull the leg straight off the ground and feel satisfied with the pose. The result is a character that would immediately fall over.

The current position of the character ignores gravity. It's impossible to stand this way. I suggest you try putting yourself in this pose; I guarantee you can't do it. The character must alter his mass to compensate for the weight shift. I'll show you how to fix it.

As the character begins to raise the leg, the hips must shift over the standing leg. This redistributes the weight and creates an equal balance along the center of gravity. The character can sustain this pose with ease. (See Figure 9.10.)

Keep in mind that this concept must be applied throughout the character. The 50% I mentioned included all parts of the body. It's important that you keep an equal distribution across that line regardless of the pose. This will ensure the character's physical appearance is true to the laws of physics and appears natural and possible.

Asymmetry

Characters often gesture with multiple appendages. Both arms might rise in triumph from a victory or extend outward to embrace a loved one. They are striving for the same goal and often end up behaving alike. This symmetry can contribute to an unnatural pose, and make the character feel wooden and stiff. A slight adjustment can make all the difference.

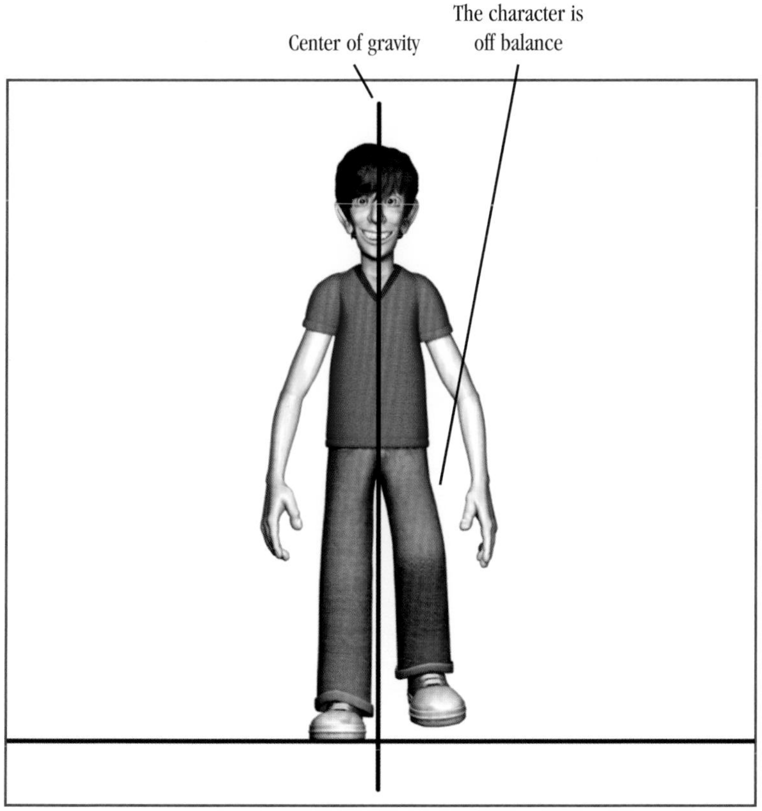

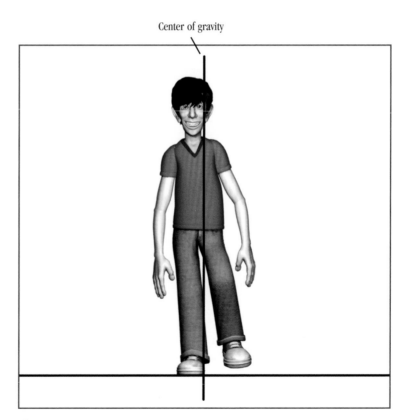

Figure 9.9
The unbalanced character would be unable to keep this stance.

Figure 9.10
The balanced character is in a more natural state.

Figure 9.11
The arms are symmetrical in their raised position.

Figure 9.12
The asymmetrical pose is more appealing.

Take the example of a character that has raised his arms protesting his innocence. He is about to deliver the line, "I didn't do it." Both arms extend from the body, and the elbows move in toward the torso. Figure 9.11 shows this gesture with both limbs in identical positions.

The pose is stiff and lifeless. It's inconceivable to think that two arms could strike and maintain the exact same pose. By repositioning one of the arms, the gesture becomes much more natural. The character's body has a sense of asymmetry and is more lifelike. (See Figure 9.12.) Although these examples involve static poses, it's absolutely necessary to be conscious of symmetry when moving in and out of a gesture.

Watch for Twinning

When two appendages hit a pose on the exact same frame, it's referred to as *twinning*. Arms, for example, often mirror each other's action as they move in and out of a pose. It is highly unlikely that the human body could replicate this amount of symmetry while performing a motion. This movement is abnormal and helps to create an unbelievable character. A minor adjustment can make the flow between poses much more effective.

Offsetting the point when two arms reach an extreme key frame is crucial. That value could be as small as three or four frames. The difference doesn't sound like much, but will dramatically affect the look of your motion. This small separation takes away the robotic appearance that's often encountered in digital animation.

Let's say a character is cheering at the scoring of a touchdown. He thrusts both arms toward the sky as the player crosses the goal line. Offsetting the arms by a minor amount will remove the twinning aspect. Having the right arm hit at frame 15 and the left at frame 18 will assist in a more natural stopping of the character's movement. (See Figure 9.13.)

Exercise: Silhouettes

I mentioned the necessity of having strong poses earlier in this chapter. A strong silhouette provides readability and ensures the character is posing and staging the action in the best possible way. This exercise isolates an action into a single pose and forces the reader to clearly demonstrate a specific emotion while using a silhouette. I find this exercise especially useful when working with a new character. It provides a great opportunity to warm up with a new figure and provides a quick way to practice getting some key emotions into a pose.

The exercise entails creating four individual poses. Each pose should have a distinct emotion associated with it. The character should be manipulated and then rendered as a silhouette. The successful image will communicate a recognizable emotion. Having that sentiment read in the simplest of forms will ensure that the attitude of the character is communicated.

I asked a colleague to complete this exercise. Jason is relatively new to the profession and is always looking for methods to improve his skill set. After his initial pass was complete, we discussed each pose and modified it accordingly. The first poses, comments given, and revised pass are presented in the following figures. I'm a firm believer in the learning ability of the critiquing process. Not only can an animator improve from having his own work commented on, he can also learn a great deal from other animators involved in the process.

Frame 15

Frame 18

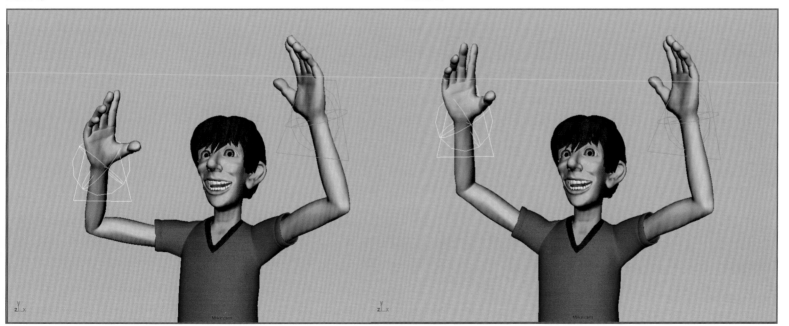

Figure 9.13
The right arm hits at frame 15, the left at frame 18.

Figures 9.14, 9.15, and 9.16 are the results of Jason's first pose.

Initial comments: This image actually worked quite well. It is obvious that the character is in a confident and happy emotional state. The pose has been staged in an optimum direction toward the camera. Details such as the backward curve in the spine, arms, and legs, and the head tilting backward read very well. The extremities are unobstructed, and that gives the viewer a clear understanding of their intent. The balance works well. The animator shifted the hips over the right foot just enough to compensate for the upper body leaning backward.

Changes requested: Although minimal, I felt that two changes were in order. The arms have a small amount of twinning in their current state. I'd move the right wrist up a small amount to break the symmetry. In addition, I think the head could be rotated more to the character's right. There is a hint of facial expression in the current render. Pushing the turn should create a more definitive opening between the upper and lower jaw.

Figure 9.14
The initial silhouette.

Figure 9.15
The revised silhouette.

Figure 9.16
The final render of the confident/happy character.

Figures 9.17, 9.18, and 9.19 are Jason's second emotion.

Initial comments: As the first image, this pose is pretty clear. The character's slumped nature and dangling arms suggest a very sad figure. The staging clearly shows the curve created in the spine. This slouch is a big clue in revealing the emotion of the character.

Changes requested: This pose does contain some symmetry problems. The arms are hanging at the exact same length. Slightly raising the left arm will create a more appealing pose. I'd also suggest adding some rotation to the character's right arm. Currently, the arm appears very linear. Pulling the elbow outward and rotating the hand will give a much better indication of what that arm is actually doing.

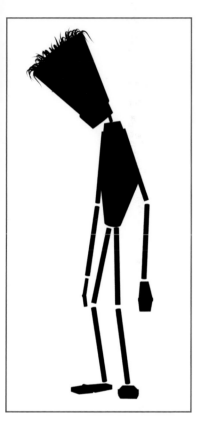

Figure 9.17
The initial sad silhouette.

Figure 9.18
The revised pose.

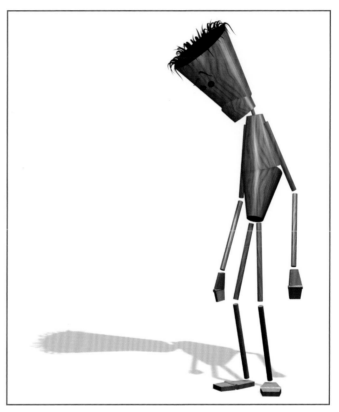

Figure 9.19
A final render or our sorrowed character.

Figures 9.20, 9.21, and 9.22 represent the third emotion.

Initial comments: This pose is fairly dynamic. Again, I was able to recognize the emotion being presented with relative ease. The arms have a nice amount of exaggeration and the legs are properly positioned to support the upper body. The head is staged to show the open mouth, which helps sell the scared nature of the character.

Changes requested: I felt the main area of improvement was in the arms. Once again, they feel very linear in their presentation. The elbows need to give a better indication of the orientation of the arm. In addition, the wrists would be better suited if they were rotated up. This would put the character in a more defensive position and assist in the frightened feeling of the pose.

Figure 9.20
The first pass at a scared character.

Figure 9.21
The revised silhouette addressing the arm and wrist concerns.

Figure 9.22
A final render of the terrified figure.

Figures 9.23, 9.24, and 9.25 are Jason's final attempt.

Initial comments: This was the weakest pose. I had difficulty deciding on what the intent actually was. After revealing the emotion, I could see what the animator was trying to achieve. He was going for "anger" and wanted to portray a character pointing aggressively toward another person. I think he succeeded in staging the character to best present the gesture, but didn't make the pose strong enough to reveal the emotion.

Changes requested: I think Jason should try the clinched fist approach for this emotion. Adding a bend in both arms would help intensify the character's feelings. In addition, exaggerating the lean forward will make the figure appear more assertive in his delivery. I'd also make the jaw opening very apparent. Any character in this state of mind would definitely be yelling.

Figure 9.23
An obscure figure.

Figure 9.24
The revisions clearly denote an angry character.

Figure 9.25
The full rendered version.

It's absolutely necessary that animators place a high priority on creating successful poses. The slightest obscurity from your character can hamper the intent of a scene. The next chapter is a discussion with Sean Mullen. He's a traditionally trained animator who has an excellent understanding of the importance of posing.

chapter 10
An Interview with Sean Mullen

Sean Mullen is currently a lead animator at Sony Imageworks in Culver City, California. He has a unique style of working that incorporates many techniques from the traditional hand-drawn world of animation. The following is an interview with Sean in which he discusses his approach to animation.

KYLE: *What is your background and how did you end up at Imageworks?*

SEAN: I was born in Massachusetts and grew up there. I started really drawing in the 3rd grade and got interested in becoming an animator just a couple years after that. A family friend named Susan Nichols, who was an animator at Disney and was going to California Institute of the Arts at the time, told me about the school and suggested I focus on life-drawing and basic design fundamentals if I wanted to try to get in there. So I took weekend life-drawing classes taught by an incredible artist named Tom Haxo at UMass all through high school. (See Figure 10.1.) I also spent my summer between junior and senior year in a life-drawing and design program at Pratt Institute. I applied at Cal Arts and started the year after I graduated high school. (See Figure 10.2.) I ended up leaving after two years because it was more affordable to get a job than it was to stay in school.

Figure 10.1
A drawing from Sean's high school days.

111

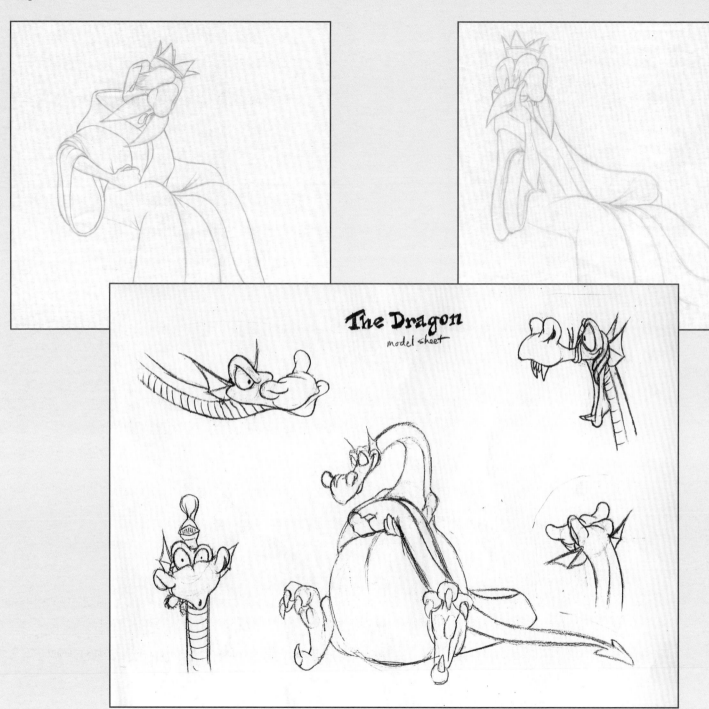

Figure 10.2
A few drawings from Sean's Cal Arts days.

KYLE: *Where was your first job after leaving school?*

SEAN: My first job was at a commercial place called Duck Soup in 1993 working as a clean-up artist. I worked on several commercials for clients such as Charmin, 7 UP, and Pupperoni. The first thing I animated professionally was a J.C. Penney commercial for a summer sale with all these little ants running around in picnic settings. The first half of my career was in commercials and all traditional. One of the best things that came out of that was dealing with the deadlines in commercial production. It conditioned me to try and nail a shot on the first pass. I think I've probably lost some of the speed I had back then when I started working on features where the deadlines are a little longer.

KYLE: *By nailing things the first time, did you rely on a stronger sense of planning?*

SEAN: I don't know if it was really more planning, but rather trying to economize your energy. It forced you to think simply and clearly. That's the way you should really think about a scene even if you have a long time to do it. You have to figure out the core idea behind a scene and make sure everything in the scene is focused on that idea. It keeps you from going off on a tangent that would make you waste too much time and, more importantly, miss the point of the scene.

> You have to figure out the core idea behind a scene and make sure everything in the scene is focused on that idea.

KYLE: *Did you take full advantage of the resources Cal Arts had to offer?*

SEAN: I didn't really, but I can't say I regret it. The reason I didn't take full advantage is because it was my first time away from home and I was a little overwhelmed by being on my own. The reason I don't regret that trade-off is that it was a rare chance to experience some unique situations that I'll probably never get to experience again. But I wouldn't recommend to people that they squander an opportunity like learning animation at Cal Arts. I did work and learn a lot while I was there, but I certainly could've worked harder. After working at Duck Soup, I landed a job at Baer Animation working for Dale Baer as an assistant on the farmed-out portions of *The Lion King*. About a year after that project, Dale left Baer Animation and started a new studio called High Horse Animation. He gave me my first real job as an animator there. It was just he and I at that studio. He had gotten his start at Disney as an assistant until he got a chance to start animating on the film *Robin Hood*. He learned from the "nine old men" while he was there, so I couldn't have asked for a

better mentor. Working with him is what really made me a better animator. It wasn't that he sat down and gave me lessons in animation; it was more about my trying to measure up to the quality of work he was producing. I would have to credit that with 90% of what I know about animation now.

Here's another interesting thing about Dale. Back in 1983, when I was 11 years old Disney put out a television special called *Mickey's Christmas Carol*. I was always excited to see any Disney cartoon, so of course I made sure to watch it. I loved it, and thought the scenes with the ghost of Christmas future were the greatest thing ever. So I tried to duplicate one of the scenes from that section of the show myself on a newsprint drawing pad with magic markers. It was the first thing I ever tried to animate. Then, in 1996, 13 years later while I was working for Dale, I mentioned this to him in one of our conversations. It turned out that he had animated most of the Christmas future sequence, including the scene that I had tried to copy back when I was 11. I was just blown away to find out that I was learning to animate from the guy who had done the scene that had played such a big part in my wanting to be an animator when I was a little kid.

KYLE: *That's why young animators who can find their way into a studio can quickly add to their skill set. If the bar is set fairly high, you're driven to at least match that level of quality.*

SEAN: Definitely. Even after I left that studio and started doing freelance on *The King and I*, I would sit there and ask myself what my scene would look like if Dale was animating it to get an idea of where to start.

KYLE: *So then you went to Sony?*

SEAN: Yeah. From there I went directly to Sony. There wasn't any particular reason I switched to CG. I had a friend over there and they were starting *Stuart Little*. I'd read the book when I was a kid and was really interested in working on the project. It ended up working out a lot better than I thought. Working on the computer revived my interest in drawing and really defined my style.

KYLE: *When you made the jump from traditional to computer, what did you find most difficult?*

SEAN: The most difficult thing was getting the technical and creative elements to work together. It got pretty bad in the first few weeks when I was learning the animation controls. I would start trying to do a simple piece of animation to get used to the controls and it would look horrible. I realized that I was focusing so much on the technical stuff that I was completely forgetting all the basic animation principles. I went back to a process I used to use when I first started doing traditional animation to get back on track. I made photocopies of all the lists of animation principles from *The Illusion of Life* and pasted them right by my computer screen. I'd have to constantly be looking at them to remind myself of the basics. It seems pretty elementary, but it really helped me when a scene wasn't working.

KYLE: *Was there a particular technical hurdle that you had to overcome?*

SEAN: The biggest thing was my fear of the computer. I'd never really worked on computers. I didn't own one yet and I hadn't even played around on one, really. It was pretty intimidating. Once I got past the fear, and realized all I had to concentrate on were the tools that I'd always be using, it wasn't too bad.

KYLE: *I know you have a CG working style that relies heavily upon the things you've learned in the traditional world. How about taking us through a shot you've completed and explaining your process.*

SEAN: There is a shot in *Stuart Little* with the Stouts, Stuart's fake parents. It had some fun acting and involved multiple characters. (See Figures 10.3 through 10.8.) I approached it exactly like I do a traditional scene. When working in 2D, I'd do one drawing from the scene to establish the overall feeling of the character's emotional state and use that as the starting point. I do the same thing when posing in the computer. I do everything from the facial expression to the fingers. I get the whole pose worked out so I can look at it and see that I'm on the right track. If it's a subtle acting situation, you're pretty much going to be working in and out of that pose. If you get that one nailed down, the rest of the scene is going to be a lot easier. Action scenes will require more poses since the character will be moving more broadly, but even they can still be kept to a minimum. A good example of what I'm talking about is any Norman Rockwell painting. One frame can illustrate an entire situation, from a character's movement all the way to their emotional state.

KYLE: *That one pose is the main benchmark for the entire scene even though the scene may require many poses to communicate the emotions. That pose essentially summarizes that scene.*

SEAN: Right. Even if there is a change of emotion, which most times there will be, usually there is an emphasis on one emotion or another. In the Stout scene, for example, when Mr. Stout goes from being preoccupied with a peanut to faking shame about having given Stuart up for adoption, the point of the scene is him faking shame. So I'd focus on that second emotion.

KYLE: *So there's one idea in a scene that you are trying to convey?*

SEAN: Yeah. That's what I was referring to in our discussion about commercials. The short deadlines really made me focus on that one central point. I still try to do that. Also, to a certain degree, and this probably just comes from experience and

really knowing the characters I'm working with, I don't put as much thought into a scene as you might expect. Once I've got that central idea, I tend to go more with my instincts.

KYLE: *So it's similar to working straight ahead. You're looking for that spark?*

SEAN: Yeah. I will think about the scene when it's first given to me to figure out the overall performance and how I want to achieve it. But that's maybe in the first day or so. After that I really just focus on sticking to that one idea. I try not to over-think things while I'm working on the scene. So with Mr. Stout in this example, I took into account the fact that he was a life-long, second-rate hustler who was trying to convince Stuart and the Littles that Stu was actually his son. And the real trick was getting that across somewhat subtly so that I wouldn't give away the fact that it was a scam too early in the film. Mrs. Stout was also involved in the scam, but she approached it differently. First of all, she's pretty ditzy, but she has a truly loving personality. She liked the idea of being a mom so much that she had essentially convinced herself that this was actually real. So I played her much straighter. She's not trying to "act" as much as Mr. Stout. So keeping these things in mind, I listen to the dialogue over and over while I picture what their performances might look like in my head. Once I decide on something I'm happy with, I create that first pose. Then it's just a matter of following through with the rest of the idea and not getting off track or second-guessing myself.

KYLE: *Once you've created a pose for each of those characters, what is the next step?*

SEAN: The next step is setting what you would consider to be normal key poses. Just an overall road map of where I want the scene to go. Both spatially, where they are going to start and finish within the confines of the frame, as well as emotionally. This is where I'd start establishing that change of emotion if there is one. So focusing on Mr. Stout in the scene, we first see him as he's about to take a bite of the peanut. Stuart asks Mr. Stout why they didn't want him, and Mr. Stout pulls his attention away from the peanut to answer him. Then he goes into delivering his sob story. Some of the key extremes would be the pose where he's about to bite the peanut (see Figure 10.3), the poses where he looks at Stuart and his mind is scrambling to come up with the sob story (see Figures 10.4 and 10.5), and a few poses of extremes, such as pointing at Stuart with the peanut to accent a word and slumping over, covering his face in shame at the end of the scene. (See Figures 10.6 and 10.7.) The completed set of images side by side is shown in Figure 10.8.

At this point I'm still not really worrying about movement. Of course, I'm keeping it in mind, but the actual movement of the character is focused on later, at the point where I'm doing breakdowns.

Figure 10.3
Mr. Stout admires his snack. "STUART LITTLE" © 2002 Columbia Pictures Industries, Inc. All Rights Reserved. Courtesy of Columbia Pictures.

STUART...

Figure 10.4
Mr. Stout thinks of an excuse. "STUART LITTLE" © 2002 Columbia Pictures Industries, Inc. All Rights Reserved. Courtesy of Columbia Pictures.

10. An Interview with Sean Mullen

IT SHAMES ME TO SAY THIS...

Figure 10.5
Mr. Stout looks away in shame. "STUART LITTLE" © 2002 Columbia Pictures Industries, Inc. All Rights Reserved. Courtesy of Columbia Pictures.

... BUT YOU WEREN'T BORN...

Figure 10.6
The pointing of a peanut. "STUART LITTLE" © 2002 Columbia Pictures Industries, Inc. All Rights Reserved. Courtesy of Columbia Pictures.

... INTO A PROSPEROUS HOME

Figure 10.7
The slumping state as Mr. Stout finishes his speech. "STUART LITTLE" © 2002 Columbia Pictures Industries, Inc. All Rights Reserved. Courtesy of Columbia Pictures.

STUART...   IT SHAMES ME TO SAY THIS...   ... BUT YOU WEREN'T BORN...   ...INTO A PROSPEROUS HOME

Figure 10.8
The completed set of poses. "STUART LITTLE" © 2002 Columbia Pictures Industries, Inc. All Rights Reserved. Courtesy of Columbia Pictures.

10. An Interview with Sean Mullen

117

KYLE: *When you are setting these poses, are you keying facial features, fingers, everything?*

SEAN: At this point, I usually included all of the details in the pose. If it was a more action-oriented scene, I probably wouldn't. However, in a subtle acting situation I definitely do.

KYLE: *Would you show this stage of the shot to your supervisor or the director?*

SEAN: I actually start doing some breakdowns before showing it. I want to get some idea of the timing in addition to just the emotion. I'll bring it to a point where it's clear what I'm going for. That's actually a pretty important thing. A lot of people show scenes at a point where the lead or animation director has to ask "where are you with this scene?" or "what is it you're trying to get across here?" and the animator has to explain what is and isn't done yet. I don't think that's the best time to show a scene.

KYLE: *I might disagree there a bit. If you are dealing with a director or supervisor who has trouble projecting what they might want, you can often get some information by showing them anything. I've had several directors who wouldn't tell you what they wanted until you put a roughed-out scene in front of them. You didn't want to invest a lot of time producing an idea that was incompatible with the director's vision.*

SEAN: A director like that's going to be difficult to work with no matter how you work. I would personally always tend to lean toward not showing something you have to explain. I've found that it leaves the scene too open to interpretation and then you risk the chance of being directed along a totally different path before your ideas have been given a real chance to prove themselves. And really, setting your keys and adding some breakdowns shouldn't take that long to do. For example, the scene I'm working on now in *Stu2* is 95 frames long. Between keys and breakdowns, I probably had no more than about 9 or 10 poses and it only took a few hours to rough out. That's when I showed it for the first time. I agree with you on the idea of not investing too much time in a scene before showing it to whomever you need to show it to.

KYLE: *Getting back to the shot, when you do get ready to show a scene, don't you initially present it with step-curves turned on? And if so, why?*

Step-curves force the characters to hold a pose until the next key frame. (See Figure 10.9.) The computer then interpolates in one frame and the result is a popping action of the poses. See Chapter 4, "Tools of the Trade," for more information.

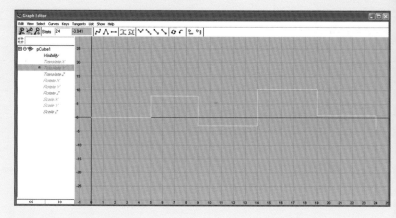

Figure 10.9
The step-curve setting in Maya.

SEAN: I prefer it that way and it's basically due to my traditional background. It looks exactly like the traditional pencil tests we used to do. I also prefer to see only what work I've done with no drifty computer in-betweens getting in the way. A lot of people will set keys and allow the computer to do its spline work between those keys. With splines, 90% of what you are looking at is the computer's work, and the majority of the time that work is going to be wrong. The stepped method lets the scene speak much more for itself.

KYLE: *You're taking the computer out of your work and just presenting the decisions you've made.*

SEAN: The only things the director, supervisor, or myself see are things that I intentionally put there. This is just what I've been used to for my entire animation career. Although I have strong convictions about working this way, I can legitimately see people working in other methods and being successful.

KYLE: *Everyone has a style that's influenced by his or her prior experiences. However, I think there's plenty of room to bring in elements from other styles. It's a constant refinement process. I have a different approach than this but I might be able to take small parts of that process and work them into my own routine.*

SEAN: That's definitely one of the advantages of the computer.

> The only things the director, supervisor, or myself see are things that I intentionally put there.

KYLE: *So at this stage of the shot are you just going to continue adding break-down key frames between your initial pass of poses?*

SEAN: I've only in the last few months settled into a comfortable working method for this stage. For me, it's always been the most painful portion of the process. I used to take my scenes down to fours, sixes, or eights, meaning that I'd save a pose on every fourth, sixth, or eighth frame, depending on the action. From there I'd switch to spline curves and start fixing all the inaccurate in-betweens the computer was inserting. This was so tedious and painful for me that I would have trouble concentrating on the scene. So now, I like to bring the scene all the way down to twos or threes while still using stepped curves. This way, when the curves are switched to splines, there's much less room for error in the computer's in-betweens. There's not much tweaking of things necessary at all when I do it this way. The only time I don't bring it down this far is on something like a moving hold that doesn't need to be broken down very much.

KYLE: *By tweaking things are you setting additional keys or are you adjusting the curves?*

SEAN: More often it would involve working with the poses themselves, interacting directly with the character. I tend to avoid any of the technical editors and curves until I need to use them for something specific. It's in the same line of thinking as only wanting to see what I've intentionally done when showing a scene. I'd rather work with the pose itself than mess around with some curve and then have to go back to see how it affected my pose. The way I look at it, no audience is ever going to see my curves on screen, so I don't really care what they look like. All anyone is ever going to see is the character, so that's where I direct my attention. I will use the graph editor, but it's just usually to help me figure out what's causing something weird to happen, such as a pop in the arm.

KYLE: *You're using those tools as a clean-up device.*

SEAN: Yes. It's really just that. I'll take the scene down to twos or threes by interacting directly with the model rather than refining movements by working with the curves.

KYLE: *You're setting keys every two or three frames for every part of the body?*

SEAN: Not necessarily every part, but every part that needs something done to it. Say the character's body is standing relatively still but they are doing a broad sweeping motion with their arm. The body might stay on fours but the arm will end up going to twos to keep it on arc. It's a matter of only setting as many keys as you need.

KYLE: *It's essentially putting keys where you need more control.*

SEAN: Right. And I've found that when I work things down to twos or threes and switch to the spline curve, 95% of the time it's essentially done.

KYLE: *How do you deal with changes once you've gotten to this stage? For example, I'm the director and look at your scene in a 98% completed state. I decided to have the character jump up and down in the middle of the shot as opposed to just standing there. What happens now?*

SEAN: If it's a significant change, I basically go in and start blowing away sections of keys. It's easier just to start over on a section of the scene than it is to try and rework what you already have there.

KYLE: *It's difficult to salvage something with that many keys. It's often just too laborious.*

SEAN: Right. But that's why it's important to get the blocking approved. Ideally, you would show your scene in the early blocking stage, and then a second time at a point about halfway through, when the idea is completely clear. You would ensure that the direction you are moving in is correct, and then finish the scene. Hopefully, you get any director comments in those first two stages before breaking it down to that many keys.

KYLE: *So what advice can you offer to people looking to become stronger at posing their characters?*

SEAN: I would put a really strong emphasis on getting classical training. Learn life-drawing, learn what a strong silhouette is, learn design, and all the basics that are constantly being harped on. (See Figure 10.10.) To me, the most important aspect of a good pose is that it should look natural. Don't do anything with the character that looks like it would really hurt or maybe even break a bone if you tried to do it in real life. *The Illusion of Life* is another great reference for posing tips, too. Also, keep in mind that 3D animation presents some new challenges, at least for 2D animators. One of the biggest for me to get used to was the idea that your character is actually three-dimensional, so even though it will only be seen from a specific angle in a scene, you should do your best to make it work from all angles. For example, if the character is leaning over toward the camera, the pose will tend to look more natural if the character is balanced when you look at it from the side as well. If it looks off-balance from the side, chances are it will look a little odd in the camera view. And remember, just because the computer appears that it can do a lot of stuff for you, doesn't mean that it's doing the right stuff. You really have to control it.

> **The most important aspect of a good pose is that it should look natural.**

KYLE: *If a person is not good at performance, do you think he can learn it?*

SEAN: To a certain degree I think you can. In the larger sense, I believe it's a gift. For some people it definitely comes much more natural. Some people just have a knack for that. But there are a few specific things you can keep in mind to create an interesting performance. I feel it's really important to know the character's back-story. Not just knowing that a character acts a certain way in a particular situation, but knowing *why* they would act that way in a situation. It's like knowing your wife and why she reacts to things the way she does. If you know the character that strongly, it's like animating a friend. I also think it's important to put yourself in the character's situation. You can definitely tell the people who are doing a scene thinking, "what would a cartoon character do here?" versus the people who are thinking about what they might actually feel if they were in that situation. The people who apply the character's emotional state to themselves deliver much more natural performances.

KYLE: *The result is a less clichéd approach to the shot.*

SEAN: Absolutely. That's a huge thing. Once you have an idea how you would act if you were in the character's shoes, you can go on to exaggerate it however you want. This ties in to my belief about getting classical training to help learn animation. Obviously, movement in animation is a caricature of movement in real life, and you need to know the fundamentals of real life before you can caricature it. It's the same with the emotional performance. Figure out an emotionally realistic approach to the scene and what would happen if you were in that situation, and then you can caricature it as much as you need to. Also, keep in mind where the character is going in the context of the overall film. The character should be growing over time, so they'll most likely act differently at different points in the story.

KYLE: *Any last words for our readers?*

SEAN: To sum it all up, the most important single word I can stress is "natural." I personally believe that the most important elements of a successful animated scene are a natural emotional per-

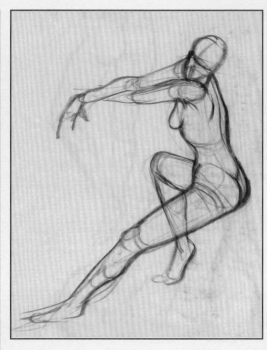

Figure 10.10
Life-drawing has been an integral part of Sean's learning process.

> **Movement in animation is a caricature of movement in real life, and you need to know the fundamentals of real life before you can caricature it.**

formance and natural movement from an entertaining charactezr. These few, simple elements rely heavily on each other to truly work. Nice movement alone is only a visual novelty and gets boring pretty quickly without a feeling, interesting character behind it. A strong emotional statement can get lost behind unnatural or elaborate but unnecessary movements. And even the most interesting character can be uninteresting if it's not clearly emoting or moving well. But if you can get all these elements working together naturally, the result will be a performance that audiences will believe and enjoy.

chapter 11
Arcs and In-Betweens

This chapter will focus on the fundamental and technical aspects of creating effective arcs in your actions. I'll discuss their relationship to actual performance in Chapters 17 and 18 later in this book. One must understand both the technical and artistic nature of animation in order to produce quality work.

The fundamental theory regarding arcs took a strong hold in the animation community and became a standard for all traditional 2D and stop-motion artists. Those traditional artists know the importance of maintaining this principle in order to produce quality work. This fundamental remains an important part of the current processes. However, its translation into digital technology hasn't been an easy one. As you'll see, managing this important aspect of character movement isn't that easy.

There is a certain amount of laziness in letting the computer do the work because it is relatively easy to get something to move. If you think in terms of the traditional animator, he does not have this luxury; he must draw every arc needed. There is a lesson to be learned from this approach. I've seen both novice computer animators and seasoned industry veterans fail to pay attention to their arcs. To be honest, I've done it myself more often than I'd like to admit. Taking a lesson from the traditional animators, I learned to set a few more key frames, because if I fail to pay attention to the arcs that create a natural sense of movement in my characters, the performance suffers.

Different actions have different degrees of arcs in their motions. For example, the swinging of an arm has a fairly noticeable arc between its forward position and rear position. Conversely, a head turning from side to side has a much more subtle degree of an arc as it traverses. I'll break down some of these exercises in greater detail later in the chapter, and give you some examples of how I use these different types of arcs in my animated characters. First, I'll show you what arcs are and how they apply to animation.

> **arc** n.
> A curved or semicircular line, or direction of movement, or arrangement of items.

Arcs

According to *Webster's Dictionary*, an arc is simply "a continuous portion of a curved line." When most people think of an arc, they think of the perfect 180 degree arch on a building, but an arc can also be represented by a figure-eight or just about any other continuous curved line.

The discovery of arcs in human movement can be traced back to the early 16th century and the master artist, scientist, and inventor, Leonardo da Vinci. Through careful dissection, da Vinci was able to uncover the true shapes and internal workings of the human body. More importantly, however (at least for our discussion), Leonardo did not simply observe these structures; he became obsessed with how they worked. This led to the first accurate knowledge of body mechanics and human movement. Because all animation is created with movement, you can see the importance of this work.

By analyzing how the bones attached themselves, the idea of arcs in motion was uncovered. da Vinci observed that the limbs and spine, like any moving object, attached at one end (similar to a pendulum) and moved around the axis of its attachment. Because the joints of the body are attached with a ball and socket (able to rotate on all axes) or hinge joint (only able to rotate along one axis), the resulting path of movement would be curved in nature. The spine is the exception because it derives its movement from a series of specialized joints "compressing" on discs allowing it limited but flexible motion. Another revelation that came out of this tendency toward curves (and one that applies directly to high impact animation) is that these joints were simply unable to make angular, linear motions. Again, LIVING OBJECTS CANNOT PERFORM ANGULAR LINEAR MOVEMENTS.

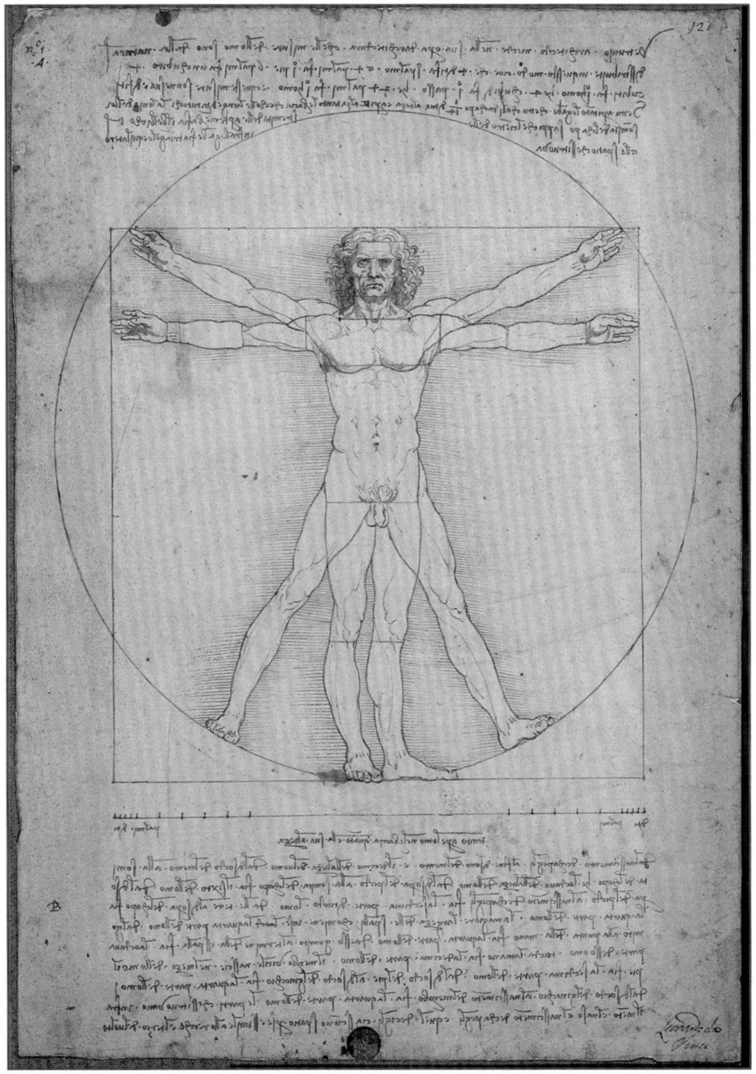

Figure 11.1
This drawing was intended to show human proportions as well as illustrate the fact that the movement of the limbs can be defined by curved paths or arcs. Leonardo da Vinci (1452-1519). The Vitruvian Man, ca. 1492. Copyright Cameraphoto / Art Resource, NY, Accademia, Venice, Italy.

Leonardo attempted to illustrate this concept in his famous drawing titled *Vitruvian Man*. (See Figure 11.1.)

To illustrate a ball and socket joint, simply stand with your arm fully extended at your side, with your palm facing your thigh. Keeping your arm fully extended, lift your arm perpendicular to your body with your palm facing the ground. If you were to draw a line tracking the movement of the fingertips, you would notice that the path in which your hand traveled can be drawn as a 45 degree arc. For a hinge joint, lay your arm out in front of you with your palm facing up, and bend your elbow toward your shoulder. This motion also creates an arc defining the movement of the hand.

The non-linear path an object takes from one position to another can be defined visually by the representation of an arc. (See Figure 11.2.) This arc, or curved segment, is present in large movements as well as the slightest motions. From the swaying action of a blade of grass to the sweeping movements of an elephant's trunk, every character or object that maintains an organic sense of motion incorporates arcs.

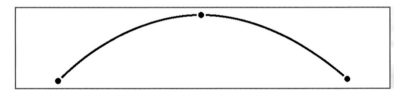

Figure 11.2
A simple arc diagram.

There are exceptions to the rule, of course. Remember, I said anything "natural" operates with the use of arcs. Things that are mechanical have the ability to move in a linear fashion. The pistons in a car engine, the needle of a sewing machine, and the shaft of a drill press all move in a straight line. These devices have structural restrictions and a set of hand-made devices that force their motion along one axis. It's important to understand the limitations of mechanical movement, but it is equally important to understand that an object that possesses life will never be able to move in such a way. The objects and characters discussed here will be organic and, therefore, move along arcs.

As animators strive to create more believable characters in films, games, commercials, and shorts, they must be careful to replicate the organic movements they observe every day. The circular path created from a turning head or a swinging arm is a detail that must be incorporated into an animated scene.

11. Arcs and In-Betweens

The concept of arcs dates back to the earliest days of Disney animation when the animators discovered that their characters took on a whole new sense of realism when proper arcs were followed on all moving parts. They began charting and planning their keys with notations included for arcs to ensure their performances maintained the genuine motion they so desired. (See Figure 11.3.)

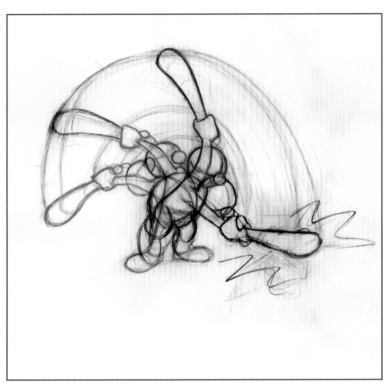

Figure 11.3
The plotting and drawing of arcs helped the animators stay on the proper path.

The Computer and Arcs

Although 3D technology has many great things to offer, one of the things it doesn't have an easy solution for is proper motion arcs. Artists can't rely on software by itself to generate acceptable paths between key frames. When two key frames are set, the computer creates the shortest path between those points. The software is designed to specifically translate between two given values. It's solving that equa-tion in the most efficient manner possible. Obviously, animation isn't about effi-ciency, it's about making choices that will create a performance or an action. You're looking to solve that space in between two key frames in the most natural and artistic way, regardless of the effort. By paying attention to the path along which an object moves, you can correct the computer's tendency to create linear paths.

I'll give you an example: I'm going to animate a character throwing a Frisbee. His right arm needs to make a smooth arc as he swings to release the disc. I've set a key at the beginning and end positions, frames 1 and 32 respectively. (See Figure 11.4.) The top view provides an excellent place to watch the resulting action. As I scrub through the scene, the computer calculates the resulting path that the arm will take. A snapshot from the middle of the action clearly shows that the computer has made an undesirable path of motion. (See Figure 11.5.)

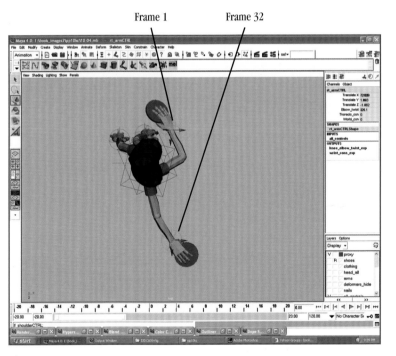

Frame 1   Frame 32

Figure 11.4
The first and last keys of the Frisbee throw.

Frame 1   Computer created a key that's on a   Frame 32
straight line between frames 1 and 32

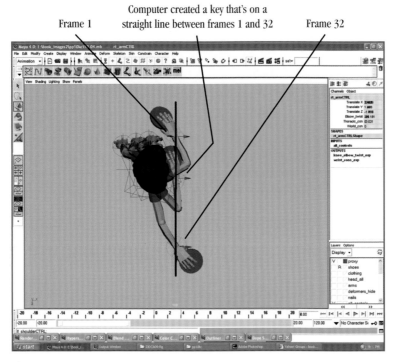

Figure 11.5
The undesirable path created by the 3D software.

The new position at frame 16 will give
Frame 1   the arm swing a more natural arc   Frame 32

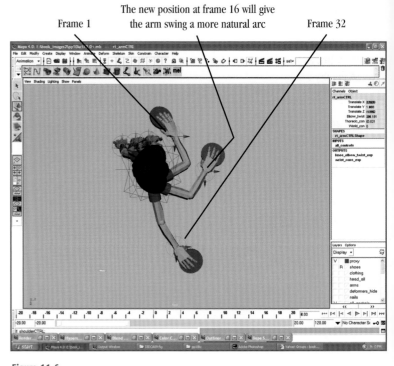

Figure 11.6
A key at frame 16 helps the arm swing in a circular fashion.

The solution to this problem is actually quite easy. If I add a few extra keys, the arm will swing in a more natural arc as it releases the disc. I'll begin by setting an additional key on the wrist controller at frame 16. (The proper placement of this in-between pose will be discussed later. This position is just to demonstrate the idea of generating an arc.) Extending the hand outward at the frame will result in a more natural translation between the first and last keys. (See Figure 11.6.)

Ultimately, this action will require additional keys in order to achieve the optimum arc. However, it's clear that the computer alone cannot create this motion (at least not yet). One additional key frame makes a significant difference. Several more and the character will swing his arm in a fluid, organic motion. Now, let me show you how proper arcs are determined.

How to Track Arcs

Many off-the-shelf packages have utilities or techniques for tracking the path of action. Chapter 4, "Tools of the Trade," discusses some of the options that exist in

3D animation packages. There is, however, a simple and efficient way to accurately trace the route an organic object should travel.

This approach does not employ technology, but instead uses the method that I prefer over any script, plug-in, or custom utility. It begins with the use of a dry erase marker, which is an inexpensive pen that can be bought at most office supplies stores. The dry erase marker originally was developed to write on erasable white boards, but can be used on any smooth surface. The ink can easily be removed with a dry towel. I'm going to be marking on the computer monitor with these pens and it's imperative that you use this type of marker. Trust me, you won't be happy (nor will the studio) if you use a permanent marker.

Take the example of a character waving his hand to get someone's attention. This is a broad motion that has a well-defined arc. The hand will require some special attention and several keys to keep the path of action desirable. The dry erase marker will assist in this process and ensure that the animator doesn't stray from her goal.

I'll begin by setting the two extreme poses. These keys will involve one pose at the left of the wave and one at the right. As with the Frisbee toss, scrubbing through the scene shows a hand traveling along an inaccurate trajectory. This is not difficult to correct. Just as a traditional animator might sketch in the arcs for his assistant, I can use the dry erase pen to indicate where the next set of key frames needs to be set. (See Figure 11.7.)

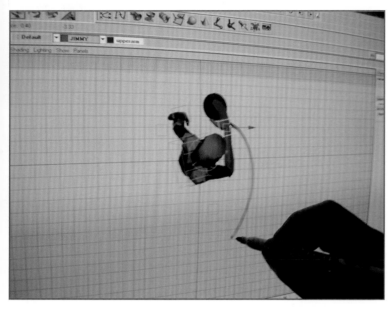

Figure 11.7
The arc is indicated with a mark on the computer screen.

This mark provides a template for the remaining keys that will be set. I can begin setting the in-between poses making the wrist conform to the sketch on the screen. In addition, tick marks at the various key frames give me an indication of the spacing of my poses. Each time a key is added, I'll make an additional tick mark with the pen. Now there is a visual representation of how the arm is articulating and I can adjust the keys accordingly. (See Figure 11.8.)

As you can see, having the proper arcs and paths of action (especially in computer animation) is crucial. Setting those additional keys in-between major poses is essential. In-betweens put the control in the animator's hands, where it belongs, and as I will show you next, impact the accuracy with which the characters move.

Figure 11.8
The poses are set in accordance with the sketch. Tick marks provide additional information to the whereabouts of my keys.

The In-Between

To accomplish the refined movements of the characters I'm animating, it's important to understand the term "in-between." This term refers to the parts of animation that occur between the defining poses of a scene. Animators can set these additional keys or the computer can interpolate and create the motion for you. Regardless of their origin, these in-between key frames directly affect how the motion appears.

Like many of the other fundamentals discussed, this technique dates back to the early days of hand-drawn animation where the animator would lay out the key or extreme poses. After those drawings are completed, a second artist would be responsible for adding the in-between drawings based on timing charts and notes from the animator. These additional drawings created the necessary transitions to create a fluid movement with natural arcs. (See Figure 11.9.)

As you can see in Figure 11.9, the in-between poses influence the quality of arcs that characters and objects move along. The examples, however, have yet to take into consideration the sense of weight and timing. In-betweens have a direct effect on both.

A

B

C

D

Figure 11.9
The in-between drawings in a traditional scene are shown above. The first and last images are the keys and the two drawings in the middle are the in-betweens.

11. Arcs and In-Betweens

I discussed the idea of timing in Chapter 8, "Timing," and laid out the fundamentals behind creating strong arcs in the previous section. It's now time to consider both aspects of motion and begin to unravel how the two co-exist in the same scene. To do this, I look to the in-between.

Referring back to the Frisbee throw from the previous section, I remember the computer's inability to create ideal arcs. The next step was setting a few extra keys so the hand would have a natural feel as it propelled the disc forward. Although the hand now traveled on a more favorable path, it lacked the necessary force to give it a sense of weight.

In-betweens, if properly placed, can create both a circular path and a believable amount of force. Characters need a certain amount of time to begin and end an action. This particular scene doesn't call for an excessive amount of time to move the arm forward, but will most certainly require a "weighting" of the keys at the beginning of the motion.

The in-betweens need to be placed so that the accelerating arm will ease out of its initial starting position before thrusting forward and releasing the Frisbee. The current keys are set at frame 1 and frame 32. I'm going to place an in-between key at frame 16. However, instead of placing the arm directly between the first and last positions, I'm going to place it toward frame 1. (See Figure 11.10.)

The key will result in the arm taking half of the 32 frames to move 1/3 the total distance. This will create an easing out of the move and will give the perception of the body actually projecting an object that has some sense of mass and a deliberate force behind it. How much force will depend on the character, of course. A different character of the same size, throwing the same object will have a new set of in-betweens, arcs, and timings. This example is not intended to be a timing lesson; rather, it is intended to show how the in-between keys will have an effect on both the timing and arcs in a motion. Although this one additional key has an impression on the action, a few more are required.

The shot is now approaching a somewhat desirable result. However, the computer still has too much influence on the throw. The arcs aren't quite right, and the timing is a bit flat. The next in-between I'll set will occur at frame 6. I'm placing this key closer to frame 1 to continue with the concept of easing out, and to help watch the arc that's required. I'll also need to place another key between frames 16 and 32 for the same timing and arc control. (See Figure 11.11.)

Weighting frame 16 toward the frame 1 will create more acceleration for the remainder of the throw

Two more keys help control arcs and timing

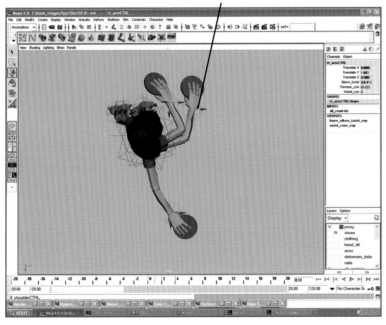

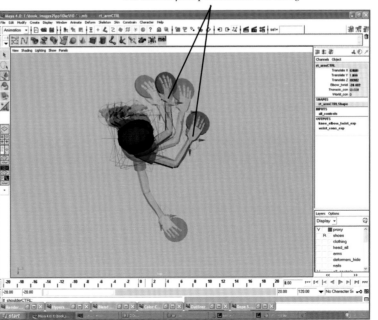

Figure 11.10
The first in-between is placed near the beginning pose of the Frisbee throw.

Figure 11.11
A key at frame 5 helps to better control the arc and impacts the timing as the arm speeds up.

This trend would continue until the desired animation was achieved. The coupling of both arcs and timing is a constant factor when animating a scene. Both must constantly be monitored in order to achieve the best results. By approaching a more complicated action from start to finish, I can get a complete picture of the importance these fundamentals have. The next section takes a look at such an example.

Exercise: The Arm Swing

One thing you can always count on in animation is the character walk cycle. (See Chapter 14, "Walks," for a complete discussion.) One of the most difficult parts of a walk is the arm swing. It's a complex motion that relies on a complete understanding of the principles already discussed in order to be successful. Proper arcs, an understanding of timing, and appropriate movement along multiple axes are all equally important.

Although there are many variations on how an arm can swing, I'm going to explain a technique that I often rely on. It's referred to as the "figure-eight" due to the resulting arc generated from the hand traveling along a path of this shape. (See Figure 11.12.) This is a generic approach, but can be modified to fit most any walk.

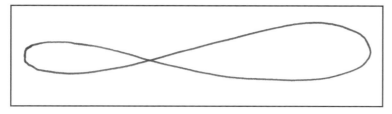

Figure 11.12
The path of an arm swing. The wrist travels in a squashed figure-eight pattern.

The example is being presented as a cycle in that the arm starts and stops at the same position. When played, the arm will appear to make a smooth transition from front to back for as long as the animator desires. This allows for proper dissection of the motion and lets the reader see both directions of the swing completely. It begins by setting a few simple keys.

The first poses that will get key frames are the two extremes. These two keys will define the farthest distance forward and backward that the arm will reach. Keeping the arms extended in these positions helps sell the "breaking" of the elbow as the arm moves in the opposite direction. In addition, these keys provide a framework for the subsequent in-between poses. (See Figure 11.13.)

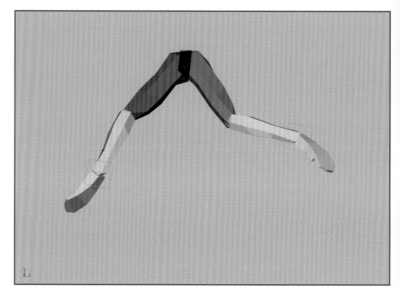

Figure 11.13
The two extreme poses for the arm swing. The back positions are keyed at frame 1 and frame 24. The forward position is set at frame 12.

The main positional keys are being set on the wrist controller of the arm. The arm setup contains the same controller configuration as discussed in Chapter 4, "Tools of the Trade."

The next step is starting to layer in a few in-between keys. Their position is determined by the distance the arm will have to travel and the amount of acceleration and weight that is desired. Remember, the heavier an object, the more effort it takes to get it to move; therefore, it takes longer to get it moving. For this character, I've chosen to place the first set of in-betweens at frame 6 and frame 18. (See Figure 11.14.) These two positions are a quarter of the way toward their goal in half the time they have to move that direction. The result is an arm that eases out then accelerates quickly to its target.

Frame 1 Frame 6 Frame 12 Frame 18

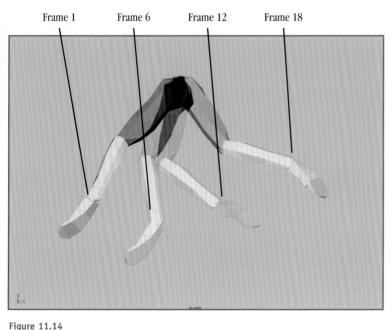

Figure 11.14
The first two in-betweens at frame 6 and frame 18.

Along with this relation to distance, I must not forget to keep the keys on the proper arc. They currently lie on a sweeping path from front to back. Minor adjustment might be necessary after future keys are layered in. However, they are positioned at a good starting point. (See Figure 11.15.)

Frame 1 Frame 6 Frame 12 Frame 18

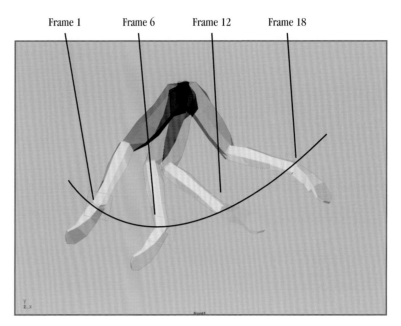

Figure 11.15
The arc created by the first four keys.

The current keys have established a basic standard of timing. Their position is creating the proper ease out and acceleration when moving from both front to back and back to front. As I continue to layer in additional in-between keys, it becomes increasingly necessary to concentrate on the path of action the arm is taking. The next few steps are a bit more complex but are needed to create a proper arm swing.

As the arm swings forward, it must continue on a circular path. The arm continues on an upward motion as it breaks back toward the body. This is a big point of confusion for many people. This action starts the first breaking of joints as the limb begins its back swing. The following image shows a sequence of keys that illustrate this point. (See Figure 11.16.)

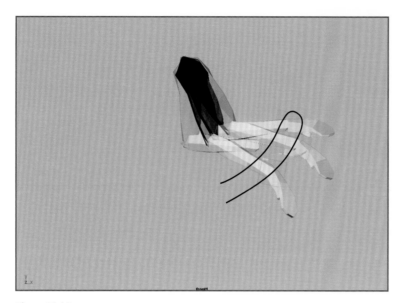

Figure 11.16
The circular path created as the swing changes direction.

A similar arc occurs at the high point of the back swing. The arm makes a small circle as it begins moving back toward the front. Two in-betweens are required to make the tight transition. I've placed them at frames 2 and 4.

The arm swing now has all the necessary elements of a believable action. The hand swings along a rounded, organic path and the proper in-betweens give the appearance of weight and acceleration.

Arcs and in-betweens are key fundamentals to keep in mind when animating your scenes. They must be implemented in order to create refined and believable animation. There is little room for shortcuts when entering this level of refinement so you must take control of the software and prevent the computer from making decisions for you. Be conscious of the effort and attention to detail required to produce a believable performance, both physically and emotionally and, of course, the most important rule … make it perfect.

chapter 12
Anticipation and Exaggeration

by Steve Harwood

In this chapter, I will explain two important ingredients needed to provide clarity and add the unique expressive quality of movement that is a hallmark of great animation: anticipation and exaggeration. By ignoring these fundamental concepts, you run the risk of producing work that lacks realism and subtlety and is difficult for the audience to follow, depriving them of the experience they have come to expect from animated entertainment. I'll begin with anticipation.

Anticipation

In human movement (and the movements of most living organisms of noticeable weight), a certain degree of momentum is needed to shift the weight of our bodies, raise our limbs, or jump up off the ground. To generate this momentum, almost all action is preceded by a smaller action in the opposite direction. In animation, this smaller movement is known as an anticipation or "antic" and can be illustrated quite easily by simply clapping your hands.

The obvious point of this action is to accelerate your palms together so that a loud noise is produced. To create the desired effect, you must generate enough force and speed in each hand so that when they collide you are able to create the needed amount of noise. To do this you must first move your hands apart. This movement is the anticipation or antic for the main action, which is the actual impact of the palms.

Try reaching for something.

Look to your left.

Did you notice your body preparing for the move by anticipating in the opposite direction and generating momentum? You may not have, but it *is* there. Your body actually geared up to reach for the item. Antics can be very subtle as in the preceding examples, or they can be very obvious and involve many parts of the body, like when you are preparing to jump over a gaping hole in the ground or similar physical actions.

The bottom line, however, is the sooner you learn this concept, the sooner you will be able to inject your animation with a new sense of subtlety and believability. This especially applies to 3D computer animation where the characters are already much more realistic and the audience expects them to move with a certain degree of fluidity and balance.

Why Do I Need Anticipation?

If you were to take the antics out of organic movement, most actions will immediately seem unnatural and mechanical as the character robotically shifts from one pose to the next. There are some instances, however, where anticipation is not required or even desirable. Objects such as machinery don't require movements to generate momentum even though it is absolutely necessary to include it in your work if you're animating living creatures, especially those that are anthropomorphic. You can always tone down your antics or remove them if they don't feel right.

Equally important to adding realism, anticipation serves as a tool the animator can use to enhance the experience had by the audience when watching their characters. The animator does this by following these guidelines:

1. **Preparing the audience for an action.** By clearly anticipating an action, you create audience expectation, a small moment of suspense before executing your more important poses and making the point of the scene.

2. **Allowing the audience to easily follow the action.** Like an actor, an animator wants to make sure that the audience receives the important information in each scene. Antics can effectively draw the attention of the audience to

131

a specific character at a specific time ensuring that they don't get lost or miss an important piece of information.

3. **Enhancing big actions and violent physical movements.** When performing large violent movements, such as the classic mallet over the head or the big knock-out punch, a strong anticipation goes a long way to add energy to the action by implying a much larger degree of force being generated. It is important to keep in mind, however, that the bigger the anticipation, the bigger the expectation the audience has and they will feel cheated if you fail to deliver. Generally speaking: the bigger the antic, the BIGGER the move.

Now I'll show you how to apply this concept to a character of your own.

Example: The Table Pound

In this exercise, I am going to show you how to apply the concept of anticipation using my good friend, Charlie. I assume you are familiar with posing your characters, so I will not go into detail about selecting individual controllers, and so on. In this exercise, poor Charlie has just watched his favorite team lose by one point and he isn't happy about it. I will attempt to relate this by having him slam his hand down on the tabletop. The basic poses/actions needed are as follows:

1. Observing.
2. Anticipating the table pound by bringing his arm up and behind his body.
3. Accelerating the hand down onto the surface of the table.
4. Settle.

Create a simple piece of geometry for a table and pose the character in front of it. I've placed both hands of the character on the table, palms down. The character is currently in his observation stage. He just watched his team lose and will shortly begin the process of venting that frustration on the table. (See Figure 12.1.)

Next comes the antic. The character needs to raise his arm for the pound. This draws back the chest, shoulder, and arm so that enough force can be generated in the hand as it is thrust onto the surface of the table and prepares the audience for the violent reaction that is about to take place. If this anticipation did not occur, it is unlikely that our character could strike the table in a manner that clearly demonstrated his frustration and anger. (See Figure 12.2.)

Now that the character has an antic, I want to position the character in an action pose: the impact of the hand on the table. This will be the main action of the

Figure 12.1
Charlie has mentally processed the loss and is about to strike the surface.

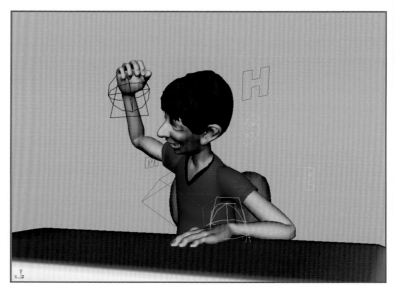

Figure 12.2
The anticipation pose lets the audience follow the action much clearer.

Figure 12.3
The contact frame.

Figure 12.4
The character settles into his final pose.

exercise. The character strikes the table with a closed fist, straightening his arm and rotating his chest and head upright, applying all the force that can be obtained from the antic position. This creates an angular positioning of the body that is characteristic of someone in an angry or agitated state and makes the point of the scene: Charlie is angered by his team losing. (See Figure 12.3.)

For the last pose the body is "settled" back toward the default position. The character has made his point and is now contemplating his next action. This pose also serves as a hold and provides a beat for the action to register with the audience. (See Figure 12.4.)

These poses clearly show the beats necessary to create a forceful slamming fist. The character uses the position in Figure 12.1 to prepare the audience for the violent action that followed. In addition, the level at which our character raised his wrist made the action more effective. This brings me to the next topic of discussion: exaggeration.

Exaggeration

The concept of exaggeration is an easy one to grasp. To exaggerate something is to embellish or overemphasize it to the point of being almost beyond belief. In animation, this is achieved through poses and timings that, depending on the amount of exaggerated movement you are looking for, overstate and draw attention to a character's actions. Like anticipation, exaggeration has a wide range of intensities. For example, photo-real characters such as those from *Stuart Little* and *The Mummy* have a minimal amount of exaggeration. (See Figure 12.5.) The characters are interacting with the subtleties of human actors, and the style of motion needs to match.

Exaggeration can be applied much more liberally in the fully animated environment. Tex Avery, the creator of such classically exaggerated personalities as Daffy Duck, Porky Pig, and the legendary Bugs Bunny, perfected this concept. Avery is considered by many to be the master of exaggeration, and his style continues to influence today's animation. Just take a look at an episode of *Ren & Stimpy* or the feature film *The Mask* (in which Avery's work is the basis for the wild transformations of Stanley Ipkiss). (See Figure 12.6.)

Figure 12.5
Stuart from *Stuart Little* ("STUART LITTLE" © 2002 Columbia Pictures Industries, Inc. All Rights Reserved. Courtesy of Columbia Pictures.) and the digital Imhotep in *The Mummy* (Copyright © 2002 by Universal Studios. Courtesy of Universal Studios Publishing Rights, a Division of Universal Studios Licensing, Inc. All rights reserved.) are both good examples of characters with very little exaggeration.

Figure 12.6
Exaggeration can be pushed to the extreme as with this character from *The Mask*. "THE MASK." © 1994, New Line Productions, Inc. All rights reserved. Photo appears courtesy of New Line Productions, Inc. and Industrial Light & Magic.

12. Anticipation and Exaggeration

134

Exaggeration also has its roots in the early acting styles of people, such as Buster Keaton and Charlie Chaplin. (See Figure 12.7.) If you have never viewed their work, I recommend that you try to obtain a copy and pay attention to the use of body language. Because these films are silent, the actors were forced to get the story points and characterizations across purely through pantomime. As a result, the acting is exaggerated so that the points of the scenes can be clearly made and there is very little room for confusion by the audience. The modern day equivalent of this approach can be seen in the work of Jim Carrey in such films as *The Mask* and *Ace Ventura*. The ability to tell stories without dialogue is at the core of producing great animation and is definitely a valuable skill to master.

Why Do I Need to Use Exaggeration?

Perhaps the most important benefit that exaggeration provides is clarity. Without exaggerating the movement and poses to some degree, you risk winding up with animation that is not only flat and boring but that is also difficult to follow (especially if your shot does not include dialogue). With that in mind, I think most animators will agree that some amount of exaggeration is needed to create an interesting and appealing performance that is easily understandable. Additionally, exaggeration can also provide the following:

◆ **Enhancement of large moves and violent actions.** This is where anticipation and exaggeration reveal their importance to each other. Because a big antic implies a big move, it seems natural that an exaggerated action needs to be executed. Remember: The bigger the anticipation, the BIGGER the move and thus, the BIGGER the exaggeration (generally speaking).

◆ **A unique style of movement and increased entertainment value.** Take a look at the film *Final Fantasy*. The movement lacks any kind of exaggeration and mirrors the motion of actual human beings. In contrast, take a look at one of my favorite scenes in Walt Disney Picture's *Toy Story*: The scene underneath the truck where Woody and Buzz have their final argument concerning the fact that Buzz is only a toy. The differences should appear obvious. Notice the exaggerated movements. These are characteristic of the Pixar style and add a quality of acting and life to the characters without throwing you out of the film by over-exaggerating or boring you with mundane acting—a difficult task indeed.

Are there times when you should not use exaggeration or tone it down so that it isn't as noticeable? Of course. This depends on several factors, including the character you are animating, the style of the studio, and your own preferences in your work.

Figure 12.7
Exaggeration as an acting technique can be traced back to such silent era stars as Charlie Chaplin. Charlie Chaplin ™ Bubbles, Inc. SA

Figure 12.8
The right amount of exaggeration can go a long way in creating a unique, entertaining style and adding extra life to your characters. © DISNEY ENTERPRISES, INC./Pixar Animation Studios

I was recently discussing the character Stuart Little with one of the senior leads on that particular show and mentioned the fact that he lacks a lot of obvious anticipation and exaggeration. He said that although Stuart is a mouse and an animated character, in the film he exists in the real world and is looked upon as being equal to a human being, so it is important that he behaves like one. Therefore, too much anticipation and exaggeration draws attention to the fact that he's animated. It would be like having a sign saying, "Hey look, I'm an animated character" every time he performed an action. If you take a look at the film, you will occasionally see some exaggeration and a noticeable antic or two, but for the most part, these moves go unnoticed because there is a conscious effort to tone them down.

In the end, it will be largely dictated by the environment variables mentioned previously. Unless, of course, you are doing the work

Make it twice as big as you think it should be and you're halfway there.

on your own, in which case you may want to consider a bit of wisdom handed down by my former animation teacher when referring to the amount of exaggeration an animator should try to achieve: Make it twice as big as you think it should be and you're halfway there. Artists tend to underestimate how big a pose or action should be. I often have to go back and push things to read much larger. Don't be afraid to go over the top; you can always tone it down.

The Role of Squash and Stretch

Because we are on the topic of exaggeration, I'll take a moment and look at a companion principle that is often employed with anticipation and exaggeration: squash and stretch. This concept has its origins in traditional hand-drawn animation and is primarily used to add impact and fluidity to a motion. However, it also has other applications, such as explosive movements or just about any situation where an anticipation followed by an exaggerated move is needed.

I am sure most of you have seen the classic bouncing ball tutorial (see Figure 12.9). In this demonstration, a ball is shown bouncing off the ground and the appropriate squash and stretch is applied to key poses in the movement.

> When animating in 3D, make sure that you "squash" your ball in all three axes to achieve the proper effect.

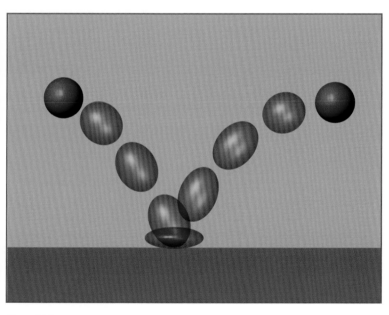

Figure 12.9
The squash and stretch of a ball bounce.

Notice how the ball elongates as it approaches the contact position, squashes from the impact, and stretches again as it leaves the ground. The compression (or squash) helps sell the ball's contact with the surface, and the extension (or stretch) shows the driving force upward. It also gives the ball a rubbery feel.

Now I'll show you how this same concept applies to a human character in the act of jumping off the ground using my simple character. From a standing position, he anticipates the jump by crouching down to generate the force needed to leave the ground, essentially squashing his body into position (see Figure 12.10). The curvature of the spine also helps create an opposing curve against the ground plane and acts as a visual cue that the mass has changed.

Figure 12.10
Squashing the body down to create the necessary force.

For the jump, the body stretches out as the thrust from his legs sends it upward and out (see Figure 12.11). The extension of both legs and arms presents a visual stretching of the character. In addition, the spine and head have straightened. This position has a strong similarity to the elongated nature of the ball as it leaves the surface.

Figure 12.11
Stretching the body upward.

Figure 12.12
Compressing the legs at the high point of the jump.

At the top of the move, the legs are brought up so that the knees approach the chest, squashing his body back into a ball (see Figure 12.12). You can see the reappearance of a curved spine and tucked head. These shapes once again oppose the ground plane.

As he descends, the legs extend and stretch the body out to prepare for landing. The body then squashes once more to absorb the impact and support the weight of the body. (See Figure 12.13.)

With this simple example, you can see that squash and stretch can be applied to just about any character or object that you animate, and can help to add energy to a large move where the body is shifting between two very different poses.

Obviously, there are no steadfast rules when it comes to this, but it is something to pay attention to when working in 3D photo-real environments. There are many things that you can get away with in drawings that you cannot on the computer.

Figure 12.13
Unraveling the legs to catch the weight of the body and then absorbing the impact.

Because the computer is incredibly accurate at portraying real-life objects and materials, you must be cautious in what you choose to squash and stretch. The viewer will subconsciously expect a ball that appears to be made of steel to not squash or stretch at all. If it does, all of a sudden you have a viewer who is saying to himself, "that metal ball doesn't look right" instead of being engaged by your animation. A racquetball, on the other hand, is going to have a great deal of squash and stretch simply because that's what it is expected to do. Remove that element and you no longer have a ball made of highly elastic rubber.

Putting It All Together: The Take

Now for the fun part. In this exercise, I will show you how to combine the ideas discussed in this chapter into one of the more entertaining actions in animation: the double take—or the Take. When executing a Take, you can use any degree of exaggeration depending on the amount of emphasis you are trying to achieve. A Take can be a simple second look or can be pushed to the extreme with your characters' jaws on the table, eyes popping out of their heads, and bodies twisted into impossible poses. (See Figure 12.14.)

Figure 12.14
A classic Take.

For this exercise, my simple character is going to be innocently standing on the train tracks when he hears a whistle, looks up, and reacts to the oncoming train approaching. The poses include:

1. Relaxed position.
2. Looking up in reaction to the whistle.
3. Anticipation for the Take.
4. The Take.
5. The settle.

First I will have him standing and looking down at the ground. At frame 1 I'll position the body so that it is similar to the image shown in Figure 12.15. This relaxed state provides a calm, neutral frame of mind that will contrast with the Take. Again, I am assuming you are familiar with how to move the various body parts and set key frames on them.

At frame 8 I am going to execute the look up in reaction to the train whistle. At this point, the character has heard the whistle and turns his attention to the general direction that it came from (see Figure 12.16). This action is slower since Charlie doesn't yet know that a train is barreling toward him. I achieved this pose by rotating the chest around a small amount and sold the action primarily by rotating the head and neck. The pose should appear something like this:

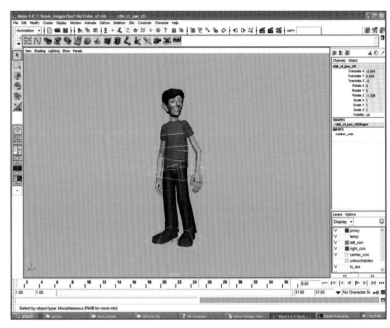

Figure 12.16
Charlie looks up in response to the whistle.

Hold this pose for 10 frames to give a beat so that the look registers with the viewer. Moving the time slider to frame 18, I will set keys on the chest, arms, and head while leaving them in the same position.

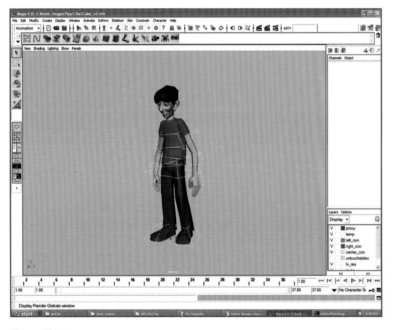

Figure 12.15
The relaxed pose.

Next is the anticipation for the Take. Charlie CG fully realizes that it is, in fact, a train moving in his direction that is responsible for the whistle. The natural response is one of surprise and terror and will require a large move and, therefore, needs the proper amount of momentum. The spine curves downward and the arms raise to provide the momentum needed to "explode" into the main action (which you will see in the next step). Depending on how violent you want the Take to be, you can adjust the position of your antic. I'm going for a decent size Take; at frame 25 I'll involve a curvature of the spine and a large arm movement (see Figure 12.17).

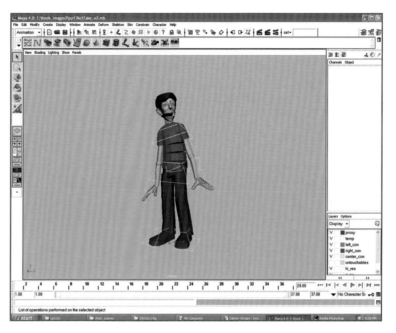

Figure 12.18
The Take pose.

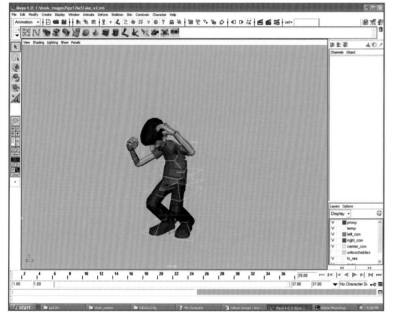

Figure 12.17
Anticipating the movement upward.

Now for the main action: the Take position (see Figure 12.18). Through body language, Charlie is going to communicate to the audience surprise and terror. The Take pose will take place on frame 29 to give it a quicker timing in contrast to the antic. I am looking to stretch the body out in the *opposite* direction of the antic and overemphasize the reaction to the train.

Finally, Charlie will settle (see Figure 12.19). At this point, Charlie has communicated his reaction and his body relaxes slightly but maintains a posture of fear and amazement. This serves two purposes: It allows him a second to think about what to do next, and it allows the audience a beat to absorb and enjoy the action. This pose is a bit less extreme than the Take itself but should maintain the same emotional state.

Once again, this animation isn't going to screen at SIGGRAPH, but it helps to demonstrate what a little bit of exaggeration can do for your actions. Practice different variations by adding and moving in-betweens for proper arcs and altering the poses and timings. As you will soon realize, the possibilities are endless.

12. Anticipation and Exaggeration

141

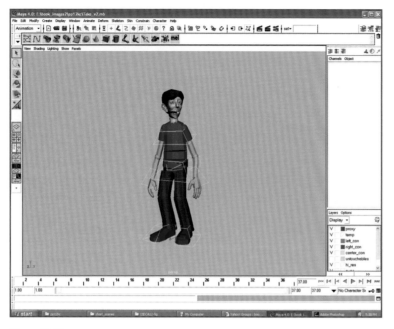

Figure 12.19
The settle.

A great exercise for the imagination is to try to come up with crazy and unique new takes with your characters. Pop in an episode of *Ren & Stimpy* or *Red Hot Riding Hood* and use Tex Avery's wolf for inspiration and you will see what I mean. One of the most enjoyable things about watching these shows is waiting to see what the animators will come up with next as they try to outdo themselves with each Take.

Again, the use of these concepts is going to differ from studio to studio and super-visor to supervisor. Many believe that anticipation, exaggeration, squash and stretch, Takes, and the like should be reserved for cartoons (something animated filmmakers make an effort to distance their work from). You shouldn't let this stop you, however, from experimenting with and using these tools in your own work. You may just discover something new and exciting. If you're lucky, you might even discover your own style.

chapter 13
An Interview with Mike Belzer

Mike Belzer began his career when he was 12. He was doing stop-motion in a middle-school class that was taught by Dave Master. Years later, a student from that class, who knew Gumby creator Art Clokey, had heard he was developing a revival Gumby TV show in San Francisco. That was where Mike landed his first job in animation. After the TV show, Art started the feature (*Gumby: The Movie*) which Mike worked on briefly. Beyond that, he worked at Colossal Pictures and did a variety of commercials including the Pillsbury Doughboy and Hershey's Kisses. It was around that time that Tim Burton approached Henry Selick about the project and asked him to assemble the crew. After completing that, Mike went over to Pixar for a year and a half, and then back to Skellington for *James and the Giant Peach*. At the end of *James*, it was then down to L.A. to work at Disney on *Dinosaur*. Recently, Mike has been working on a Jerry Bruckheimer film called *Down Under*, a 3D theme park film called *Mickey's Phillharmagic*, and will soon be moving on to a new Disney feature.

KYLE: *Is the Disney feature a mixture of 2D and 3D?*

MIKE: Yeah. It's primarily being done in Florida. Some of the primary characters are 3D. I'm heading up a sequence with a crew in the L.A. facility to work on some of the sequences.

KYLE: *Is your role similar to that on* Dinosaur?

MIKE: With production happening across 3,000 miles, we've adopted a new philosophy. Instead of the standard role as a character lead or supervisor, we're using more of a Pixar method and handling the entire sequences and all of the characters contained within them. It just seemed too difficult to share scenes and information that far apart.

KYLE: *That's the model I'm more familiar with. I think the visual effects facilities tend to lean that direction when setting up their productions. It seems to help with the continuity between shots.*

MIKE: Yeah, there are positives and negatives to both.

KYLE: *What are some of the positives to the "single character" approach used in* Dinosaur?

MIKE: Well, you get to concentrate and put your entire effort into one character. Just like Jack Nicholson would get into a role, the animators can start to associate with the character. You can even write up a back-story and develop the way a character would approach a situation. Hopefully, if the director is good and open to ideas, he'll listen to those suggestions.

KYLE: *How was your transition from stop-motion to CG?*

MIKE: It went very well. It was an exciting time for computers. Tippett had just lost *Jurassic Park* to ILM and stop-motion animators were walking around with their tongues on the ground. (See Figure 13.1.) It was like going over to the dark side to make the switch. It was very similar to what's happening in the 2D world right now. A guy's gotta eat, and I had a great opportunity at Pixar, so I gave it a try. I went to work in the commercial division at Pixar. They were just beginning the process of *Toy Story*. However, they didn't have PU (Pixar University) set up at the time, so it was a lot of looking at the computer screen and saying, "How does this work?" Just like anything, though, they throw you in the deep end and you either sink or swim. Eventually you just get a grasp on it. I think my experience from working in traditional 3D medium really helped out. Unlike 2D animators who can often cheat perspective, I was used to making that work in an actual 3D setting.

> **You get to concentrate and put your entire effort into one character. Just like Jack Nicholson would get into a role, the animators can start to associate with the character.**

Figure 13.1
Jurassic Park marked a milestone in computer-generated animation. Copyright © 2002 by Universal Studios. Courtesy of Universal Studios Publishing Rights, a Division of Universal Studios Licensing, Inc. All rights reserved.

KYLE: *Do you still work in the straight-ahead mode that stop-motion demands or have you adopted a more layered approach?*

MIKE: I think the computer forces you to work in more of a layering method. Changes are inevitable. You get some directors that want to make changes into the eleventh hour. In stop-motion, when you did a scene, that was it. What you shoot is what you get. There wasn't the ability to go back and edit. The director either approved, bit his lip, and let it slip by, or you did a re-shoot. In CG, you just can't manage the changes if you've placed a key on every controller at every frame. It becomes too time-consuming and too messy. It's best to create strong poses and go in with a layering approach and offset things and tweak overlap and arcs.

KYLE: *I'm curious how you approach things like offsets. Do you generally incorporate a great amount of detail in each pose?*

MIKE: I find it depends on the style of the animation. If I'm doing something very cartoony, I find posing out everything and working your overlaps in on the actual pose is the best way to go. Things are snappy and moving in a quick motion between keys. The viewer gets a lot more information from the pose. Cartoons are very graphical. To put all the information in one pose is a better way to work. However, the reverse of that is doing something very realistic. I just got done animating a

There's not necessarily one way to work. You need to be able to adapt. Diversification is always good.

144

photo-real kangaroo. I still posed the scene out, but in terms of getting the overlap and delaying certain things, it is easier to go into the graph editor and slip things around. There's not necessarily one way to work. You need to be able to adapt. Diversification is always good.

KYLE: *I think one of the biggest benefits from animating in stop-motion is learning how to incorporate lead and follow into every pose you create. The medium just doesn't allow for an artist to go back and "layer" in some drag on the arm or wrist. Any thoughts on how artists without stop-motion experience can learn to adopt that way of thinking?*

MIKE: Good question. One of the problems I see with inexperienced animators is the lack of intent in their scenes. They don't really think about how the character is going to move and just start pushing things around. They take the layering attitude and start with the hips, then shoulders, arms, and so on. When the shot is done, it lacks any continuity. The sections of the body are so far removed from each other. It's like an animatronic puppet. You get some really talented artist to create a creature that can blink and move and twitch and looks really amazing. However, you throw eight guys together to make it move and it just looks off. Things just don't seem right. People get too caught up in letting the computer generate their in-betweens instead of working on strong poses and putting in the breakdowns you want.

> People get too caught up in letting the computer generate their in-betweens instead of working on strong poses and putting in the breakdowns you want.

KYLE: *You mention planning and its importance. What are your planning rituals?*

MIKE: I think thumbnails are an excellent idea. That's where the 2D guys have a big edge over 3D people. They can effectively communicate their ideas in a short amount of time. Things that would take me all day to generate on the computer, they can quickly do in an hour or two. I'm not a strong illustrator and can't rely on my drawing skills to generate ideas. I have to do it on the computer. However, I'm always trying to get better at my drawings.

KYLE: *So do you actually make drawings or just use the computer?*

MIKE: Given that my background is in 3D, I can usually create poses very quickly. I don't necessarily worry about the details, but quickly think through my ideas and create those in the computer.

KYLE: *So you are basically doing a quick pass to see if your idea will work or not?*

MIKE: Yes.

KYLE: *Stop-motion animators also seem to develop a sense of timing much quicker than people who just spend time in front of the computer. Do you have any tips for helping animators grasp the idea of how long things take to get from point A to point B?*

MIKE: Timing is definitely an elusive concept. I think it's something you get with experience. However, no matter how long you work, you never develop perfect timing. I bet if you asked Glen Keane, he would say that he wrestles with timing every now and then. As far as learning the craft, I think a stopwatch is the best choice. I still have one in my desk. It's an easy method to figure out that a pencil dropping on the desk takes half a second. Once you get that generic number, you can figure out the minor details of how fast it starts and stops. That's where the animation comes in.

KYLE: *So do you just work on getting that generic framework or do you try and figure out the more intricate motions? If you're timing the opening of a door, do you try and break down the ease out as it swings open?*

MIKE: It depends on the motion. If it's something basic like a door opening, I think the generic timings work. More complicated motions, however, might require some additional timing. I don't think it's necessary to get too technical with it.

KYLE: *Chapter 14 will discuss walks. Every new animator wants to start with a walk cycle. They think that's the first thing they need to do. I personally think it's one of the most difficult things to do well in any medium. Do you have a particular approach to nailing that perfect walk?*

MIKE: Avoid it. (Laughs.) I agree with you. Getting a walk is very difficult. You are not just walking a character. You look at anyone walking and they all have a distinct walk. A lot of times it's on subtle levels, but it's displaying personality right there. It's exactly what we were talking about with the stopwatch. You can time out point A to point B for footfalls and it's going to be 12 frames. But what is happening to the hips shifting, the overlapping of the belly, and the position of the arms? All of those little nuances are the things that you strive for. That's the fun part of it. It's not just making a character walk; it's making him walk different. It's bringing in emotion while doing something we do on a daily basis. You see people walk every day. When we mimic that, people judge it so quickly. It's a hard thing to nail.

KYLE: *Anticipation and exaggeration play a huge part in animated medium. It obviously depends on the style you're working in. How did you determine the right amount of each for shows like* Nightmare *and* Dino?

MIKE: Number one, you have to look at what the director is wanting. You are trying to please him, because he knows the big picture. Once you tap into that style that he's looking for, you are halfway there. Nailing that style also builds trust. If you build that trust up quickly, you might have a little bit more room to explore. In terms of knowing where that's at, it's all artistic licenses. In a film like *Dinosaur*, we had to sell the fact that these creatures were extremely large. My character, Baylene, was 70 tons. (See Figure 13.2.) If you've ever watched an elephant get up off the desert floor, it takes a LONG time. I only had, maybe, 150 frames in a shot to show that. I had to take some artistic license and push the envelope, but do it in a realistic fashion. Look at a shot like the one done in *Jumanji* with the elephants

running over the cars. Could an elephant actually run over a car like that? It looked like it. You bought into it. They made it look like an elephant but added the entertainment value to it.

KYLE: *They definitely took some liberties, but it seemed to serve the purpose well. How about* Nightmare? *What challenges did it bring in terms of anticipation and exaggeration?*

MIKE: In *Nightmare*, Jack Skellington was very long and slim. You didn't want to make him move too fast because he was a stick figure and he might get lost in the background. He was a little more fluid and poetic in his motions to get a better read. This was in contrast to Oogie Boogie, who could move very quickly across the screen in terms of distance, due to his size.

Figure 13.2
A still from Walt Disney Pictures' *Dinosaur*. © DISNEY ENTERPRISES, INC.

KYLE: *Finding that level comes from working with the character. You have to spend time with the character to understand what the limitations are.*

MIKE: Yeah, and look at a lot of reference, too. I remember for a sequence with Jack dancing around the Christmas tree I watched Fred Astaire films, because I can't dance very well. Jack needed to be graceful, and Fred and Ginger provided some excellent tips.

KYLE: *When you are looking at reference, do you store that away as a mental image or do you make drawings and notes?*

MIKE: Going back to my inability for illustration, it's more of a mental note. I will write down things if I see something specific. Maybe if I'm looking at it frame by frame, I'll jot down what happens to the foot. Other notes such as if the head is following the body are also beneficial. You just categorize things in your mind. Watch a little two-year-old walking in the playground and you can modify that into a drunken, little person in animation. You just soak those things up and store them away.

KYLE: *If I find a specific piece of reference, say the dancing of Fred Astaire, that I'm not that familiar with, I'll keep that tape handy. I might look at it multiple times to look back and see what some of the nuances are.*

MIKE: Yeah. Sometimes that stuff is really beneficial for pumping out shots for Saturday morning television. To get the nuances out of what's happening when Fred is dancing, you definitely need to watch the tape. However, I think you just take it to a point and then let the character take over. What Jack Skellington has in terms of appendages and clothing might be different than what Fred has. You want to tie in your own animation sensibilities with the character you are working on.

KYLE: *You mention pumping out shots for Saturday morning. In the production world, animating fast, to some degree, is a factor. How fast you can work makes a difference. Did working on projects like* Gumby: The Movie *really help you develop your speed?*

MIKE: Yeah. You get any job where you are cranking out seven seconds a day, and you learn quickly what works and what doesn't. You also learn shortcuts. It might not be what you want to do, but that's just one of the painful parts of that production environment. You get a job and are being paid to pump things out quickly, but as an artist you want to labor over it and make it your own. However, you can't. What I always tell people is burn through 90% of your shots but single out a shot that you kind of like. Try to get through the other shots as fast as possible, so you have some extra time to give to that one shot. As an artist you can come away with something you feel good about.

KYLE: *Do you have any last bits of advice for anyone wanting to get started in the industry?*

MIKE: Do it because you want to do it. That's my biggest tip. When I started, computers weren't really on the scene. Stop-motion wasn't that popular. There wasn't much work out there. I got into the medium because I truly loved it. It was okay if I had to eat Top Ramen for a week, because I was doing what I wanted to do. It pisses me off when people come out of animation school with their certificate and want to use animation as a steppingstone to be the next Spielberg. Some people say, "Well, I'm going to be an animator or a baker." I say, "Go be a baker." There are plenty of people out there who want your job as an animator and are willing to sleep under their desk to get it.

> **There are plenty of people out there who want your job as an animator and are willing to sleep under their desk to get it**

chapter 14
Walks

Inevitably, a shot or scene in your animation career will involve a character walking from point A to point B. Walks provide an excellent opportunity to reveal a character's personality and attitude. Animating one, however, isn't quite as easy as you might think.

Although this is an important area of animation, I was hesitant to devote an entire chapter to it. A walk cycle is one of the most difficult motions to successfully accomplish in animation. Walks have a number of intricacies and each part of the body is dependent on another. Miss one detail and it could trigger a chain reaction that might force you to abandon countless hours of work and start over.

An animator should have a solid understanding of animation fundamentals before trying to execute proper walk cycles. I can personally attest to this because my first assignment as a professional animator was to create a character walk. Having just practiced a few walks on my own time, that initial effort was incredibly tough. Fortunately, experienced animators were on hand to pass along valuable wisdom. This chapter contains a compilation of tips, tricks, and techniques from my various work experiences that should give you a sound understanding of how to create a successful walk.

Forces at Work

To successfully create a believable walk, it's important to understand the physics involved. Chapter 6, "Force: Lead and Follow," outlined a number of influences that are at work when a character is in motion. The walk, more than most actions, has a specific set of forces that must work in harmony. The most important is the initiating force.

Picture yourself moving forward. Your back foot is the driving energy. It pushes against the ground, drives through the calf and thigh, and forces the hips upward.

This is the initiating force in a walk. (See Figure 14.1.) The composition of the ground surface and tension in the heel and calf determine the amplitude at which a human moves. Although this is the technically proper approach, I'll simplify the process in order to make it a bit easier.

Figure 14.1
The drive in a walk begins with the heel and calf.

I prefer to concentrate on the hip area when breaking down the initiating force. It is important to keep in mind the proper push from the back leg, but at this stage, the hip provides a more visual key when determining how the remaining sections of the body should move. Because the movements of the entire body "grow" from the hip area, it is the ideal component to look at first as you discover what's actually occurring through the body during a walk. So from this point on, assume that the walk's amplitude and nature is directly associated with the motion of the hips.

Using the hips as a reference, it's actually quite easy to break down the forces of the walk. The first two sections directly affected by the hips are the chest and head. The hips' motion affects the shoulder rotation and translation, and the shoulder motion then affects movement of the head. I'll keep this simplified by just talking about one axis and view of the walk. The side view serves this purpose best.

Figure 14.2 dissects the motion. Position A in Figure 14.2 shows the down position in the walk. As the hip drives upward, the shoulders delay a few frames (position B). They roll forward in anticipation of the energy from the hips. The energy from the hips takes a few frames to reach the shoulder region. Once the force reaches the shoulders, they react accordingly and roll backward. Position C shows this. Notice the character's nose is still pointing downward. The head reaction is delayed until the shoulders initiate a move. In position D, the character's shoulders have finally pulled the head so that it's looking forward.

The most important thing to remember is the "chain reaction" that's occurring when a character is walking. The hips affect the shoulder, and the shoulder affects the head. In addition, the shoulders will drive the elbows, wrists, and fingers. That has both a positive and negative aspect. The good news is once the hips' motion has been set, the remaining sections of the body are along for the ride. The bad news is any change in the hips and the remaining body parts will need to be modified. As a result, I'll be approaching the walk tutorial with the layering method in mind. I will also address more of the forces at work as you step through the process.

Personality a Plus

As you probably know by now, making an interesting character involves more than just physics and muscles. The technical aspects are certainly important; without them, a figure would move without any regard to weight or proper physicality. From a fundamental standpoint, it's necessary to discuss all these aspects in full detail. However, if you take away one piece of advice from this chapter, remember the importance of characterization when attempting a walk.

When beginning your walk, make sure you are clear on the attitude of the character. (See Figure 14.3.) I often see walks that lack any sort of emotion. When asking the artist his intentions for the walk, the usual response is, "I just created a generic walk." There is no such thing as a "generic" walk. Otherwise, you get a generic character. Keep tabs on the emotional state of your character, and respond with a motion that is typical of that condition.

Position A   Position B   Position C   Position D

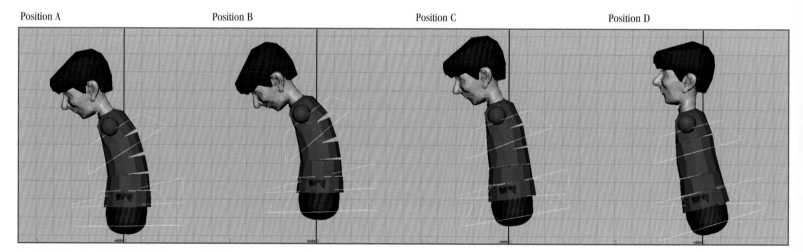

Figure 14.2
The poses show the forces at work during the up motion of a walk.

Figure 14.3
The character is undoubtedly in a happy state.

I fell into this trap during the production of *Rocky and Bullwinkle*. I had a 480-frame shot of both characters walking down the road. (See Figure 14.4.) Knowing that a cycle would be needed, I began the process of creating the walk. After a day or two of working, I showed the progress to a fellow animator. He told me that the work was flat and the personalities of the characters were absent. The scene called for a relaxed and confident stroll for Bullwinkle, and an upset and irritated canter for Rocky. I had missed on both. I was more concerned about the tight deadline and failed to really think about the true nature of the scene from a character standpoint.

Don't let yourself fall into this trap. It's very easy to "overlook" the emotion and dive right into setting key frames. The end result will suffer. If you create a strong emotion accompanying some sound technical work, your walks will have the life they deserve.

Creating the Walk

I discussed a few theoretical aspects of walking and now it's time to get down to business. The following sections are going to step through my method of creating a walk. This process is illustrated to provide the reader with a detailed list of the forces at work and how I go about implementing them. I'm using a simple character and a rig that Mike Ford and Alan Lehman built. (See *Inspired 3D Character Setup* for complete details.) It's extremely fast to work with and allows total control when layering in the various sections of the body. Keep in mind that the specified axis of rotation and translation might be specific to my setup. I'm less concerned with the technical specifics of these axes and more concerned with you understanding how and why the body moves. This tutorial will concentrate on a cycle.

Why Cycle?

An animated cycle is a motion that loops when played. That is, the first and last frames are exactly the same. When played, the motion repeats itself without a stutter. The action can play continuously until the loop is stopped. Cycles work well in instances when the motion needs to be the same. The stepping forward of legs and the swinging of arms are almost identical as the character moves across the floor. This means I only need to concentrate on creating the small amount of frames for one repetition of the motion. Fewer frames means less work. By limiting the number of frames you need to animate you can spend more time making the *quality* of the walk stronger. The ease of editing is also one of the main reasons to use a cycle. If changes are needed, they happen within a limited time range. I'd rather modify 24 frames than mine through 300 frames of a character walk.

Looping the same frames has additional benefits, as well. It allows for consistency of movement and ensures that each stride feels natural and does not vary from step to step. Timing, step length, and amplitude of the up and down are consistent as the cycle loops repeatedly allowing the character to maintain that regularity for as long as the shot requires.

Cycles can be a time-saver over distance issues as well. Often, situations require the character to travel a great distance in a shot. For example, a character might need to traverse a long hallway in the duration of a single scene. If a base cycle has been established, the animator can use that data and easily fulfill the needs of the shot. In addition, cycles can often be applied to multiple characters. If the character had twin brothers, they could all use the initial cycle. Essentially, once it is created, it can be used as many times as necessary.

14. Walks

Figure 14.4
The long walking shot from *Rocky and Bullwinkle*. Copyright © 2002 by Universal Studios. Courtesy of Universal Studios Publishing Rights, a Division of Universal Studios Licensing, Inc.
All rights reserved.

Lower Body First

I like to begin the cycle process by setting keys on the lower body. The hip timing and leg extensions will have the most direct impact on your walk. Fail to make this work properly and you'll have an awkward character moving in an unnatural manner.

When creating poses for my walks, I always set a key on every animated attribute of the character. I use the "key frame all" function primarily out of speed. I can press the "s" key much quicker than selecting an individual channel. In the end,

I'll have to edit the curves anyway. In addition, I like to isolate individual axes and views when working. By limiting the amount of data that's viewed, I can concentrate on getting the correct poses and forces from the angle I'm viewing.

This particular walk is going to encompass 24 frames. That is, frames 0 and 24 will be exactly the same. The motion of one leg passing from front to back and returning to its original position will occur during that time span. I decided on a 24x frame walk because the character needs to be upbeat and happy. With his particular build, this time frame works well.

The first step is to create the footstep extremes and relative hip heights. This is a preliminary step and will most certainly require some adjustments. For now, however, layer in a few keys to set up the major beats of the cycle. The initial pass will take place in the side view. As I stated before, I'll isolate my view to this one axis until some basic parameters have been created.

Frame 0 has the right leg forward and the left leg back. The right leg is represented by a green pant leg and the left by a blue one. (See Figure 14.5.) The hips are at a height that allows maximum extension on the front and back legs. As you'll see shortly, this extension is the foundation for a successful walk. Key frames are set for all three controllers.

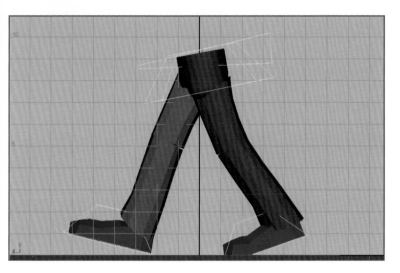

Figure 14.5
The initial key is set at frame 0.

Because I'm interested in creating a cycle, it's imperative that the first and last frames are identical. Frame 0 has key frames on both feet and the hips. I can replicate this position at frame 24 by moving the time slider without updating the scene. This particular package uses the middle mouse button. I move the slider to frame 24 and set the necessary keys. I can also copy the values from frame 0 and paste them in at frame 24. The process of replicating keys will be used on many occasions because the nature of a cycle involves repeating actions.

At this point, the initial extremes have been set. The right leg is extending out front and the left leg is extended backward. The next step is to place keys at the opposite positions. That is, the right leg needs an extreme backward, and the left leg needs an extreme forward. Those keys occur at frame 12—the halfway point in the walk. Because I've already determined an initial position for both extremes I just need to copy those values to the opposite leg. Here's a little trick to accomplish that.

Move the slider to frame 0 and allow the scene to update. The right leg is forward and the left leg is back. Take the left leg controller and move it to the exact location of the right leg. It will require both translation and rotation. Figure 14.6 shows the position. Look closely and you'll see two sets of controllers and two sets of geometry. The legs are currently overlapped. Once the left leg is in position, slide the time line with the middle mouse to frame 12. That will prevent the scene from updating and allow you to set the key for the left leg controller.

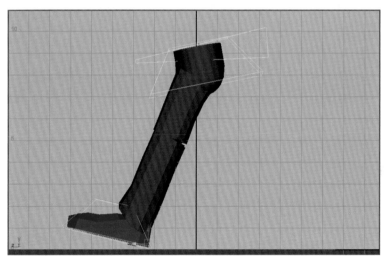

Figure 14.6
Use the right leg's extension to correctly place the left leg. This image shows frame 0. The time slider must be placed at frame 12 before a key can be set.

The same process can be applied for the right leg. Move the controller so that it mirrors the left leg's back extension at frame 0. When the right leg is in place, use the middle mouse button and slide the time line to frame 12. Set the key on the right leg controller. Playing the animation will reveal a character that slides his legs from front to back. Be sure to also set a key at frame 12 for the hips. Because I've yet to adjust that controller, its position should be the same.

I need to provide some initial up and down movement in the hips to get a better idea of how the walk is going to work. That basic motion and the simple translation of the feet should give you a good indication of how well your initial movement is working. The up keys are set at frame 0, frame 12, and frame 24. Add some down keys at frames 6 and 18. I moved the slider to frame 6 and translated the character's hips' controller down along the y-axis. (See Figure 14.7.) This same position needs to occur at frame 18. I middle mouse and move the time slider to frame 18 and set another key. The value at frame 6 is duplicated. Again, this is just a rough pass of the values and times for both hips and feet. Notice the floating feet in Figure 14.7. I know for certain that adjustments will be required. This is just a quick and dirty method to develop the outline.

Hip translation along the y-axis   Up position   Down position

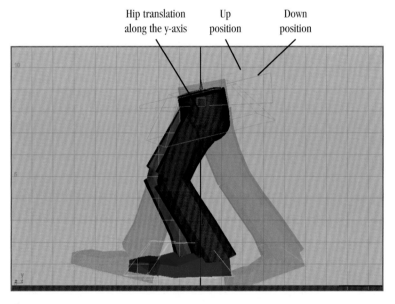

Figure 14.7
The initial pass at the down position of the hips at frames 6 and 18. The ghosted image showing extended legs is the pose at frames 0 and 24.

At this point, I also like to set a few additional keys at these two frames on the foot controllers. It's a quick way to get a little more detail in the legs. At frame 6, the right leg should be sliding backward and contacting the ground. Adjust the rotation and translation so that it sets flat against the ground plane. The left leg will be moving forward. Raise it off the ground and add a small amount of rotation. (See Figure 14.8.) Repeat these steps at frame 18 for the opposite leg. Playing the animation should give you the basic nature of the walk. There are many more keys to be set, but the initial structure is in place.

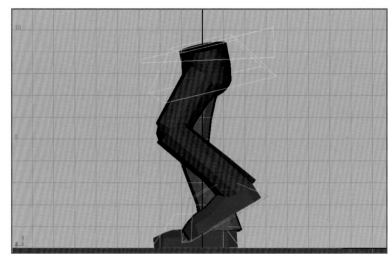

Figure 14.8
The front foot is flat on the ground, and the back foot is raised as it translates from the back. This is often referred to as the passing position.

It's now time to hone the hip and leg animation. I need the proper timings and extensions to get the feeling that my character is propelling himself along. So what's actually going on in the lower body during the walk? Well, the ankle and calf are driving the hips upward. As the hip translates up, the other leg moves forward to prepare to catch the falling body. The leg extends as the hips begin to fall and accepts the downward force of the body. The front leg bends as it accepts the weight, then straightens as it quickly begins to push the hips back up. Figure 14.9 will address these issues.

First, I know the hips need to fall a little faster than they currently do. The initial keys generated a generic up and down that's uncharacteristic of how the body will move. A new extreme down position will eliminate this problem. At frame 3, I lower the hips in Y a bit more and set a key. I'll mimic the same keys at frame 15, but use the left leg.

Because these new keys are now the low point for the hips in the cycle, frames 6 and 18 will need to rise slightly. I want the hips to accelerate downward and then bounce back from the low spot. The action is very similar to a bouncing ball. The hips rise and then quickly bounce from their low spot. I like how the sharp nature of the curve punctuates the up and down motion in the body. The Y translation curve will need some attention to make this idea complete. Figure 14.9 shows the modified graph. The quick acceleration at the bottom of the curve is generated by making the in and out tangents linear.

The up position at
frames 0, 12, and 24.

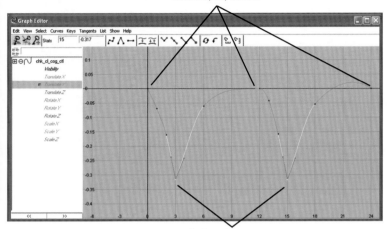

The hips down position
at frames 3 and 15.

Figure 14.9
The sharp acceleration in and out of the low point of the hips mimics that of a bouncing ball.

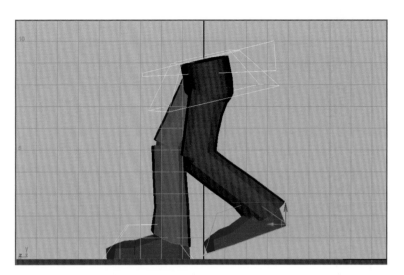

Figure 14.10
The back foot's current position at frames 6 and 18. The early lift from the ground causes the character to feel out of balance.

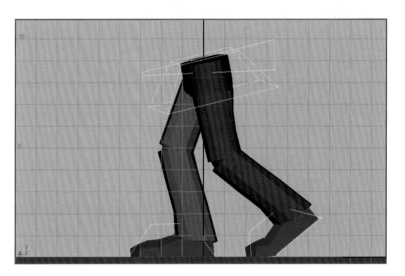

Figure 14.11
The flattening of the back foot at frames 10 and 22 helps keep the leg extended.

Now that the hips are starting to get in shape, I'll work on the back leg push. This is probably the most critical part of the walk; it's also the part that most people animate incorrectly. Not extending the back leg long enough causes the foot to translate forward too early. The result is an off-balance walk that is void of a drive. I call it the "dirty diaper walk" because the character looks as though he's moving with something in the seat of his pants. Figure 14.10 shows the incorrect pose. Obtaining the position is impossible because the character would fall over backward.

I need to pay special attention to keeping the back foot on the ground as it pushes the body forward. Maintaining contact with the surface is critical to creating the necessary force. The character must keep this position until ample weight has been transferred to the front leg. I'm going to pull the foot flat against the surface on both frames 10 and 22. This will help with the extension of the back leg and provide a better thrust for our character. Figure 14.11 shows the delayed foot.

The walk is starting to get close. Let me rephrase that—The walk is *starting* to get close on the lower body from the side view. There are many more things to add and adjust. However, getting to this point is a big part of the process. I'll continue to make adjustments to the current list of key frames as other forces and actions come into play, but there is just one more thing I'd like to change before moving on.

Attention needs to be paid to the extension on the front foot. Currently, the front leg has a nice extension at frames 0, 12, and 24. I've posed the character so that his leg is almost straight. However, that pose only lasts one frame. A few more are needed. So why the extra frames? Just as I needed the extra frames to sell the drive from the back leg, I need a couple of extra frames to reveal the front extension. Without showing that pose for at least two frames, the extension doesn't quite read. The walk looks as though the character always has a bent leg. This is another key mistake many animators make in their walks.

To fix this, I move two frames back from the extension pose keys. That means the adjustment will happen at frames 10 and 22. I don't want to copy the pose from frames 12 and 24 because this would cause a pause in the leg's motion, and the leg never completely stops. The trick is to get the most extension while maintaining some forward motion. Figure 14.12 shows the new keys set at frame 10 and a ghosted image of the already created extension at frame 12. Notice the small amount the leg actually moves.

Now it's time to start working on other aspects of the walk. I like to shift to the front view for the next few steps. The adjustments I'll make are most noticeable from that angle. Once again, isolating my efforts to one perspective helps keep things simple.

The first thing I need to focus on is the side-to-side translation of the hips. This is important because the character must maintain proper balance as he lifts one leg off the ground. Without this shift, the character would fall to the side. Frames 6 and 18 are first. This is the passing pose. One leg is supporting the weight of the entire body as the alternate leg translates forward. The hip must shift over the grounded leg in order to support the weight of the body. At frame 6, the leg is translated to the left. In addition, a rotation value in the Z direction has been applied. The force from the supporting leg pushes the pelvic bone upward. (See Figure 14.13.) The same thing occurs at frame 18; however, the hips move to the right and have an opposite rotational value.

It's important that the hip not translate until the foot accepting the weight has been planted. Key frames at 12 and 24 are required to keep this from occurring. They will delay the translation along the x-axis. The side-to-side curve will look something like Figure 14.14.

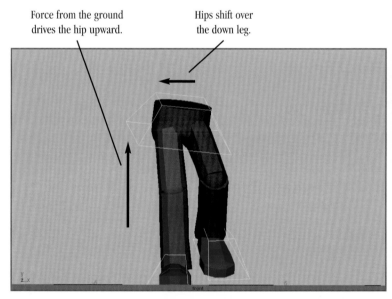

Force from the ground drives the hip upward.

Hips shift over the down leg.

Figure 14.13
The extreme rotation and translation of the hip at frame 6. The force driving from the ground pushes the pelvis bone upward.

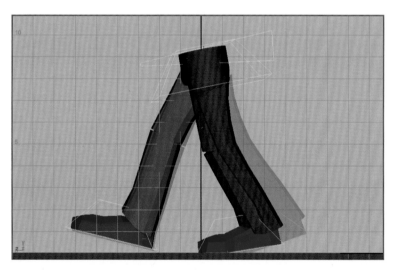

Figure 14.12
The new pose helps sell the extension on the front foot.

Keys at 12 and 24 delay the
side-to-side motion of the hips.

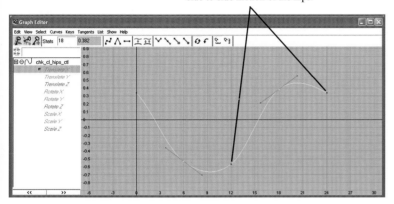

Figure 14.14
The X translation of the hip node. Delaying its motion to the opposite side ensures the foot
can accept the weight of the hip.

In addition to a hip adjustment, the feet need some work at these same two frames. They currently move in a linear motion from front to back. I'm going to rotate the foot outward at the passing pose to break up the motion. This is more of a stylistic choice and creates a more interesting translation from back to front. The knee will probably need some adjusting. I've rotated my characters outward and added a slight roll at the ankle. (See Figure 14.15.) The controller's curves will need some attention to make this transition smooth.

There is one last lower body issue to take care of. This is best addressed in the top view. The hips rotate front to back during the motion of a walk. Their rotation is in direct relation to the extended legs. If the right leg is forward, the hips will be turned in that direction. The mid-section helps pull the rear leg forward by rotating in that direction. Frames 0, 12, and 24 need the keys. (See Figure 14.16.) Make sure you look at the corresponding f-curve; it will probably need some minor tweaking.

At this point, the lower body should be pretty solid. I'll definitely have to make adjustments down the road, but I have a nice foundation to work with. Now, it's time to tackle the upper body.

Knee and foot are turned outward
as the foot moves forward.

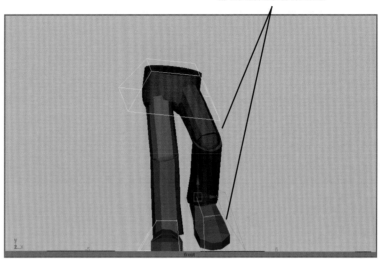

Figure 14.15
The lifted foot is rolled outward as it passes under the body.

The hips rotate along
the y-axis.

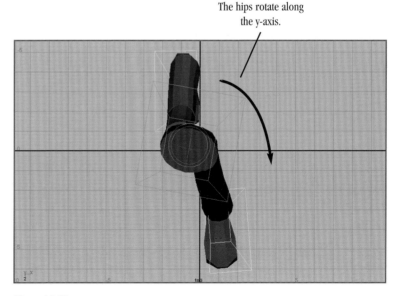

Figure 14.16
The Y rotation occurs at the extremes of the footsteps.

14. Walks

157

Add the Body Action

The hips are going to be the driving force in this walk. Significant time has been spent making sure that the hips are working correctly. That attention will pay off as I begin the process of adding the upper body. The road map has been created. It's now just a matter of following the direction that's been set. I'll reveal the remaining geometry and get started.

I like to begin the upper body motion with the chest controller. It has a direct relationship with the hips and is the foundation for everything that moves above the waist. I'll move back to the front view and begin setting a few keys.

The hips currently hit their extreme right and left positions at frames 6 and 18, respectively. This side-to-side motion is a result of the hips shifting their weight in order to keep the character in balance. As a result, I know that a similar motion is necessary in the chest. The only difference being a slight delay in the timings. The chest will slightly follow the motion in the mid region. I'm going to add another frame to the timings of the chest. The controller will also translate along the x-axis and hit extremes at frames 7 and 19.

In addition to a side-to-side translation value, the chest has a rotation from side to side. The driving of the hips causes the chest to roll from left to right. This happens along the z-axis and is opposite the hip rotation along that same axis. This countering of the hips helps balance the character. (See Figure 14.17.)

The next step involves another rotation of the chest. Just as the chest countered the pelvis's up and down motion, a similar occurrence happens as the hips rotate forward and back. The upper body is rotating in the opposite direction as the hips extended forward. (See Figure 14.18.) This provides a natural balance for the character. That extension of the front foot occurs at frames 0, 12, and 24. The chest is moving slightly behind the hips, so I'll add this rotation one frame later at frames 1, 13, and 25.

I'm hoping you're wondering why a key was set at frame 25 since this is just a 24-frame cycle. It's actually a simple trick that will make the chest behave properly. As I mentioned before, the feet extend at frames 0, 12, and 24. I want the chest controller to delay one frame from those keys. However, without generating a value for frame 24, the chest won't have enough data to cycle.

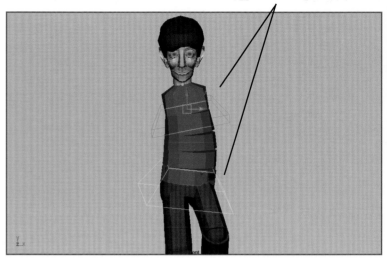

The shoulders rotate opposite of the hips.

Figure 14.17
The chest controller translates and rotates to counter the motion in the hips in this front view. Keys are set at frames 7 and 19.

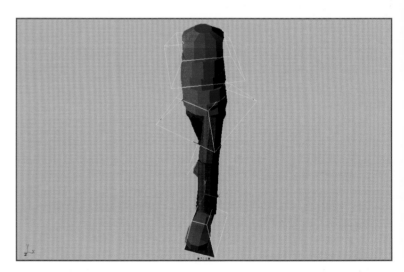

Figure 14.18
The chest counters the hips from the top view. That rotation occurs along the y-axis.

An additional key is required to complete the motion. However, this key needs to occur in the proper location. Setting a key at frame 25 keeps the 12-frame separation between keys that was established by the hip swing. However, that key is out of the limits of the cycle. The key at frame 25 generates a curve that passes through frame 24 with the proper amplitude. Once that value is created, I can set a key and copy the value to frame 0. Now I have a cyclical curve with the proper spacing. Figure 14.19 shows the pre- and post-curve. This technique should be used on all sections of the body to ensure proper cycling while maintaining overlap in the different body parts. It is important at this step to check the tangency of your first and last key frames. You want to make sure they match so that unwanted popping does not occur when your cycle repeats.

The tangent at frame 0 is different from frame 24.

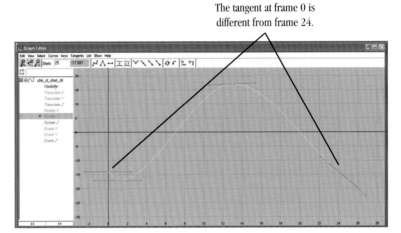

Figure 14.20
The curve doesn't ease in and ease out from frame 1 as it does at frame 13.

The value at frame 24 is copied to frame 0

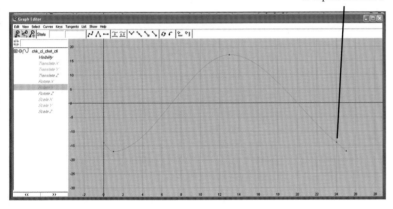

Figure 14.19
The completed curve. A key is created at frame 24 and is copied to frame 0.

The slope at frame 0 matches that of frame 25.

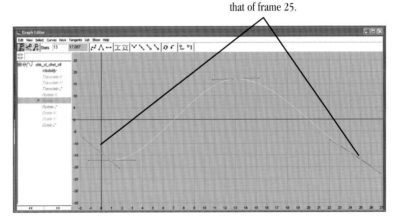

Figure 14.21
The curve now has equal slopes moving into frame 25 and out of frame 0.

It's probably a good time to mention the issue of curve clean up. Making the curves flow properly from the last frame of the cycle to the first frame is essential. You know that the key frame values must be exactly the same, but having the curves work is just as important. The previous rotations in the chest actually generated a curve like the one shown in Figure 14.20.

This can be easily remedied by adjusting the tangents on frames 0, 1, and 25. At this time, you want the curve to have an easy transition from its extreme frames. Altering the necessary tangents produces a clean and smooth transitioning curve. (See Figure 14.21.)

Now that I have all the desired twisting motion in the chest, I'll add some impact action. By impact, I'm referring to the slight chest rotation that occurs when the hips drop to their lowest position and rise to their peak. The hip impact causes the

chest and head to roll forward a small amount and then roll backward as the hips drive upward. (See Figure 14.22.) The center of gravity (COG) is the driving factor for this impact. I'll use its values to determine the chest's timing.

I've opened the Y translation curve of the COG controller. This will tell me in exactly what frames the hips hit their high and low point. The Y translation curve shows the COG hits bottom at frames 3 and 15. I'll continue with the previous standards and have the chest follow one frame behind. I'll slightly rotate the controller in the X direction and set keys at frames 4 and 16.

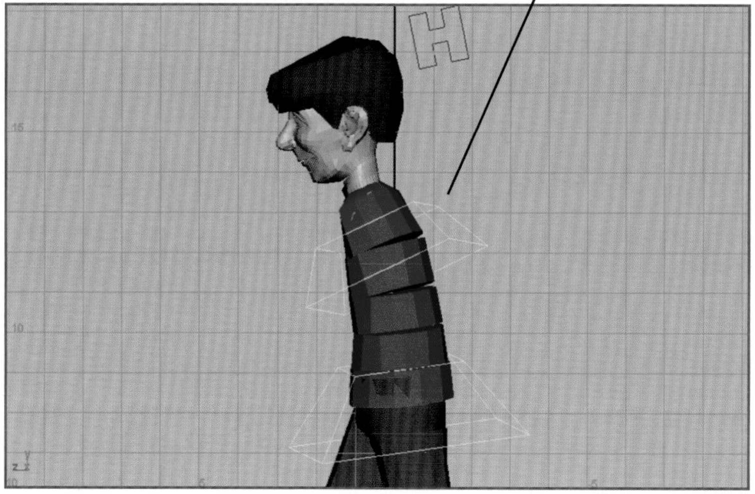

Chest rolls forward as
the hips drop down.

Figure 14.22
The chest helps indicate the body impacting the ground.

The COG rebounds from the impact at frame 6 and moves upward. It holds that position until frame 12. This same pattern occurs between frames 18 and 24. This drive upward will force the chest to roll backward. I'll place keys at frames 7, 13, 19, and 25. This will generate the necessary curve to set a key frame at 24 and 0. The resulting curve will look like Figure 14.23.

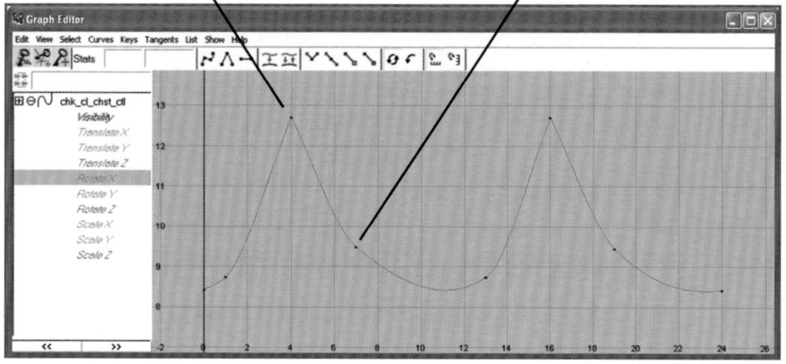

The chest is rotated
forward at this position.

The chest is rotated
backward at this position.

Figure 14.23
The X rotation curve for the chest.

This is where I begin to work on the arm animation. Chapter 11, "Arcs and In-Betweens," discusses the arm swing at length. I'll let that serve as the process for creating the proper type of swing. However, it is important to mention what will dictate how the arm moves. The rotation in the chest will decide when the arms hit their extremes. As the chest rotates along the y-axis, it drives the arms forward. (See Figure 14.24.)

Chest and arm rotate in
the same direction.

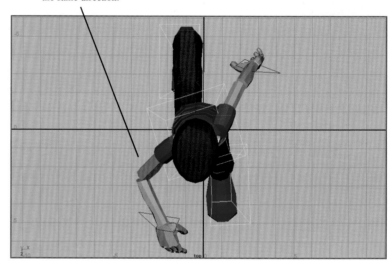

Figure 14.24
The Y rotation of the chest drives the arms.

To create the arm extremes, I'll continue the pattern and add one frame to the chest timings. Remember, the arms are following the chest, which in turn is following the hips. The chest extremes hit at frames 1 and 13. I'll set the arms to hit at frames 2 and 14. (See Figure 14.25.)

The last remaining item is the head. It is being driven by the shoulders and contains most of the same rotations but on a much smaller scale. For the first axis of emphasis, I'll move to the side view. I'm going to set the keys that show the impact of the hips. I've already created this motion for the chest and will use the curve from this controller to decide where the keys lie.

For this particular walk, I want the head to delay two frames behind the chest. This will generate a higher degree of overlap between the head and chest and give the character a loose and relaxed feel. The high point in the head rotation will occur at frames 3 and 15, and the low point will occur at frames 7 and 19.

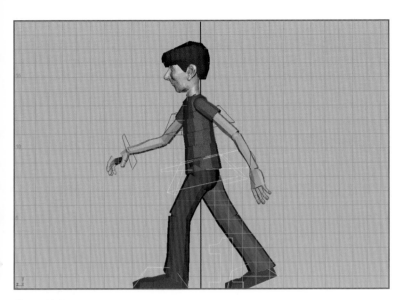

Figure 14.25
The extremes of the arm swings at frames 2 and 14.

The x-axis curves for the chest and head are almost identical. The only difference lies in the timing. The rotations occur two frames earlier. (See Figure 14.26.) This lag is due to the force traveling from chest to head. The separation created is critical in obtaining the natural movements of a walking character.

The head keys lag behind
the chest two frames.

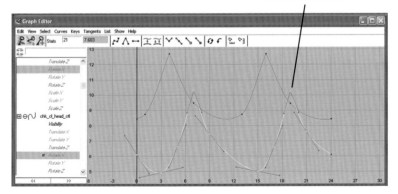

Figure 14.26
The x-axis curves of the chest and head. The head curve is highlighted in white. The chest is in red.

There is one remaining rotation to create. The side-to-side motion generated from the hips and shoulders forces the head to roll slightly from left to right. This occurs along the z-axis in the character setup. Again, I've generated this exact action with the chest. That will be the road map for the head rotations. I'll continue with the two-frame delay and set the rotation to the character's right at frame 9 and the extreme rotation to his left at frame 21. (See Figure 14.27.)

Head rolls side to side in
response to the chest motion.

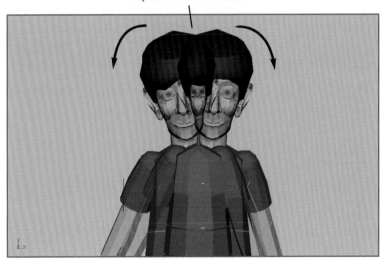

Figure 14.27
The left and right rotations for the head.

That completes the walk. Although much more time will be required to get the exact characterization you're looking for, the basic fundamentals and forces should be intact. Varying degrees of rotation and translation will generate an entirely new feel and look to the walk. Experiment with these settings as you begin creating your own version. You'll be amazed at the difference a small adjustment can make.

14. Walks

161

Move It Through Space

Now that you have a working cycle, what are you going to do with it? The character should be nicely cycling as he walks in place. However, that doesn't do you much good in a scene. Part of the lure of creating the cycle was the ability to implement it into multiple scenes over the course of a production. One more step is necessary in order to make this happen. This is a little trick I picked up early in my career and have been using ever since.

If I've done everything correctly, the character should be taking steps with the exact same stride length. Remember, I used the extreme front and back locations and transferred them to the opposite leg. This should create a consistent value for the placement of the front foot as it touches down. This will be crucial. Double-check your character to make sure it maintains that forward value for each foot.

If indeed the values for both feet are consistent, moving the ALL node for the character the proper amount will result in a character translating through space. I am essentially moving the character's entire rig just enough to remove the sliding effect of the cycled feet. This will probably be confusing at first, but should be clearer as I walk you through the process.

The first thing I'm going to do is create a simple cube. This cube will act as a marker for the placement of my front foot when I begin determining how much to move the entire rig. I'll place the right edge of the cube at the tip of the right foot on frame 0, and place a key on the ALL controller for my character. (See Figure 14.28.)

Based on the previously made decisions, the right foot travels from its extreme position at frame 0 backward until frame 12. Frame 12 is the extreme back position for the foot. Grab the ALL controller and translate it along the z-axis until the toe of the right foot once again touches the right edge of the cube. (See Figure 14.29.) Set a key on the ALL node at this frame.

Scrub through the animation. The right foot should stay fairly close to the cube as it makes a half stride in the walk. You'll probably find some slipping occurring. However, that can be managed with some curve adjustments. I'll address that in a moment. First, make this character walk until you can't see him anymore. Open the f-curve editor and look at the Z translation for the ALL controller. It should have only two key frames on it: one at frame 0 and one at frame 12. The curve needs to be linear between these two points. This ensures a constant translation as

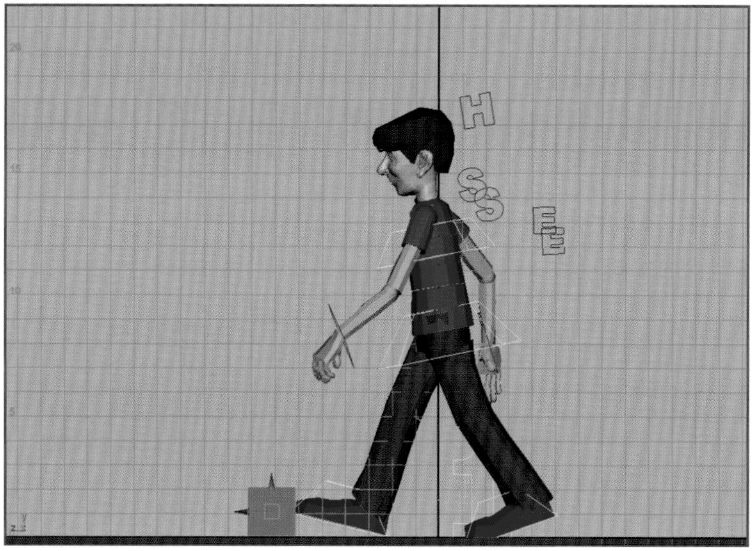

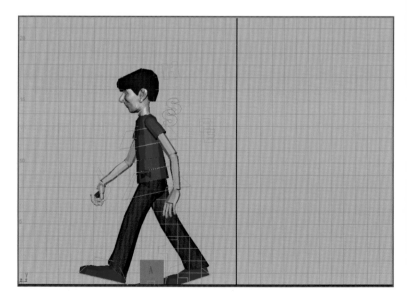

Figure 14.28
The cube acts as a marker.

Figure 14.29
The right foot now touches the cube in its extreme back position.

the character moves forward. By repeating this slope over an extended period of time, the character will continue walking.

Select the Z curve and apply a constant or gradient function to both keys. This should create a slope that is constant for the duration of the shot and provide the last remaining puzzle to getting the character to translate across screen. He should now move for as many frames as the scene file specifies. The ALL controller and feet are moving at a consistent pace and can travel indefinitely. Some fine-tuning of the curves will be necessary to keep the foot from slipping as it steps. More than likely, it's a factor of the Z translation curve. Setting the keys to interpolate in a linear fashion should solve the problem.

This provides you with a base walk. Each scene and situation will require some modification of your character's motion. It's pretty obvious that no one would walk in the exact same manner at all times. Slight head turns, variations in rotations and translations, and some altered timings can all assist in masking the cyclical nature of the walk. The last thing you want is the audience recognizing that you reused animation. Take the time to make some adjustments and you'll be much more pleased with the results.

chapter 15
Lip-Sync and Facial Animation

by Keith Lango

Since animation is a communicative language, the more you expand your understanding of how motion and pose can be applied, you will expand your vocabulary and find the necessary elements to add depth and subtlety of meaning to your communication. Facial animation is a particularly challenging aspect of character animation, primarily because it has such a demanding need for both subtlety and broadness in what is being "said."

Facial Animation

For the longest time, I relied on my innate sense of timing and expression to animate faces, relying on the gut instinct that I'd been blessed with. Unfortunately, that only carried me so far before I started falling back on old habits and patterns. I then got down to the nitty-gritty and analyzed how to approach facial animation in a moderately systematic fashion. My goal was to open up a world of principles to be used, mixed, and matched to conjure up new combinations and possibilities. Keeping the fluidity of all great facial animation at heart, I want to show you the techniques, principles, and thought processes you can experience while animating faces.

The face, perhaps more than any other part of the body, is a window into the soul of a character. As such, there is a thin line between good and bad facial animation. The margin of error in executing facial animation is slim, more so than other parts of the body. Having said that, there's plenty of room for loose interpretation in facial animation. Lip-sync and emotional posing of facial features can be as broad or as subtle as the detail of the character or the need of the moment allows. This opens doors to portray thought, motivation, and emotion in your character in rich, subtle, and powerful ways. To achieve these results, you'll have to think about facial animation in a way that is slightly different from other parts of character animation.

Singularity of Message

Animation is, at its core, a communicative language. As such, your primary goal is to clearly communicate your given message in such a way that there is no ambiguity or doubt about your character's thoughts and actions. When you're trying to convey a message, you must provide clarity. If your message lacks clarity, it becomes muddled, confused, and oftentimes unintelligible. Say only one thing at a time and make sure your whole character is saying that one thing. Your message can be simple (I'm happy) or complex (I'm happy, but not quite as happy as I thought I'd be), but it must be singular. So make sure your whole character's face is saying the same thing at the same time. (See Figures 15.1 and 15.2.)

Build on the Body

Facial animation cannot save poor body animation. You cannot hope to rescue badly timed, poorly motivated, or sloppily executed body animation with great facial animation. Unless the shot is a close-up, facial animation is more often a "flavor enhancer."

Body language accounts for 90% of the emotional communicative weight of a character. Body language can be read from afar, without a good look at a person's face. Follow the lead of the body language and make your facial animation fit the intensity, energy, tone, and tenor of the body animation (see Figure 15.3).

Strive for consistency in your message. The last thing you want to do is put "I'm happy!" facial animation on a body that's saying "I should have stayed in bed this morning" (see Figure 15.4). That is unless the situation calls for a lie to be told. All things in facial animation are relative and subject to the needs of the shot, which is why there are so few rules to go by.

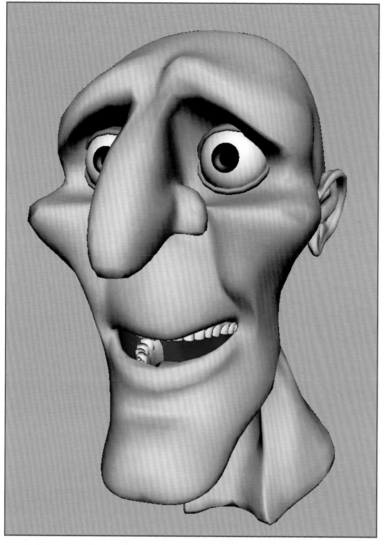

Figure 15.1
The character's smiling mouth and sad eyes are contradictory.

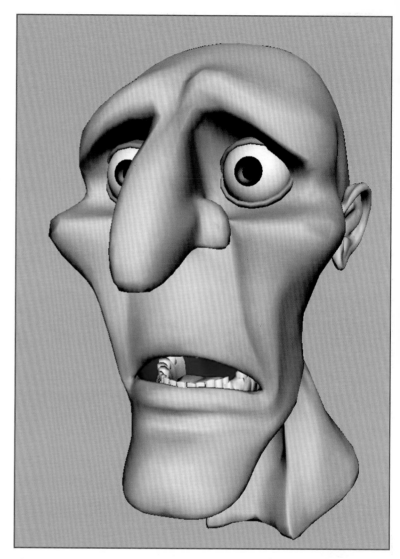

Figure 15.2
The character's sad mouth and sad eyes express the same thing.

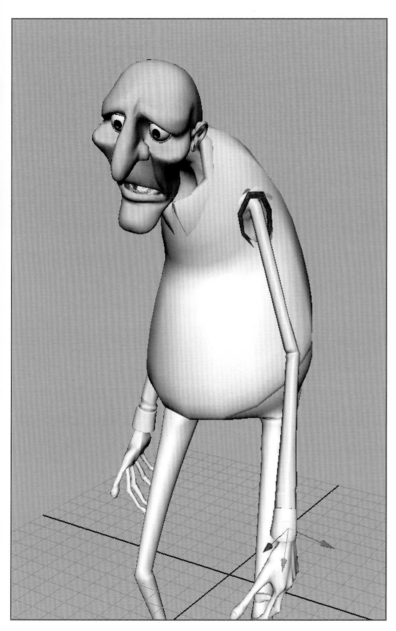

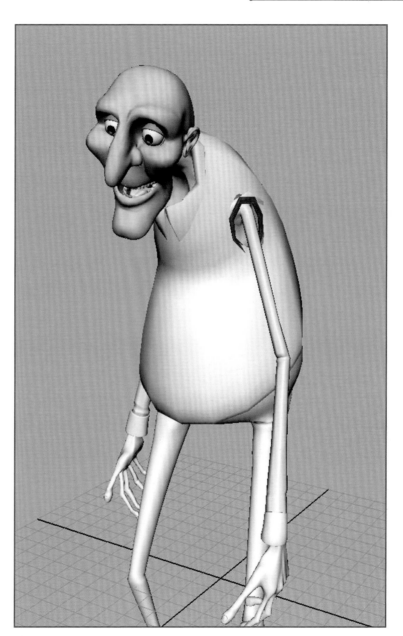

Figure 15.3
The sad pose of the body matches the sad look on his face.

Figure 15.4
The happy face is contradicting the body.

Asymmetry

The initial temptation in all animation is to be too symmetrical (see Figure 15.5). Asymmetrically animating the face creates endless possibilities for facial expressions. People's faces are bland and boring when they're symmetrical. However, raise a single eyebrow and now you have a sarcastic look, or perhaps a quizzical, cynical, or mildly surprised look.

By combining various asymmetries in your face posing, you can mix and match to capture just the right expressions to clearly communicate an idea. Rotate the jaw left and right to add flavor. Raise one eyebrow higher than the other to add punch to a facial expression. Sneer one side of the lips to break up the flat even line of the mouth. Cock a half smile on a character to hint at an underlying motive. Leave the jaw slightly more slack on one side to impress the notion of utter shock. Play around with the combos of poses and asymmetry to unlock great little gems in facial animation (see Figure 15.6).

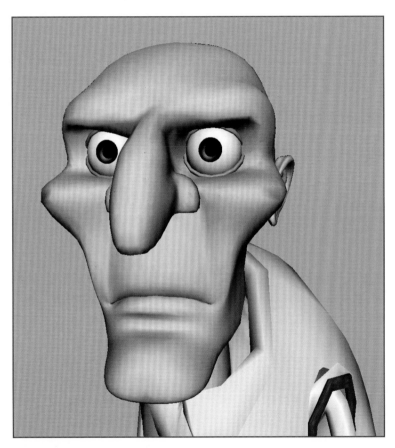

Figure 15.5
A symmetrical face.

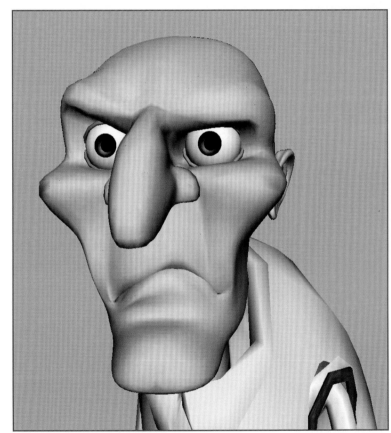

Figure 15.6
An asymmetrical gesture.

The most dramatic emotion shifts can be given higher intensity by shifting the asymmetry in reverse. For example, pretend the character is smiling out of the right side of his mouth and his right eyebrow is down. (See Figure 15.7.) Now he becomes angry and shifts to a frown on the left side of his mouth and raises the right eyebrow higher than the left. This reversal gives the character's internal emotional shift an extra kick, helping it to read more clearly.

Facial Connectors

A telltale sign of inexperienced 3D facial animation is shown when the character's mouth and eyebrows are moving, but the vast dead sea of face in between never moves. The face lacks a holistic connection within itself. Often, this disconnect between the eyes and the mouth will result in a confused message.

The trick is to think of animating the entire face as a whole, not just animating parts of the face. Because of the complex musculature of a face, it is nearly impossible to move the jaw without the muscles and skin all around it being affected, even all the way up to the eyes (see Figure 15.8). If you feel like a good lip-sync

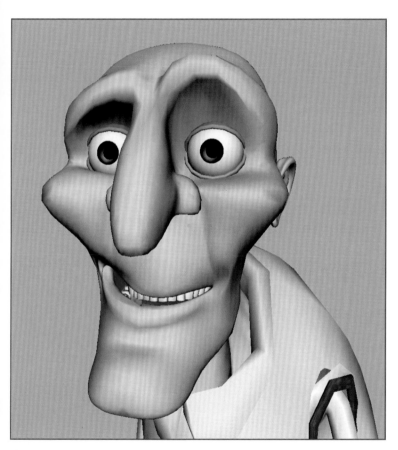

Figure 15.7
The character is smiling with an asymmetrical pose setting up the move to an angry face.

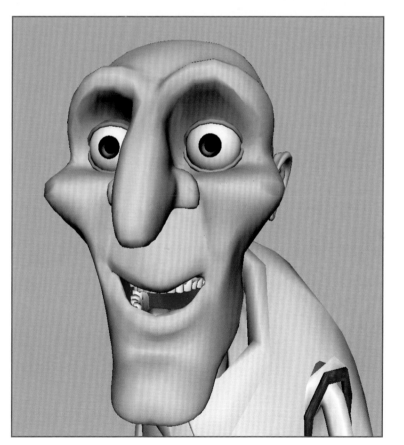

Figure 15.8
The face with the cheeks and nose NOT being used.

animator and a good eye-emotion animator, but you're looking to put your work over the top, then you're looking for connection. The primary connectors in a face are the cheeks, the nose, and the ears (see Figure 15.9).

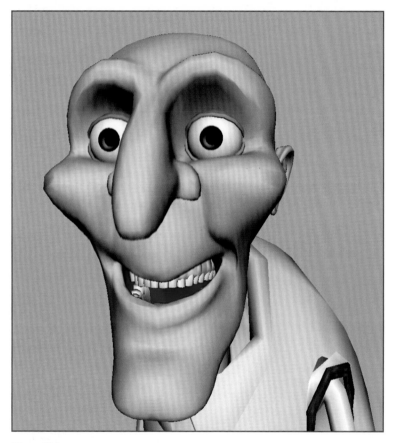

Figure 15.9
A face with the connectors tying the whole face together. The cheeks and nose are receiving the proper attention.

From a technical standpoint, you should try to build as much forethought into your facial morph targets as possible. Try to get the facial connector areas incorporated into your target building so that you're maintaining connectivity for your face. Technically, from a morph target point of view, you're going to want to make sure that you build push and pull into the nose, cheeks, and ears of a character. These face parts are highly driven by the underlying muscles used to make facial expressions. Here are a few tips to keep in mind when building your facial shapes:

◆ For the mouth corners up, make sure the ears are pulled up a bit.

◆ For the jaw open, make sure the ears are lowered a tiny bit.

◆ For the sneer, wrinkle up the nose.

◆ For the smile, make sure the cheeks rise up.

◆ For the jaw open, elongate the cheeks and slightly stretch down the base of the nose.

◆ Don't forget about the neck muscles used to move the jaw and mouth corners.

Probably the single most useful technique to getting the face to seem connected and whole is to key-frame the entire face at once. The exception is the mechanical operation of lip-sync; that is usually treated as a separate issue and will be discussed at length shortly. But for emotional and expressive posing, you can often work on top of the underlying lip-sync. A person can say "Oh, yeah, I'm doing fine" and really mean it, or he can be snipping back sarcastically. In both instances, the lip-sync execution doesn't differ much, but the entire face posing and expression is vastly different.

It's in this realm of emotional expression that I am suggesting that you pose and animate the entire face as one unit. Treat faces like body poses. Faces have distinct and clear poses just as much as the body does. Ignoring this rule may result in a face that is haphazard in regard to timing and impact. You can certainly offset the key-frames in your finessing stage, but from early on you should use broad strokes in blocking in your character's basic shifts in facial expression.

If the character is happy, key the whole face to be happy. Then, if the character shifts to sad set the whole face to be sad. (See Figure 15.10.) If you're doing lip-sync on top of this shift, treat the lip-sync as a distinct technique. Animate the lip-sync first; then go in behind it and modify the face to fit the emotion.

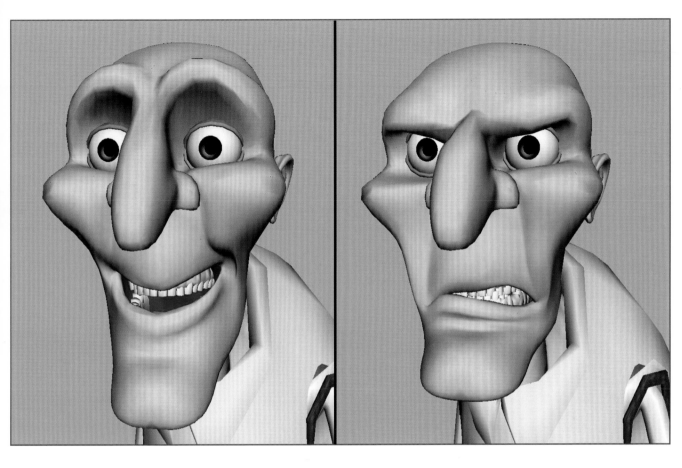

Figure 15.10
A single expression changes to another single expression.

A person's facial shift will tend to be a moment in time. There may be offsetting, especially between the eyes and the lower face, but the viewer should get the strong impression that the shift in facial expression is a very distinct and identifiable moment. The various shapes that make up an emotion will change with similar timing.

When animating the face, don't try to do too much at once. Lip-sync needs to have flow from one sound to the next, with relatively few "holds." Eyebrows and overall expressions should be singular—tending to be held until there is a solid emotional and cognitive reason to change. There's a lot of power in skillfully changing from one clear emotion to another in a shot.

The 12 Principles Applied to Faces

One of the temptations in animation is to insert the "12 principles" of animation as defined in the watershed tome, *Disney's The Illusion of Life*. These 12 principles have become a foundation for understanding animation. However, with the passage of time, they have taken on a sacred aura. As a result, many beginning animators feel they absolutely *must* insert as many aspects of the "Magic 12" as they can into each and every shot. However, merely adding overlap for overlap's sake is misguided.

It is accurate to say that all aspects of the "Magic12" have their proper place in facial animation. You do want to keep the face fluid, alive, and organic, so adding offsets and follow-through on the occasional emotion is needed. However, if you apply overlap and offset too much, the face becomes rubbery and loses its meaning. The face, more than any other part of the character, is a billboard of intent. Everything that the face does must be motivated by something. Any extraneous motion in the face will generate confusion. To do more merely for the sake of "the principle of it" is moving things without understanding why. And with facial animation, WHY is king. So as with all animation, know what you're going to apply and why; then go ahead and apply it.

Lip-Sync Animation

The single best investment you can have when animating lip-sync is a mirror. Watch yourself talking naturally—not the goofy-faced, play-acting, over-exaggerated face antics you think you should do, but the natural flowing conversation of everyday speech. Watch how your mouth shifts over sounds, seemingly skipping sounds altogether. This simple act of watching and learning how a mouth moves during speech can yield great results. It's all about observation and the incorporation of what you see into what you animate. Watch video reference and news anchors doing their nightly reports. Observe how wide and varied the mouth and face can become during speech and how much is skimmed over in pronunciation.

Interpretation

The key element in good lip-sync animation is to grasp the essential elements of the communication as recorded in the sound track. You need to "squint your ears" and try to pick up the overall *feel* of the speech rather than a slavish interpretation of what you think you hear in the dialog. I call this a kind of Impressionism, having been inspired by the Impressionist movement of the late 1800s.

For many years, up until the late 19th century, the effort in Renaissance art was the meticulous and accurate re-creation of reality in every fine detail. Realism was the goal, and literalism in interpreting a painting was the norm. Then, artists got an idea about capturing the overall essence of an image. They became less interested in capturing every leaf on a tree and began to focus on how the light, shadow, and color hues projected that tree into another realm. In this new interpretive realm, leaves didn't matter as much as form, color, tone, and contrast. Just as the Impressionist painters got away from a literal realism in capturing a picture, animators need to become impressionistic when it comes to lip-sync animation. The best place to start is with the broad strokes of your "brush," to get blocked in the very foundation of your work. The best way to do this is to nail down your mouth open and close timings.

Open or Closed?

When you begin a lip-sync task, seek at first to do nothing more than hit the primary mouth opens and closes. By focusing on this basic need, you can get nearly all you need for lip-sync. Heck, the Muppets have gotten by on that for 30+ years! These main target points are like the broad brushes in an Impressionist painting. They define shape, contrast, form, and direction. The details of texture come later with the specific choices you make on top of the broad brushed open and closed pose shapes and timings.

The opens and closes are the foundation of your more specific choices. Even if all you do is properly hit the opens, closes, and wide shapes of the mouth at the right time, you are already more than 75% of the way to great lip-sync. You can get a lot out of very little lip-sync animation. If you have any doubts about this, take a look at animated films using projected texture map mouths, such as those in *Veggietales*, which have proven that this is indeed true.

Literalism Versus Impressionism: A Case Study

In the film *Mouse Hunt*, Christopher Walken's character is mumbling about getting into the mouse's head. In this rambling, he says (in a rather understated fashion) that "you hafta get" inside the mouse's mind. "You hafta get" takes about 25 frames to say. At first look, it literally seems like there should be the following keys for the phrase:

Y (a pucker shape)

Ooo

H

Aa

V

T

Uh

G

Eh

T

That is a very literal interpretation of what it takes to show a person saying "you hafta get." However, if you key-frame the lip-sync in that manner, this will result in a very poppy or jerky mouth when animated. Some of those poses will be onscreen for only a single frame, which is entirely too much information and not enough time for the viewer to interpret it.

A quick analysis will show that you go from one mouth shape that is quite open (Ah in hafta) to a pretty closed one (the F in hafta) and then back open again (for the end of hafta). The result is the mouth popping from open to closed back to open in just three frames.

Oftentimes, beginners will make a phoneme that is an exact copy of one's face saying that single letter. So, to make "E" phonemes, you would say "E" by itself. To model "K" phonemes, you can base it off your own face in a mirror saying "kuh". At first this seems logical. The problem is that when you say the "t" sound by itself ("tuh"), your face doesn't look at all like it would if you said "skate". And that "t" in "skate" gives a face shape that is completely different from the "t" sound shapes in "pet store". And THAT "t" is very different from the "t" shape you make when you say "goatee". Figure 15.11 shows variations on the "t" shape.

As such, it's imperative to remember that mouth shapes for sounds must be animated in context. The preceding sound shape affects the current sound shape. Likewise, the following sound shape is anticipated in the current sound shape.

So, the shapes shown must all be in context with the shape/sound that precedes it and follows it. If you get stuck on the idea of making all the "t" sounds in a soundtrack the same shape, regardless of the prior or following sound/shape context in the dialogue, then you're setting yourself up for a popping mouth when you go to view your animation. Animating speech is not animating letters; it's animating the flow of shapes that are needed to make the sounds.

If you can get the major impressions across in your animation, you can let the little stuff slide. Just like the impressionist would hint at a cluster of leaves with a single daub of his brush, you too should let words and sound shapes slur into the next word or sound shape. Mix the target facial weights together to show a flow. Get away from showing leaves and start showing contrast and form. Talking is more of a flowing thought than an alliterative function of letters.

Looking again at the example phrase, "you hafta get," a more impressionistic interpretation would be to emphasize the following major accents:

Ooo

aaFF

Eh

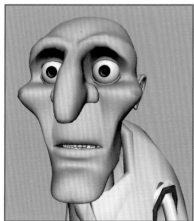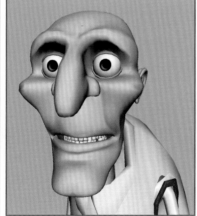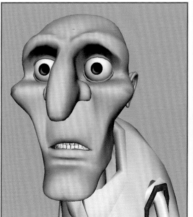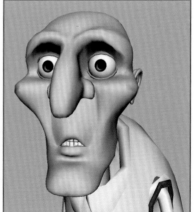

Figure 15.11
Working from left to right: the default "t" shape; the "t" shape in the word skate; the "t" shape in get; and the "t" shape in goat.

Go ahead and say that out loud. "Ooo" as in "scoop", "aaFF" as in "after", and "Eh" as in "pet".

Ooo-aaFF-Eh.

It sounds a lot like "you hafta get," doesn't it?

Now go one further. Grab a handheld mirror and say "you hafta get." Watch how your mouth looks as you say it again. Now, say "ooo-aaFF-eh" a few times. See how very close the two are in how they look? Here is another example of this same principle: Say to your mirror, "I love you." Then say to it, "elephant shoes." The two look similar, don't they? Here's a breakdown of a few specific choices.

You'll want to start by letting the "yuh" of you flow into the more open "aa" at the beginning of "hafta." Skip the specific "ooo" at the end of "you," because it is not very strong. It's there, but it gets said while the mouth is transitioning into the beginning of "hafta." Basically, it slurs into the next word. The "h" of "hafta" is buried in the back of the throat, so the lips don't really need to show it.

Picking up from the moderately strong "aa" of "hafta," hit the "f" for two frames to let it read. It's the major closed point of the phrase, so that needs to line up and read clearly. Then skip the ending "ah" of "hafta" altogether, as well as the "g" of "get". Both happen under the breath; they're slurred under the transition from "ff" to the "eh" accent of "get." Hit that last open pose of "eh." Then end with an appropriately shaped nearly closed mouth to catch the idea of a "t." You've basically now animated "Ooo-aaFF-Eht." And you know what? It flows, it feels natural, and it doesn't pop.

What about "t"s, "d"s, "n"s, and such? Well, if your character has a tongue, you can get all the inner mouth sound shapes you need with that. The inner mouth sound shapes are as follows:

L

Th

T

K

G (hard)

Add your tongue work in here, keeping it as impressionistic as everything else, and you can handle the "little stuff" quite easily. A good tip is to keep tongue movements very quick. Don't have the tongue take longer than two frames to get from one position to another (unless you have a specific reason) or it will look like your character is saying the "LL" sound—the word "bad" turns into "bald" and "good" becomes "gold." Keep the tongue light and quick.

Miscellaneous Lip-Sync Tips to Keep in Mind

The amount of data available on lip-sync and animation is quite impressive. Animation is nearly 100 years old and much has been discovered and found to be generally reliable. As an additional aide to a good lip-sync technique, here are a few miscellaneous tips that have been discovered over the years:

◆ Don't go from wide open to closed in one frame and vice versa. Definitely don't go from open to closed to open in three frames.

◆ Don't hold a mouth shape static. An "Ah" shape should shift into a slightly different "Ah" as it's being held.

◆ Keep "M"s and "F"s for two frames. If space and timing are tight, steal from the previous sound.

◆ Keep an eye on your targets and make sure they're not too linear going from one sound shape to the next. Facial animation requires all the animation techniques that are applied to the body (breakdowns, arcs, overlap).

◆ Hit the sound shape at least two frames before the sound is heard. Even if you're right on the nose, it will feel late when played at full speed. Humans process sight faster than sound, so the audience will pick up the cues from the shape *before* the sound.

◆ Break up the mouth angles. Shift the mouth up and down, tilt it left or right, and get snarls in there. Show emotion as the character speaks. The character can speak and smile, speak and frown, and speak and yawn at the same time. Build rigs that allow you to keep that kind of life in your lip-sync animation.

◆ Upper teeth do not move; they're nailed to your skull.

◆ Jaws rotate, not slide, in characters with clearly defined head/neck areas.

◆ Push your poses. Don't be afraid to go extreme. Avoid the Princess Fiona Final Fantasy Syndrome (translation: don't try to replicate photo-realism). Keep the energy of the sound track in mind when you're doing the mouth shapes. Louder sounds with more energy should be shown with the mouth open wider and sound shapes more extreme. Watch TV announcers talk; their faces are very elastic and extreme at times.

Eyes

You've heard the quote, "the eyes are the window to the soul." After the body, the eyes are key in emotional communication. If you have great body animation and great eye-emotion animation, you don't need a mouth to get the point across. So, remember that the eyes must follow the same pattern for communication as the rest of your character.

Cascading Revelation

The eyes lead the rest of the face. I refer to this as "cascading revelation." The revelation (revealing) of the change of inner emotions starts with the eyes and then cascades down the face into the mouth, then into the shoulders and spine. It's like the emotion in a character is flowing down the body, all starting with the eyes; they lead any emotional shift. Figure 15.12 shows this transformation of emotion.

The first place to get a sense of a character switching from happy to angry should be in the eyes. The rest of the face will come second, and the body will follow. From a motivational standpoint, a character must feel something before he can act something. So, you need to know what the character is feeling, then show that in animation. If a character is going to shift his feelings, you must show that inner shift in emotion in the eyes first. After that, you can move that emotional shift to the rest of the body.

Emotion

A person's eyes cannot hide the inner realities of the heart. So while a person may put up a brave front, the eyes give away the keys to the soul. The lever to subtext in animation (subtext being the unsaid truth of the moment) is to show this truth in the eyes.

If your character's eyes are missing the mark emotionally, then your character is lying. You can show a brave body, but if the eyes show fear, then fear is what is true, no matter what the bluster of the body is saying with its pose. If that's what you want to portray, that's great. The worst possible thing is to have your character's eyes be off the mark by mistake. That's akin to using words out of context. (Hey, don't jump to contusions!) For this reason, it is imperative that you study and learn the values of expression in the eyes. There are several excellent resources for facial posing for emotional impact—one of the most popular being Gary Faigin's book *The Artist's Complete Guide to Facial Expressions*. However, the best resource is studying real life. Watch people, watch good films (not junk films), and study great acting performances to instill new and varied meanings into your animation vocabulary. By expanding your vocabulary, you'll be able to broaden your ability to speak to the viewer through the eyes of your character.

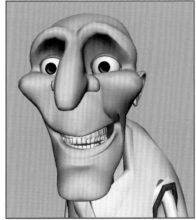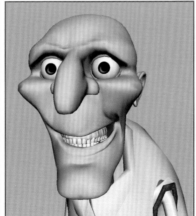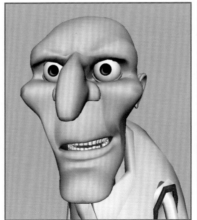

Figure 15.12
The character's face begins with a happy expression. The shift begins in his eyes, then moves to his lower face. The final expression of total anger is then revealed.

Blinks

Blinks are one of those odd areas in facial animation. There are good rules to follow, but they're never "lock solid never shall we violate these rules under penalty of death and public shame" kinds of rules. They're merely little things to keep in mind when you're animating blinks. A few of these are…

◆ blink on head turns

◆ blink on eye shifts

◆ blink once every 30 frames or so

◆ standard blinks are two frames to close, one closed, and five frames to open (on 24 fps)

Like I said, these are generalities that may or may not work. The key to blinks, like everything else, is to think about them in context. A blink can be merely a mechanical process for moistening the eyes, in which case they're unconscious and involuntary. This kind of blink shouldn't draw attention to itself; it is merely there to keep the character alive. But a blink can also be intentional and motivated. Oftentimes, the inner emotions and thoughts of a character will drive a blink or two that isn't strictly meeting a physiological eyeball-hydration need. A good example of this is a person who has just received shocking news. They may cast down their gaze in response and also blink quickly several times. This is a purely emotional, thought driven reaction. Blinks help humans make the jump from one thing to the next in the mind. Similar to a cut from shot to shot in a film, a blink is a cut from one thought or topic to another. It makes sense to blink when a character turns his head or shifts his eyes. He is "clearing the slate" in his mind. It's real-time editing in your mind. If a character is struggling to focus, or is trying to process difficult information ("Your father has just died."), he will tend to blink more often in an attempt to try to clear away the confusion and find clarity in his mind. This gives voice to the rule that a person will double-blink when lying. The person knows he is lying, and he has to work harder in his mind to gather the lie. He'll blink for clarity.

I usually create blinks last when animating a face, unless the blink is the primary action in the shot. By then your character's body, mouth, eyes, and face should be communicating very clearly what needs to be said. You don't want the audience to notice blinks, unless they're supposed to for story reasons. Blinks in face animation are a lot like seasoning. You add them to round out the flavor of the acting, not as a foundation for it. But again, this is a generality. There will always be the occasion where the blink is the primary action of the shot or has a heightened level of significance.

Workflow Checklist

Here's an example of how I generally approach facial animation. This is a "checklist" I use to complete a facial animation assignment.

◆ Planning:

1. Listen to the sound track.

2. Write down the feelings of the character at certain moments. (Know what you want to say.)

3. Watch yourself saying it.

4. Look at body poses.

5. Sketch face poses that work for that feeling. (Know what words to use to say it.)

6. Plan eye direction to match emotion.

◆ Technical Execution:

1. Key-frame eye direction.

2. Get open/close timing of jaw to match voice track.

3. Get other detailed lip-sync.

◆ Emotion:

1. Pick key moments of emotion and key-frame the face as a whole to match the emotion (whole face key-framing).

2. Modify lip-sync with emotional modifiers (happy, sad, angry, nervous).

3. Offset the animation, revealing inner realities with the eyes first, then cascading the emotion down into the lower face and then the body.

4. Do the blinks.

By planning your work and working your plan, you can bring more thought and preparation to your animation. Good planning and good execution go hand in hand in helping to achieve successful facial animation. Always remember: Failing to plan is planning to fail.

PART III

The
Production
Model

chapter 16
Getting Started: The Animated Short

The last few chapters of this text examine the production of a series of animated shots. It's an opportunity to combine the fundamentals and processes discussed throughout this book. Hopefully this will give you valuable insight on how to approach your own work and develop your own set of production processes.

I have developed a very short story and created a minimal set with one character. This basic framework should be sufficient to demonstrate the production of shots from beginning to end.

Along the way, I will implement many of the tips, tricks, and techniques specific to character animation, as well as recap some issues discussed in Chapter 5, "Approaches to Animation." In addition, I will discuss topics associated with refining the finished animation.

Storyboards

A storyboard is a two-dimensional drawing created to define the actions of a shot or scene (see Figure 16.1). These drawings are generally produced by story artists and are used to convert the written words of the script into a visual format providing a detailed description of the actions and emotions associated with the story.

Figure 16.1
A storyboard sequence.

The storyboards provide valuable insight into the script's intentions regarding action, emotion, and orientation. Multiple drawings are usually generated for each scene. This series of images provides the basic beats for the animator. Timings are generally associated with each drawing to supply the animator with a good idea of how long the character needs to perform specific actions.

Drawings generated for this project include 10 shots with 20 storyboards. These illustrations provide insight into the various beats of the story and suggest certain personality traits that might work in the scene. You will definitely want to use these images as reference.

As shown in Figure 16.2, the story artist has captured a distinct moment in the story with an expression that is characteristic of the attitude and emotion of the main character. The complete set of drawings is shown in Figure 16.3. Notice the beats the story artist chose to illustrate.

These drawings not only provide inspiration, they create the framework within which you must work. Animators rely on these drawings to define action, paint an emotional picture, and keep track of continuity. In this respect, they are crucial to digital production.

Figure 16.3
The completed sequence.

Figure 16.2
Looking tired is an important expression in this short story.

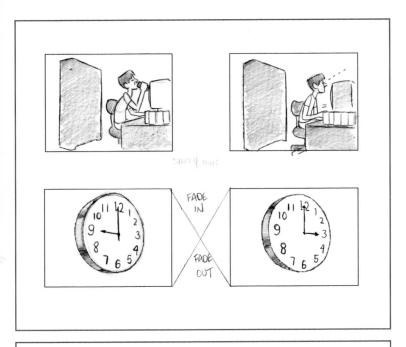

Figure 16.3
The completed sequence. (continued)

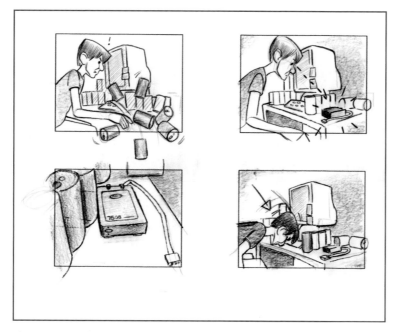

Figure 16.3
The completed sequence. (continued)

Layout

Layout is the phase of production in which the two-dimensional images and written script begin to take form in the computer. A layout artist "translates" the hand-drawn image by creating digital photos and properly placing sets and props. The proper scene lengths and sound files are loaded with the shot and saved as a complete file that will be passed on to the next stage in the pipeline. Figure 16.4 shows a storyboarded image and the layout scene generated from it.

Although layout is used most in CG productions, it also appears in commercial and feature films. An artist working on a project involving the combination of live action and CG will most likely have a camera match-move associated with each scene he is given. This file re-creates the real-world camera and set in the virtual environment. The camera's angle, size, and lens must exactly match the accompanying background plate to ensure the digital elements have proper scale and perspective.

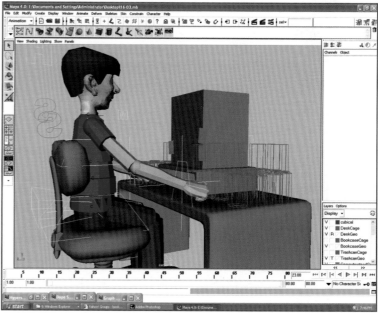

Figure 16.4
A hand-drawn image (above) and a digital representation (below).

In both types of production, the character you are animating will be placed in this file. That figure will be a static object and marks the beginning of the animator's duties. This will probably be the first file you touch. It should have all the necessary elements to complete the scene. There are, however, a few more steps before animation can begin.

Shot Turnover

The shot turnover process involves the assigning of a shot to a specific animator. A brief meeting occurs and the artist walks away with a shot or series of shots to complete. This is an opportunity for the lead or supervising animator to discuss the major beats in a scene and provide any additional information from the director or client. In addition, unusual technical considerations might be discussed, such as special character setups that are specific to the shot, as well as staging and camera issues. The animator should walk away with a thorough understanding of what is required.

Figure 16.5 shows the boards and corresponding layout file for the first three shots of the short animated film. The focus for these shots is to wake up and re-energize. The character desperately needs to finish his work and knows there is a long night ahead of him.

In addition to the attitudes the character will possess, there are technical considerations. First, the character needs to have plenty of room for his stretching routine. This will involve strategic placement of the furniture. Second, the character interacts with a few objects in each shot. Special rigs were generated to constrain his hands to both the chair and cola can. It's important to discuss these types of issues before work begins; they can influence how you approach the shot. Once these issues have been addressed, the animator can begin the process of planning her shot.

Figure 16.5
The first three shots of the short are turned over with special instructions to unique situations about the scene.

Planning

> *v.* **planned, planning**
> *v. tr.*
> 1. To have as a specific aim or purpose; intend.

Planning involves the pre-thinking of a shot. This phase occurs BEFORE you begin to set keys. It provides you with an opportunity to flesh out ideas quickly and formulate your thoughts and ideas for the shot. These can be decided upon without turning on the computer. This will ultimately make your actual key-framing efforts more effective and efficient.

Planning might be the most important step in the animation process. However, it's also one of the most overlooked. Many animators feel the pressures of production and jump right into a shot without the slightest thought being given to what they are trying to achieve. I've fallen into this trap many times as well, but I constantly try to remind myself of the consequences. My animation will take twice as long and may be five times as painful to achieve. The finished product will usually be lifeless and flat.

The most important planning process you can indulge in is thinking. It sounds simple, but again is often overlooked. Spending 15 or 20 minutes visualizing the scene can make a big difference. I often lay my head on my desk and walk through the scene in my mind. Other animators I've worked with spend an entire day thinking. Once the thinking phase has been completed, it's time to look at some references.

Video Reference

Video reference falls into two categories: The artist can shoot footage of himself performing an action or he can use pre-existing footage for guidance. The latter is particularly important when animating something that you can replicate. For example, doing a shot of a walking elephant would necessitate actual footage of an elephant walking. It would be difficult to replicate this motion on your own. Tapes like National Geographic's are easy to find in local video stores, and many studios keep their own libraries of this type of material. I also recommend beginning a collection of your own.

When dealing with human motion, shooting video of yourself or another animator can be beneficial and very simple. The only equipment needed is a cheap video camera. Spending big dollars on a high-end camera isn't necessary. The main objective is to generate a reference moves that you can study. These images can provide crucial clues to how the body actually moves during an action. In addition, nuances you might not have thought of will be realized while studying this footage.

The subtleties of human motion are amazing. Incorporating those details can make a good shot great. Consider the following example.

The three shots we are currently dealing with could use some help from the video camera. The motions that are supposed to occur are fairly complicated, and although I've gotten in and out of a chair many times, I've never studied the mechanics involved. The camera will shed some light on this. I found an open area, placed the camera on a tripod, and found a chair of similar style. I also tried to match the shot's camera angle. Although I couldn't match it exactly, getting as close as possible provides me with a more accurate account of how the shot will ultimately look.

Once the camera began to roll, I acted out the motion in a variety of ways. This process required doing a number of takes or versions of the action (see Figure 16.6). Even though it's likely that no one will be watching, it might take a while to become comfortable in front of the camera. It's important to remember that you are trying to capture a performance with this reference. Your performance must match the personality of the character you're animating and come across on tape as natural as possible. Animation is acting, and this is the first step down that path.

There are a couple of important points about this reference. First, the shots had specific frame counts associated with them. This means that I must fit all actions into that time range. As mentioned in Chapter 8, "Timing," a stopwatch is an excellent device to help determine your timings. I used the stopwatch during the first few attempts. Second, I shot video for all three shots at the same time. This was necessary to maintain continuity between actions. (I'll discuss this concept in more detail in a few paragraphs.)

After shooting several minutes of footage, I sat down to analyze the tape. While studying the footage, I made some interesting discoveries. These scenes involve a person who's exceptionally tired. I shot the reference at a late hour and tried to envision my mindset after a 14-hour stint in front of the computer. I found myself yawning and rubbing my eyes. A few shakes of the head were also necessary to wake up. This took care of the first two shots; getting into the chair was a different story.

I wanted to try something dynamic for the character's approach and sitting movement. I'd originally thought it would be interesting to have him spin around once before settling in front of the desk. I thought this might play on his young and whimsical nature. It was definitely more interesting than just walking around the chair and plopping down, but didn't entirely fit the scene. The character is supposed to be at the end of a long day. The amount of energy required to make the spin move just didn't fit.

Figure 16.6
Some stills from my video reference.

The solution occurred while the camera was rolling. I'd finished a take or attempt at the scene and was preparing to stand up and try the scene again. I noticed the natural progression was to spin the base halfway around to place me closer to the starting point in the cubicle. I left the chair in this position and attempted another take. The tired state of my body and the inviting seat worked perfectly. I plopped down on the chair and allowed the momentum to spin my body the half turn required to meet the desk. Done. Figure 16.7 shows the corresponding frames. The next step is to transfer these ideas to paper.

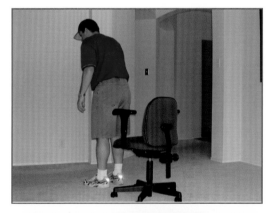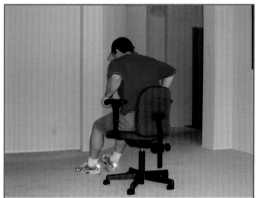

Thumbnails

Thumbnails have been mentioned several times over the course of this text. It's a popular method among veteran animators and a process that I strongly support. This simple step can save hours of wasted effort. The only requirement is the ability to pick up a pencil and draw, no matter your skill level.

Thumbnails are small drawings that are generated very quickly and serve as a vehicle to experiment with poses and ideas. Depending on the artist's skills, they can be polished characters,

Figure 16.7
The revised seating scheme.

185

stick figures, or scribbles on a page. The level of artistry isn't important. It's the visual cue the illustration provides you with. Even if it's only understood by the artist generating it. Don't be afraid of putting your ideas on paper. If *you* understand them, they will be effective.

I began this phase of the planning process after spending time studying the video reference. I have around 10 minutes of footage that needs to be ordered. In addition to experimenting with ideas, the drawings initially serve as an organizational device to assemble the more successful parts of each action being performed.

The first two areas of focus were the actions occurring at the beginning of the shot. I found an interesting take toward the end of my video that involved me turning halfway around while standing in place. This felt natural and was an excellent way to reveal the character. In addition, it was a unique way of performing the action. I combined this move with a yawn from an earlier take on the tape and began the process of sketching some thumbnails of the action. Figure 16.8 shows the results. With this initial pass, I literally tried to replicate the posture from the reference video to get a good starting point.

If you look closely at Figure 16.8, you'll notice some timing notes associated with each drawing. This is a terrific opportunity to begin formalizing some of the key frame locations. If necessary, I'll use a stopwatch to help make decisions. More than likely, I'll modify these at a later stage in the production, but they give me a reliable foundation when I start setting keys in the computer. Now back to drawing.

After completing the sketches for the stretch and yawn portions of the shot sequence, I started working on the approach, positioning, and sitting in the chair sequence.

Continuity

Continuity is critical in filmmaking. It ensures consistency of all the major elements throughout the film. Directors, producers, writers, and designers strive to develop unique environments and personalities in their productions. They associate colors, lights, actions, and emotions to those settings. Those elements must maintain some uniformity throughout or the audience will easily get lost.

As an animator, the primary focus is motion, and the most critical continuity for an animator is the matching of action and poses between shots. The character must maintain a similar gesture and position relative to camera as it cuts in, out, and around the scene. This is especially important when two shots need to correspond exactly. Such is the case with the short project discussed here.

Figure 16.5 shows the series of shots. Shot one involves the stretching motion, shot two is a match cut to the character's face, and shot three has him sitting in the chair. In reality, it's one action with three different cameras. For the action to flow effectively, the character must maintain continuity as the camera cuts into the face, and then back to the full body.

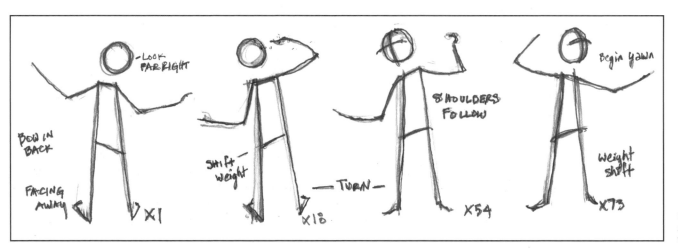

Figure 16.8
A few sketches from my thumbnailing pass.

chapter 17
Blocking Your Animation

I n this chapter, you'll look at the first stages of creating animation in the computer. With proper planning, I can now begin setting actual key frames on my character. This initial process begins with very fast manipulation of characters and ends with a series of poses that accurately reveal the intent of the scene and combine the fundamentals, tools, animation processes, and acting.

Blocking

The term *blocking* refers to the initial stages of a shot in which the action is roughed or "blocked" in. After the blocking pass is finished, the motions will still need to be finessed but the shot contains the basic movements and timings. You might equate this with a sculptor working on a bust of a famous figure; he has generated the entire form for his statue but still needs to add details, such as eyes, nostrils, lips, and ears. The form is recognizable but lacks sophistication and artistry. Blocking in animation is similar to this in that it gives the animator, supervisor, and director an idea of the artist's direction and approach. The animator should wind up with a piece of animation that has clarity and strong poses but lacks the refinement needed to meet the quality desired by the director and the expectations of the audience.

This is also the place in which the majority of revisions occur. The blocking pass will also allow the director to see a version of your shot that can be easily modified before a great deal of time has been spent on a scene. Unfortunately, change is inevitable in any form of digital production. I'd much rather make corrections on a motion that has a few keys rather than after I have sweated through modifying and offsetting every finger.

This method ultimately assists in the overall efficiency of a production. As I've said before, animation is time intensive. The last thing you want a crew to do is spend valuable workdays producing content that is unusable. If an effort is going to be made, why not make sure you're going down the right path? Blocking limits the amount of wasted time and usually keeps the animator focused on the necessary goal. Now I'll discuss the various stages of this process.

The Quick Pass

I start each shot by making a quick pass of the major actions. I use the COG and feet controllers and hit the key moments in the shot. (See Chapter 4, "Tools of the Trade," for a diagram of the character rig being used.) I'm not concerned with specific poses and I often hide the arms to simplify the character. There's no up and down motion on the character; he glides around as he steps through the various marks in the shot. I also make a habit of keeping all keys for every controller on the same frame. For example, if a key is set at frame 15 for the COG, I'll also place a key at that location for any other controllers that are being modified. This will dramatically shorten the time needed to make changes when timing modifications are needed.

Although this stage lacks detailed animation, I am referencing the timing notes made during the planning stage. For example, if the character stands facing the wall for 30 frames before moving, I'll use the COG controller and match that motion. This process will allow me to hit the important beats in a minimal amount of time. In fact, I should be able to complete this phase for three shots in about an hour. The focus is on making sure that the gestures and movements chosen can occur in the space provided by the set and camera view.

Because this sequence of shots is tightly connected, I'm going to work through all three at the same time. I need to be absolutely sure that the action flows naturally between cuts. I've labeled the series sf01, sf02, and sf03. These abbreviations serve to mark shot number one, shot number two, and shot number three, respectively. Most productions will have some sort of shot-naming convention. I'll also add a version number based on the phase of the shot. For example, the quick pass I'm making here will be labeled sf01_v1, whereas the same finished product might have a _v30 associated with it. Again, this is just for organizational purposes and to prevent overwriting old versions of the shot. A new version will be associated with each pass of the scene. Now it's time to get started!

Shot one, or sf01, is first. The shot begins with the character facing away from the camera. He pauses briefly and then turns around while making a few stretching motions. The first step is setting his starting position. Figure 17.1 shows the initial frame. I place him at the proper distance from the desk and with enough room between his body and the wall to make the turn. The ALL node is used for his translation and the COG and feet nodes rotate the body. This allows for the most flexibility when I begin breaking up the body as it turns around. Using the ALL node to rotate the character entails counter-animating the feet. Remember, the ALL node affects everything.

Now that the first position is set, I need to add a few more beats. I want the character to briefly pause before he begins the turn, so I select the COG and feet controllers and copy the pose from frame 1 and paste it at frame 18. (I could have also held down the middle mouse button and slid the time line. This would have prevented the scene from updating and allowed me to set a key without the character moving.) Once the pause is generated, I need to create the turn. I want a slow rotation and have chosen frame 74 as the last frame. The same controllers are chosen and key frames are created. Figure 17.2 shows the first two poses.

The next step is the stretching action. I'm going to continue setting keys on just the COG and feet during this stage, although I will likely remove the side-to-side rotation being set on the COG. I'd rather use the chest and hip controllers to get that pose. This is a quick and dirty way to see whether the generic action is going to work.

As the character finishes his turn at frame 74, he makes a motion to his right (screen left). I've placed the key at frame 83 and held that position until frame 95. (I again copy the value pose at 83 and use it to hold the character until frame 95.) He then leans toward his left (screen right) with a similar stretching motion. That

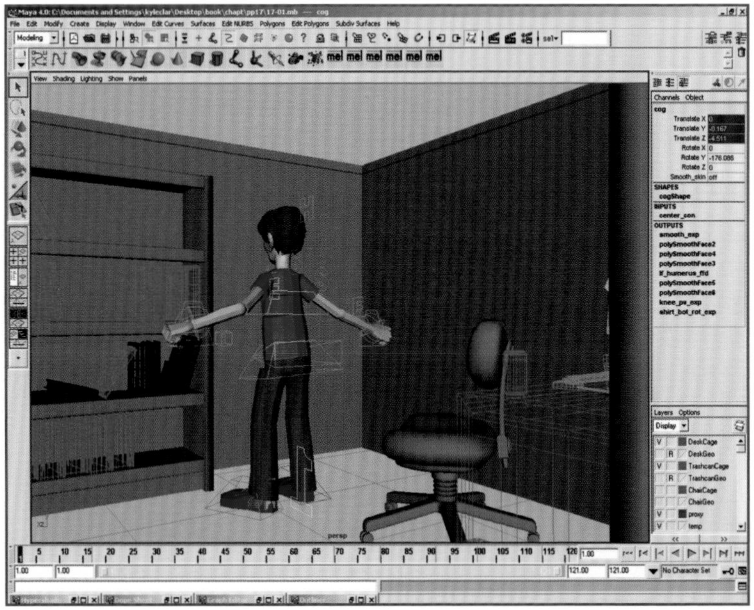

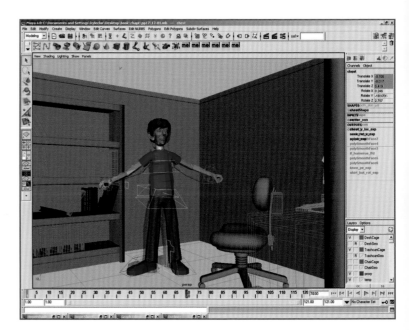

Figure 17.1
Frame 1 of the shot, sf01. The starting position was generated by moving the ALL node and rotating the COG and feet controller.

Figure 17.2
The pause and turn frames for shot sf01.

Figure 17.3
The rough stretching sequence.

pose occurs at frame 101 and lasts until frame 115. There is a slight recovery to his original position (frame 74) that ends at frame 121. Figure 17.3 shows the sequence of images.

It's time to check the animation with a quick render. As expected, some minor changes need to occur. The transition from screen left to screen right (frames 95 through 101) is happening too quickly. I'm limited to the 121 frames of shot length and need to "borrow" a few frames from another part of the shot to slow this motion down. I feel the turn (frames 18 through 74) could lose a small amount of time and still be effective.

The scene summary in the dope sheet allows me to move the range of keys to add an additional three frames to the transition from screen left to right. I'll select the keys at frames 74, 83, and 95 and shift them backward three frames. That makes the new stretching transition 9 frames.

After reviewing a fast render of the 121 frames, I'm satisfied with the initial pass on this shot. I've hit the major beats and I'm comfortable that the actions planned will work sufficiently. This process needs to continue with the two remaining shots. Shot number two, sf02, is a close-up and primarily involves one major position. I'll address more of the details in a later section in this chapter. Now on to the third shot in the sequence—it has a bit more complexity due to the difficulties of walking and entering the chair.

As a starting point, I'm using the last frame from shot sf01. That gives me the generic starting position of the character and should match closely enough for this first phase. I also need to adjust the chair position. It wasn't placed properly in the layout scene. Figure 17.4 shows the initial frame.

The first order of business is a pause at the beginning of the shot. For the first half of this shot, I'm going to continue with my pattern of using the feet and COG controllers. I've selected both sets of IK handles and generated a key at frame 12, exactly like frame 1. Remember, some modifications might be necessary depending on the curve type you have set as default. The standard curve setting will probably generate a bubble between these two frames that might cause unwanted movement.

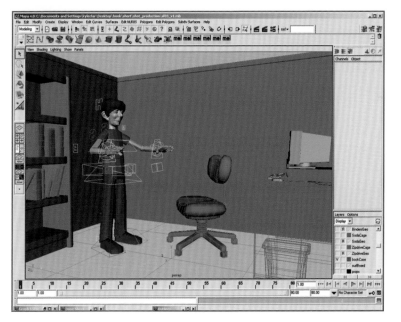

Figure 17.4
The starting point for shot sf02.

The next step is roughing in the character sitting down in his chair and sliding toward the desk. I placed keys at frames 37, 45, and 53. That provided 25 frames to make two steps (the move between frame 12 and frame 37), 8 frames of anticipation before sitting (holding the pose between frame 37 and frame 45), and 8 frames to land in the chair (the move from frame 45 to frame 53). Figure 17.5 shows the sequence of character placement.

Now that the character is seated in the chair, I need to slide him toward the desk and add the beats as he begins to work on the computer. The choice of controllers needs to be modified at this point. It will be necessary to add the chair control and

the right and left hands. It would be difficult to portray the character working on his machine without the use of arms.

The character is currently sitting down at frame 53 in the animation. I need to place a key on the chair controller at that moment before I begin moving it around. The next pose occurs at frame 65. This provides 12 frames for the character to spin toward the desk. Frame 75 should be enough time for the character to position himself against the desk. Keys are placed on the chair, feet, COG, and hands at that location. Figure 17.6 shows the progression.

Frames 12–37   Frame 45   Frame 53

Figure 17.5
The character approaches, anticipates, and then sits in the chair.

Frame 53   Frame 65   Frame 75

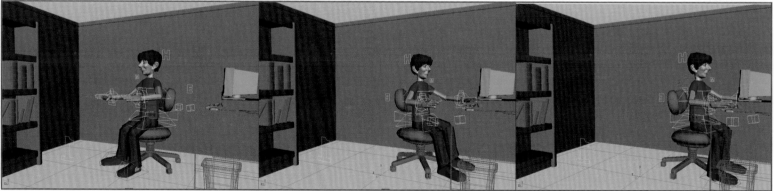

Figure 17.6
The spin and approach to the desk.

I'm going to forego the remaining steps to complete the scene in order to provide some feedback. I'm more concerned with you understanding the process, so walking through the remainder of the poses is unnecessary.

Shot sf03 did require a few timing changes. The 12 frames allowed for the character to turn in his chair weren't sufficient. I needed to add four frames to that section. I selected all the controllers in the scene and used the dope sheet to adjust timings. Additional changes will be necessary, but this animation should serve as an initial pass for the three shots.

Although I've answered a few necessary questions about the scene, it doesn't contain enough information to explain the point of the scene. If you remember the advice that Sean Mullen gave in his interview in Chapter 10, he suggests not showing a piece of animation until you are absolutely certain that it can explain itself. It isn't in your best interest to show your work if the director or supervisor can't understand what you are trying to achieve. That is exactly why some additional elements are required to complete the blocking phase.

Adding More Information

The next part of this process incorporates a more refined level of animation. It's going to build on the quick pass and create animation that clearly defines the intentions of the scene

To get the desired quality of animation, I'll need to add details to the gestures of this scene. The first pass generally concentrated on a small number of controllers. For the most part, I left the arms, head, and chest in the default position. This stage requires setting keys on most major skeletal attributes. These additional keys will not only refine the level of poses, but will also allow me to precisely delineate the timings of the scene. These polished timings should bring a sense of weight, emotion, and intent to the 3D character.

Although I am adding a large amount of detail to the previous pass, it is important to remember that this is the blocking phase of animation. The scene is still in its infancy and changes are going to happen. Staying away from the intricate details of poses will ensure that modifications can be made easily. Items such as fingers, facial features, and clothing shouldn't be introduced until the base layer of motion is established. (Unless these items are crucial to the shot.) In addition, keeping a certain degree of "tidiness" to your scene is important. By keeping the data organized, making timing adjustments will be much easier.

I'm going to start by working on the initial 18 frames of the shot. The quick pass consisted of only two frames and some additional info is necessary. The character is in mid-stretch during this time. I'm going to have him complete the end of a stretch and then hold that pose for six frames. He'll move a short distance between frames 1 and 12 and then drift slightly to frame 18. The small difference between the poses at frames 12 and 18 (the drift area) will keep the character "alive." Figure 17.7 shows the three frames.

Frame 1   Frame 12   Frame 18

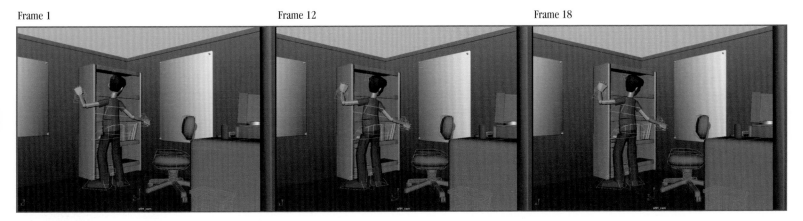

Figure 17.7
Frames 1 through 12 finish the stretch while frames 12 through 18 keep the character slightly moving. The small change between 12 and 18 provides a nice drift for the character.

On a quick side note, some extra consideration was necessary for this first shot. The geometry of the set was moved around. This required the beginning position of my character to change slightly. It also forced me to pay attention to the bookcase in the scene. I'll have to watch my poses as the character begins his next set of actions.

The next beat from the blocking is frame 74—the ending point for our character's turn. Looking through my thumbnails and video reference, I notice the character needs to make a 100-degree rotation. This requires small steps from both the left and right leg, so the majority of my initial efforts will be spent getting this action correct. I'll add upper-body poses at a later stage. I don't want to spend too much time working on the shoulders and head when the hips and feet haven't been addressed. Those lower-body sections drive the animation for this scene.

I begin by getting the feet and corresponding hip locations laid out. A complicated action such as this requires me to get up and down from my chair for additional research on how the body is behaving as it turns. I also have to keep in mind that the character is somewhat groggy. That tired feeling is going to affect the timings of the turn. The character's left foot moves first. It lifts up at frame 24 and then plants at frame 31. The right foot remains planted until frame 31, then lifts to frame 40, and plants at frame 50. The left foot has one small step that begins at frame 50, lifts to frame 55, and plants at frame 60. The body finishes its rotation by frame 74. Figure 17.8 shows the sequence of poses.

While the steps were being placed, I paid special attention to the location of the hips. Although fast, I want this phase of the animation to be as clear as possible. If you refer to the previous figure, you'll notice that the hips remain over the static leg when the character lifts a foot to step. In frame 55, for example, the weight is over the character's right foot until the left foot is planted. The hips will move after the left foot is touching the ground at frame 60. Keeping the proper balance at an early stage helps to better communicate the physicality of the character. The more believable the character is, the better the impression a director or supervisor can get from your work.

A quick render shows that the timings and locations are pretty close. Although a lot of work remains to be done on the feet and hips, this should be a good start. It's time to add some upper body poses for the turn. The scene currently has keys at frames 1, 17, 24, 31, 40, 50, 55, and 60. I'm going to generate keys on the chest, head, and arms at those same frames. This should keep my keys consistent, which again will help me if future changes are required.

As I begin to create poses, special consideration is given to the idea of "lead and follow." As discussed in Chapter 6, "Force: Lead and Follow," every action has a driving or initiating force and a complementing reactionary force. In the case of this turn, the hips are leading the chest, which in turn is driving the head and hands. If I keep that concept in mind when setting key frames, the character will be more believable.

Figure 17.9 shows two upper body poses for the turn. Notice the lead and follow built into each pose. For example, frame 31 shows the hips already beginning their turn while the shoulders drag behind. You can see that same idea applied at frame 60. The arms are swinging around as the chest is slowing to a rest.

Try to keep track of the arcs associated with each pose. Making the arms flow correctly between each frame is important. I must continually switch between the top, side, front, and perspective views to ensure that the wrists stay on track.

The turn is nearing a level of quality that I can live with. It's time to complete the blocking portion of this shot and move on to sf02 and sf03. The remaining 47 frames of this shot are a bit less complicated. I have the stretching motion to screen left and then a stretching motion to the right. I'm going to spend a little time creating poses for both actions. Similar to the first few frames, there is a long pause at both of these positions. It's basically another moving hold. Based on the timings from the quick pass, I'll add keys to controllers at frames 80, 90, 101, 115, and 121. Figure 17.10 shows the two major poses.

Figure 17.8
The step and turn poses for the lower body.

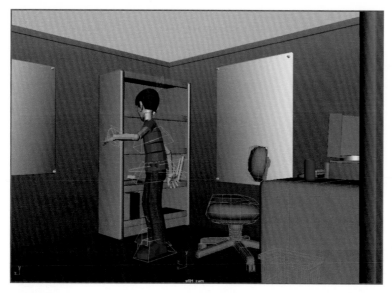

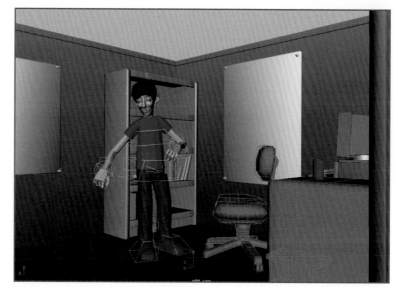

Figure 17.9
Frames 31 and 60.

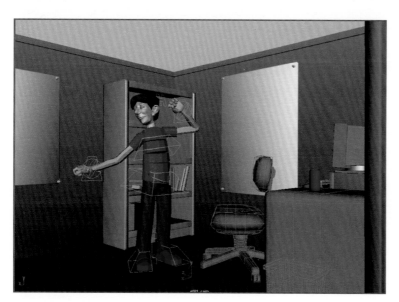

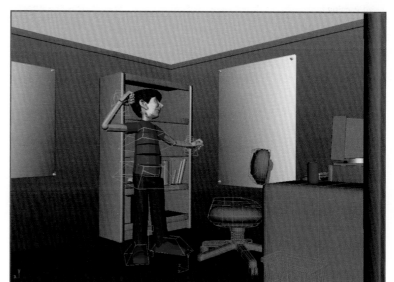

Figure 17.10
The stretching frames.

I've tried to push the exaggeration on both sides of the stretch. However, I usually find myself not going far enough. I'll probably end up working a bit more on the pose when I move into the refinement stage. Also, as these keys are being created on the low-res character, I'm not necessarily seeing the exact representation as it will appear in the high-res rig. I've also paid attention to the silhouettes created with these two frames, and I've even taken some of the cube geometry into consideration. I don't want the character's hands or head conflicting with anything from the background. Now on to the close-up shot.

This particular shot didn't receive much attention during the blocking pass. However, setting a few keys will be necessary here. You might wonder why the character is going through a yawn motion without closing his eyes. This shot will eventually require facial animation (I'll talk about the specifics in Chapter 18). For now, however, I'm going to concentrate on getting the head and chest working. I'll begin with the last frame from sf01. Remember, I'm cutting on action and need the shot to sync up.

The initial motion of the head is screen right to screen left. The character is starting a big yawn at the beginning of the scene. His head begins at frame 1 and travels to its extreme left position by frame 32. These two keys would certainly create a head turning from left to right, but you know from the chapter on arcs that organic objects don't travel in a straight line. I'm going to add a key at frame 17 to create a more natural shift in the head. This additional key will also allow me to create a more believable ease out from the head's starting frame. I'll rotate the head so it favors the initial position instead of the halfway point the computer created.

Now that the head has reached its extreme rotation toward screen left, I'm going to add 12 frames of moving hold. That means I'll adjust the head a small amount so that it continues moving just enough to keep it alive. The head should continue to travel in the direction it was going. Figure 17.11 shows the first four keys in this motion. In addition to creating the slight drift, these 12 frames serve an even bigger purpose: They prepare the audience for the large headshake that follows.

One of the biggest considerations for this shot is the anticipation for the violent action. I'm going to be shaking the character's head back and forth in an effort to wake him up. A large exaggerated motion such as this demands plenty of anticipation. Remember, the bigger the action, the bigger the anticipation. Nine frames should be ample given the context of the scene.

The headshake begins at frame 44. The head is currently rotated to its extreme screen left position. The first move occurs in 4 frames and hits on frame 48. This action is relatively quick and includes a sizable move. To lessen the abruptness, I've placed a key at frame 50 that's slightly different from 48, which helps soften the drastic change.

The head moves back to the character's left at frame 54 and back to the character's right at frame 58. These two positions are followed by keys at 62 (character's left) and 65 (character's right). Notice I didn't include the two-frame buffer that was placed on the initial rotation from frame 44 to 48. These successive motions aren't nearly as large. In fact, each transition from left to right is smaller with each successive shake. The result is a "fading out" of the shaking.

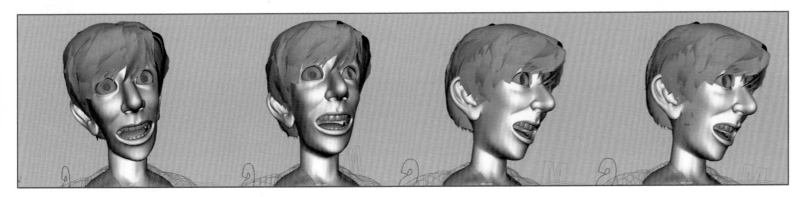

Figure 17.11
The head moves on a slight arc as it travels from right to left.

As with the previous shot, I'm also paying attention to the forces involved. Although they are not as visible as the character's turning body, they are just as important. There is actually a large contrast in the two shots in terms of which section is leading the movement. In sf01, the hips were in charge. They pulled the shoulders and head around as the body twisted. In sf02, however, the head is driving the action. It's pulling the shoulders as it traverses back and forth. That means I'll have a slight delay in the chest region. If the head reaches its extreme at frame 44, the shoulder will follow behind and hit at frame 47. The end result is an overlapping of action between the two sections creating a more organic and natural movement.

Sf03 will receive similar treatment creating more refined poses, attention to forces, arcs, and refined timing. One thing to note about this shot was the addition of a leap as the character enters the chair. Storyboards, reference video, thumbnails, and quick pass all called for a traditional method to sit in the chair. However, after beginning the scene, I felt it could use some more exaggeration. Figure 17.12 shows the results of that change. I will go into further detail with this shot in Chapter 18, "The Finishing Touches."

Figure 17.12
The new method for sitting down incorporates a jump.

Now that you've worked through the three actions, I'd like to point out a few things. The first is the complexity of the actual scene file. I've stripped this scene down to its basic components in order to render and update the shot more efficiently. There are minimal props, and the character still remains in the lowest detail possible. These items don't affect the current state of the animation and enable me to quickly render the scene for viewing.

Second, I'm working fairly quickly as I place the character in each position. The resulting poses will require some modifications and I should have plenty of time to include further detail during the refinement stage. I'm mainly interested in communicating my intentions for the scene and generating enough information to show the character's emotions.

Third, I'm not paying too much attention to the curves these key frames are creating. With the exception of a few minor tweaks to avoid slipping, I rarely open the editor and adjust the values. I'm concentrating on modifying timings in the dope sheet and relying on the perspective, front, side, and top camera views.

When your shots clearly show all the elements given to you during turnover, the director, supervisor, or lead will begin to see your work. It is here that the changes begin. This is a common part of production and one that all artists and animators must expect. If you've approached your shots as described in this chapter, you should be in a position to make changes quickly. There will definitely be times when entire shots need to be re-worked. Often this occurs after you have just saved what you thought was the final version. Understanding that change is likely and keeping your scenes well organized will allow you to easily address both minor and major changes in direction.

Now it's time to add the finishing touches in the following chapter.

chapter 18
The Finishing Touches

This chapter provides the necessary elements to add the finishing touches to a shot. It continues with the discussion of sf01, sf02, and sf03 and chronicles the additional key frames and issues related to completing your final version. This phase begins with the blocking elements from the previous chapters, with an emphasis on attention to detail.

Finaled

After putting in the amount of time needed to finish your work, the word "finaled" is music to the ears. At this point, all elements have been finessed and the shot is ready to be cut into the film.

The level of detail in a completed shot varies from project to project with the director's, producer's, and supervisor's different aesthetic tastes. Their vision and knowledge of schedules and budget will be the guide to deciding when a shot is completed. Many times I have felt that a shot needed more work, but there just wasn't enough time allowed by the schedule for additional changes. Conversely, I have had shots assigned to me that just wouldn't go away. Here are the key things I focus on when finishing up a scene.

The most important thing for me during the final stages is ensuring that the timing and gestures established during the blocking phase are maintained. Minute detail and subtlety amount to nothing if the basic intent of the scene is lost. It's very easy to get caught up chasing the perfect overlap in a long coat or tweaking the swing of a tail (see Figure 18.1). Make the acting and emotion your priority.

As a shot progresses to the final stages, I want to ensure that all parts of the body have been addressed. This may seem logical, but often minor items, such as fingers or feet, haven't been given the same attention as the major controllers. Every section of the body needs to maintain the fundamentals of force, arcs, timing, and overlap. This is an excellent time to fine-tune those elements.

Technical considerations, such as collision of geometry, must also be addressed. If a character's bicep penetrates his chest, slight adjustments will need to be made. In addition, feet and hands need to properly contact their respective props in order to keep lighting and shadows consistent. (I'll discuss this in greater detail later in this chapter.) Now I'll look back at my sequence of shots and see what is needed to get them finaled.

Refine the Body

My first step in completing these shots is fine-tuning the body. By body, I'm referring to the torso and appendages. This includes the hips, chest, head, legs, feet, arms, wrists, and fingers. These things combined define the character's performance in the shot, and drive the items I'll discuss in the next section. This entails making additions and modifications.

As I begin, the once tidy and well-kept scene will turn into a tangled web of key frames. It is, however, a necessary evil. I can't make the required adjustments to the character without breaking away from the rigidity of the blocking pass. Keys need to be offset, moved, and added to get the level of detail the motion requires.

18. The Finishing Touches

Figure 18.1
Don't let the details derail your original intent. Copyright © 2002 by Universal Studios. Courtesy of Universal Studios Publishing Rights, a Division of Universal Studios Licensing, Inc.
All rights reserved.

Begin by looking at the shot sf03. I used two approaches when animating it. I began the scene by using a straight-ahead approach. If you remember in Chapter 5, "Approaches to Animation," physical actions oftentimes lend themselves to this method. It's easier to track the complicated positions of the body by working every two or three frames. As I stated in Chapter 4, editing this motion was more difficult. However, for an action like this, it seems to work better for me. After I generated the turn, I moved on to a combination of layering and pose-to-pose approaches.

The blocking of sf03 provided a sound base for the overall motions of turning to mount the chair. However, the body needs extra attention. Proper feet push, knee rotations, hip rotations, wrist rotations, and finger poses haven't been addressed. Figure 18.2 shows a frame that needed some adjustment.

The character's left foot needs several rotations. The toe should drop as the foot is lifted off the ground. It will also slightly roll inward. In addition, the hips need some minor rotation. The character is supporting his entire weight on his right leg. That would force his hips upward and cause the knee to turn inward a small amount. Figure 18.3 shows the corrected pose.

After the turn is refined, it's time to address a portion of the jump into the seat. The anticipation and launch need to be precise to give the character proper sense of weight. One of the most critical parts of that launch is the feet. The blocking pass for this shot has enough information to sell the action, but it is lacking in detail. The feet were modified so they remained on the floor until the legs were fully extended. That extension is critical to obtaining the proper amount of thrust to push the body upward. Figure 18.4 shows the blocking pass feet and the refined version.

Figure 18.2
Here the feet, hips, and knees need concentration. In addition, the finger and wrist haven't been refined.

Figure 18.4
Frame 46 from the blocking pass (above) and the modified leg extensions (below).

Figure 18.3
The character is now pushing from the back leg and the force from his supporting leg is positioned correctly.

Also, notice the modified wrists, fingers, and elbows in Figure 18.4. I added the necessary lead and follow and refined the poses. This violent push upward will definitely require the hands to trail behind. Figure 18.5 shows the modified sequence with details added to the feet, hands, fingers, and head.

The character lands from his launch and spins 180 degrees in his chair. The blocking phase took into account the necessary forces and timings. However, I'd like to expand the amount of overlap or delay in the head, chest, wrist, and fingers during this motion. The chair is receiving a significant amount of force from the jumping character. The result is a fast spinning seat and a set of appendages that get left behind. Figure 18.5 shows a frame from the middle of the chair spin.

The character is now positioned in front of the computer and begins typing. He pauses for a brief moment to grab a drink of soda. This area needed some additional tweaking to the arm and hand that reach out for the can. The previous pass didn't incorporate enough lead and follow in the shoulder, elbow, and wrist. As discussed in Chapter 6, "Force: Lead and Follow," the motion of raising an arm begins in the shoulder. I need to add this level of detail to this section of the animation in order to reach maximum quality.

Figure 18.5
The extra drag in the upper body helps sell the force from the fast-moving chair.

This should take care of the body refinements for this shot. The animation quality has been dramatically increased with these additions. Proper forces have been incorporated and additional exaggeration and refinement of poses have given the motion that extra spark. A similar treatment will be applied to sf01 and sf02. Although these shots are fairly representative of the final version, an additional step is needed to add further details.

Adding the Details

Details are the last remaining item on your road to an animation final. These modifications are tedious and time-consuming, but can make the difference between a good shot and a great shot. They need to be added at the right stage, however, and should only be addressed once the body is complete.

Accessories

Oftentimes, scenes have props or accessories that the character interacts with. A floppy hat, a flowing robe, or the wheels on a bike are all examples that will need animation; they don't affect the emotion or action of a shot but do provide an extra layer of subtlety and nuance.

The chair in this scene, sf03, falls under the category of an accessory and needs additional motion. In its current state, rotations and translation exist only on the main node. However, the character landing actually causes a number of things to happen that will affect the parts of the chair. I need compression in the stem, a slight rotation in the seat, and some secondary action in the backrest. These elements are all reactionary movements to the landing character. I'll use his landing and impact timings to create the necessary keys for the chair parts.

Taking another look at the scene, I see that the character is typing on the keyboard. I need to animate the keys and a small amount of movement on the board when his arms come into contact with it. In addition, items such as cola cans, mouse cord, and post-it notes will all require key-frames. (These show up later in the short and will receive similar consideration to the props in the first three shots.)

Contact and Intersection of Geometry

As props begin to play an important role in the actions of a scene, special consideration must be given to making sure contact between characters and objects is handled correctly. Intersection of geometry is something you definitely want to avoid. A hand can't pierce through a doorknob, and a foot can't slice through the ground. As soon as you violate the laws of physics, the animation will not be believable. Remember, because the computer can re-create realistic materials, the audience will expect something solid to behave realistically. In addition, final lighting treatments will reveal shadows that are inaccurate.

In shot sf03, the first area of focus is the character's interaction with the chair. Proper contact needs to occur as his pants touch the seat. I need to spend time making sure that the intersection between the two objects are kept to a minimum. Up to this point, I've primarily been working with the low-resolution animation character. Although effective for the majority of body animation, this rig does not have enough detail for this refinement. I'll need to use the high-res geometry to ensure that I'm seeing the actual representation of the model. After that has been taken care of, I select the COG and adjust the Y translation until the pants are barely intersecting the seat. Moving this node preserves the majority of my animation.

Similar situations occur with the keyboard and soda can. Both props have contact with the fingers and hands of our character. Ample time needs to be spent making sure these elements are working suitably. Figure 18.6 shows the hand grabbing the can from the blocking pass, and the corrected pose with fingers just touching the geometry. Although I didn't switch to a high-res model for this refinement, it is often necessary to do so. Ultimately, the pose needs to work with the geometry used for rendering. If your animation rig doesn't have enough detail to make these adjustments, editing the pose with the final character geometry will be necessary.

Notice the camera angle from Figure 18.6. They don't resemble anything you've seen from the current list of shots. The dedicated camera angle made it difficult to fine-tune the movement and contacts. I switched to an alternate camera and zoomed in to better frame the objects. Although these modifications get me closer to being finaled, there is one step left to address.

Facial

Facial animation is the last step in the process of completing shots. As discussed in Chapter 15, "Facial Animation," elements such as lips, eyes, brows, nostrils, and tongue all fall under this category. I personally prefer to complete this stage of animation at the very end. It allows me the opportunity to place everything relating to the body in the back of my mind and solely concentrate on delivering emotion through the face. Shot sf02 is a perfect place to start the facial pass.

The second shot is a close-up of the face. The character is in the middle of a big yawn and is trying to revive himself. The blocking phase incorporated the head and body turn but ignored the facial expressions. I'll need the high-resolution geometry to accurately see the poses. I'll make that switch and add in a few details.

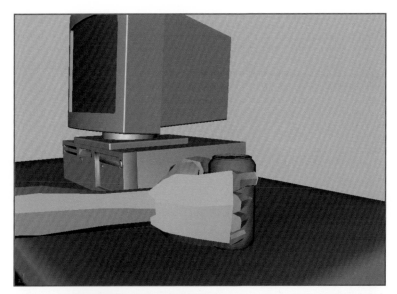

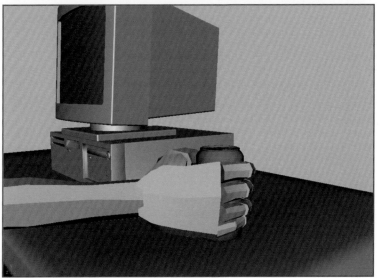

Figure 18.6
The soda can must make proper contact with the hands. Minor modifications were necessary on the hand poses to achieve this.

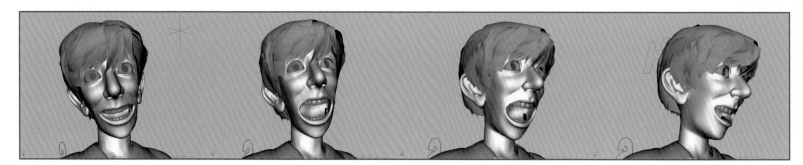

Figure 18.7
The jaw opening poses.

I'll begin by refining the jaw. For this shot, it's the driving factor of all the facial features. Rotational values are necessary on two different axes. The Y-rotation controls the opening, and the X-rotation controls the side-to-side motion. I'm exaggerating both directions for animated effect. Figure 18.7 shows the sequence of poses.

The next area of focus is the eye region. The lids, brows, and cheeks will all compress as the mouth opens wide. This action slightly follows the jaw. For example, if the extreme opening for the mouth is frame 24, the extreme pose for the face will be frame 28. The character is fighting the tired state and trying to keep his eyes open. Another thing to note is the asymmetry in the shapes. I've taken special care to differ the amount of compression on the left and right side of the character. As discussed in Chapter 11, this gives the animation a more organic feel.

The last area to consider is the mouth. As the jaw transverses from open to closed and left to right, the mouth needs to respond accordingly. I'll use the jaw keys to mark specific areas for adjustment. I'll also differ the shapes on opposite sides of the opening for variety. Just as the left and right side of the eye area have asymmetry, the mouth needs the same consideration. (See Figure 18.8.)

At this point, the animation for the three-shot sequence should be completed. I've given the character a high level of physicality, emotion, and nuance. The steps taken from the quick pass to blocking firmed up the character's timings and forces and showed intent and emotion. The refinement pass cleaned up the blocking phase, and added the final details resulting in a production-quality shot.

The animation files are handed off to a technical director to add lighting and textures. That person is responsible for the completed renders. Figure 18.9 shows a still from sf01. Figure 18.10 is a frame from sf02, and Figure 18.11 is a still from sf03. It's nice to finally see the character with completed textures in refined environment.

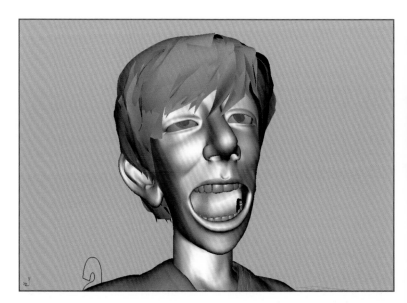

Figure 18.8
A frame from the yawn.

This process has been developed over a number of years working in a variety of formats and facilities. It's an efficient method for animating in all mediums. I'm not suggesting that you change your current approach to mirror mine, because, as Mike Belzer states in his Chapter 13 interview, "every animator has a unique way of solving a scene." Hopefully, this text will open your eyes to some of the various methods that are available to you.

Figure 18.9
A still from the first shot, sf01.

Figure 18.10
A still from the second shot, sf02.

Figure 18.11
A still from the third shot, sf03.

Glossary

The following terms are defined with respect to their use in this book. More comprehensive glossaries of lighting and effects terms can be found in *Visual Effects in a Digital World* by Karen Goulekas and *CG101* by Terrence Masson.

Symbols

2D. *See* two-dimensional.

3D. *See* three-dimensional.

A

animate. The change or motion from frame to frame; to give life to.

animation curve. *See* function curve.

animation supervisor. A person overseeing a portion or all of the animation for a project.

anticipation. An action that prepares the audience for a bigger motion in the opposite direction.

arc. The curved path an object takes when moving between two points.

aspect ratio. The ratio of width/height of an image plane.

attribute. A parameter of an object that can be modified or animated.

axis. A straight line passing through the origin that indicates direction in the coordinate space.

B

background. The part of the scene farthest away from the viewer in front of which the main action happens.

biped. A creature that walks on two legs; for example, humans, kangaroos, and the Iron Giant.

bones. A visual extension of joints when joints are in a hierarchy.

C

camera. An object that determines what is captured in an image and through which action is viewed.

Cartesian Coordinate System. A system in which a point is located in space by a set of three coordinates representing the distance along three mutually perpendicular axes usually labeled X, Y, and Z.

CG supervisor. *See* computer graphics supervisor.

chain. A series of joints in a hierarchy.

character rig. The internal skeleton and controls that enable you to manipulate and animate a character.

cheat. A technique used to sell an action or object in which obvious flaws are hidden from the camera view.

child. An object in a hierarchy that is connected beneath another and inherits the information of the object above it.

computer graphics supervisor. The person responsible for the quality and efficiency of the 3D work on a project.

constraint. Generally a direct connection of an attribute on one object to the corresponding attribute on another object.

continuity. Seamless assembly and natural flow of scenes with respect to time, space, color, and direction.

contrast. The ratio of bright to dark values in an image.

coordinate space. The location in 3D space as defined by the x-, y-, and z-axes.

counter animation. Altering a section of a character or an object in response to its influence from an object above it in the hierarchy.

curve. *See* function curve.

cycle. An animation that can seamlessly repeat an infinite number of times.

D

dailies. The daily screening of the previous day's work for review by directors and supervisors.

default pose. A neutral position for a character, which serves as a starting point to begin rigging.

depth of field. The range of distances in front of a camera in which objects will remain in focus.

digital effects supervisor. The person responsible for creation of all digital effects on a production.

director. The person responsible for creating the final realization of the production.

director of photography (cinematographer). The person responsible for all lighting and photography on a production based on the vision of the director.

dopesheet. An animation editor in which keyframes are represented by individual bars that can be moved and scaled in time.

D.P. *See* director of photography.

E

ease in. The gradual speeding up of an object as it begins moving from a resting state.

ease out. The gradual slowing down of an object as it begins moving toward a resting state.

element. An individual part of a scene, a character, or an image, which is combined with others to create a final version.

exposure sheet. *See* x-sheet.

F

field of view (FOV). The horizontal or vertical angle viewed through the camera lens.

final. A shot that has been approved as complete by the director.

FK. *See* Forward Kinematics.

focal distance. The distance from the camera image/film plane at which there is sharpest focus.

focus. 1. The emphasis of the scene or image. 2. The adjustment on a camera to set the distance that appears sharpest in view.

Forward Kinematics. The method of animating skeletons in which each bone is individually rotated.

frame. A single image in a sequence.

frame range. The total number of frames in a series expressed as a start frame, an end frame, and frame increment. For example, frames 5 through 49 by 2s.

frame rate. The rate at which frames are played back to produce moving pictures; for example, 24 frames per second (fps) for 35 mm film.

function curve. A graphical representation of the computer's interpolation between keyframes; often simply referred to as a curve.

function curve editor. *See* graph editor.

G

geometry. A NURBS surface, a NURBS curve, or a polygonal surface.

gesture. The positioning of a character to express an emotion or a thought.

Gimbal lock. When two of the true rotation axes of an object converge.

global. Manipulates an object with an axis of the same orientation as the world, regardless of the hierarchy.

graph editor. Animation editor in which motion and time are manipulated through modification of spline curves.

ground plane. The reference surface in a scene indicating the floor. Often used to receive shadows.

GUI. Graphical User Interface.

H

handles. The control points that modify the tangents in the function curve editor.

hardware render. A rendering process that uses the computer hardware's graphics card to quickly create shaded images or frames.

hierarchy. A series of nodes that are connected to each other in a parent/child relationship.

hi–res. High resolution.

hotkeys. User-defined shortcuts assigned to keys on the keyboard to automate frequently used tasks and increase workflow. For example, to print you press Alt+F, Alt+P.

I

IK. *See* Inverse Kinematics.

in-between. A pose created between two extreme or "key" poses in a scene. Use to control timing and arcs as a character transitions from keyframe to keyframe.

interpolation. Calculating intermediate values between two or more previously determined values.

Inverse Kinematics. The method of animating skeletons in which the computer solves the bending of a joint, such as an elbow or a knee, based on the position of one object, usually an IK handle.

J

joint. The building block of a skeleton, which determines the pivot point of a bone.

K

keyframe. A frame at which important position, rotation, scaling, intensity, blur size, and so on are saved to preserve and define the movement or performance of an animated object or character.

kinematics. The mechanics of motion.

L

lo–res. Low resolution.

looping. Playing an animation repeatedly.

M

manipulator. A control handle to alter object transforms in 3D space.

maquette. A smallscale practical model used as a 3D reference for character design.

match. *See* matchmove.

matchmove. The process of extracting the frame-by-frame camera and/or object motion from a live-action plate by hand/eye so that computer-generated elements appear to move properly in the scene.

motion blur. The smearing of an object in an image based on its motion relative to the camera. As the shutter exposes the film for a specific period of time, any motion occurring during that period is captured in a single frame.

N

node. A representation of an object or set of objects in which all information for that object(s) is referenced.

O

object. Any entity in a scene.

origin. The center of world space, the point at which all world space coordinates are at zero.

P

pan. Rotation of the camera about its vertical axis.

parent. To attach a node above another in a hierarchy. The node directly above another in a hierarchy.

path. A line used to control an object's direction and speed of movement.

pipeline. A sequence of steps defining the workflow of a show or series of shots from conception to final output.

pivot point. The location from which an object will rotate.

pixel. The smallest discreet unit in a digital image.

plate. The selected film footage scanned into the computer for use in digital compositing.

plug–in. An additional piece of software that can be integrated to existing software to enhance capabilities and features.

pose. The gesture or posture of a character at a given time.

prop. An object in a scene that remains static or with which a character interacts.

proxy. A low-resolution stand–in image or object used to increase interactivity.

R

real time. Relating to actual time, where 24 frames will play in one second on your computer.

rendering. The process of calculating an image from all scene information (cameras, objects, materials, lights).

resolution. The horizontal and vertical number of pixels used to define an image.

rig. Any geometrical architecture designed to place and control nodes.

roll. Rotation of the camera along its viewing axis.

root joint. The highest joint in a chain's hierarchy; there can be only one root joint in a chain.

rotation. Changing an object's rotation in world space.

rotoscope. The process of creating mattes or animation for each frame of a sequence of images by tracing the object by hand.

S

scene. The contents of a file which contains all the data that is created in a software package.

scrubbing/scrub. The process of viewing animation by left-clicking and dragging the time slider at the desired rate.

sequence. A series of related shots and scenes.

sequence supervisor. The person responsible for quality and continuity of work created for a particular sequence.

settings. The info about the working environment: units of measurement, playback speed, frame range, to name a few.

shot. A single camera view of action without interruption.

skinning. A process of attaching geometry to bones, which will allow the geometry to deform based on the movements of the joints.

space. *See* coordinate space.

spline. A curve using control vertices (not necessarily on the curve) to define its shape. Types of splines include Bézier, B-spline (generalized Bézier-spline), non-periodic B-spline, uniform B-spline, NURBS (non-uniform rational B-spline), and Hermite-spline.

squash and stretch. The modification of an object to indicate impact or acceleration.

storyboard. A series of drawings illustrating the key moments in a scene, sequence, and film.

subject. The person or object being photographed.

T

TD. *See* technical director.

technical director. The person in charge of rendering and combining the elements of a computer graphics shot. The definition of this term varies among different studios from a pure graphics programmer to a pure 2D artist.

three-dimensional (3D). Having dimensions in width, height, and depth. A 3D object can be rendered from different viewing angles.

timing. The reference to how long an object or a character takes to perform an action.

top node. The highest node in a hierarchy.

torso. The portion of a character above the waist excluding the arms, neck, and head.

track. *See* tracking.

tracking. Recording the position (2D or 3D) of a particular feature for every frame of a shot. 2D tracking results in the pixel positions per frame. 3D tracking results in the camera and object positions and camera settings per frame.

transformations. Operations of translating, rotating, or scaling.

translation. Changing an object's position in world space.

tweak. Adjust or adjustment.

two-dimensional (2D). Constrained to a plane having dimensions in only width and height; can only be viewed orthogonally.

U

UNIX. A common computer operating system developed by AT&T/Bell Laboratories.

V

vertex. A point in 3D space used to define an edge or a curve.

vfx supervisor. *See* visual effects supervisor.

visual effects supervisor. The person responsible for all visual effects utilizing any technique required to best realize the director's vision.

W

wireframe. The basic representation of an object in a 3D environment excluding all shading, lighting, and texture information.

X

x-sheet. Used to plan animation. Contains columns to record dialogue, scene notes, frame counts, and camera movement.

Z

Zero Out. The process of returning all objects and attributes to their default or "zero" positions.

Index

W

walking example of motion, 44
    back foot, pushing from, 149
    body action, 158–161
    hip movement, 150
    lower body, 152–157
    personality, adding to walk, 150
    side-to-side motion of hips, 47–48
    stepping forward of legs and swinging arm motion, 151
    walking cycle, 162–163
Warner Brothers, 75
White, Larry, 25
Wilderman, Todd, 17
wind blowing, forces in animation example, 66
wrist movement, 37–38

X

X translation curve, 42–43

Y

Y translation curve, 42–44

Z

z-axis movement, 47